Biological Weapons

Clay Farris Naff, *Book Editor*

Bruce Glassman, *Vice President*
Bonnie Szumski, *Publisher*
Helen Cothran, *Managing Editor*
David M. Haugen, *Series Editor*

Contemporary Issues
Companion

GREENHAVEN PRESS
An imprint of Thomson Gale, a part of The Thomson Corporation

THOMSON
™
GALE

Detroit • New York • San Francisco • San Diego • New Haven, Conn.
Waterville, Maine • London • Munich

© 2006 Thomson Gale, a part of The Thomson Corporation.

Thomson and Star Logo are trademarks and Gale and Greenhaven Press are registered trademarks used herein under license.

For more information, contact
Greenhaven Press
27500 Drake Rd.
Farmington Hills, MI 48331-3535
Or you can visit our Internet site at http://www.gale.com

LIBRARY OF CONGRESS CATALOGING-IN-PUBLICATION DATA

Biological weapons / Clay Farris Naff, book editor.
    p. cm. — (Contemporary issues companion)
    Includes bibliographical references and index.
    ISBN 0-7377-3182-6 (lib. bdg. : alk. paper) —
    ISBN 0-7377-3183-4 (pbk. : alk. paper)
    1. Biological weapons. I. Naff, Clay Farris. II. Series.
UG447.8.B573 2006
358'.3882—dc22   2005045118

Printed in the United States of America

CONTENTS

Foreword   5

Introduction   7

Chapter 1: The Origins and History of Bioweapons

1. The Early History of Bioweapons   14
   British Medical Association
2. Japan's Unit 731 Program   19
   Greg Goebel
3. British, U.S., and Canadian Bioweapons Collaborations   25
   Wendy Barnaby
4. Cold War Bioweapons Programs and Their Legacy   33
   Alexandra M. Lord

Chapter 2: Types of Bioweapons

1. An Overview of Weapons-Ready Pathogens   42
   Colleen M. Davenport
2. Anthrax   47
   Sallie Baliunas
3. Smallpox   51
   Donald A. Henderson et al.
4. Ricin   60
   Doug Hanson
5. Tularemia   67
   Gretchen Vogel
6. Plague   71
   Institute for Biosecurity

Chapter 3: Encounters with Bioweapons

1. Japan's Experiments on Prisoners   76
   Yoshio Shinozuka
2. Working in the Soviet Bioweapons Program   81
   Ken Alibek
3. Anthrax Attack on the Capitol   87
   Bill Frist
4. An Anthrax Victim Struggles to Recover   95
   Angela Rucker

Chapter 4: Defending Against Bioweapons Attacks

1. Emergency Vaccine Programs   100
   Mark B. McClellan and Anthony S. Fauci

2. Bioweapons Detectors   109
   Margaret E. Kosal
3. A Military View of Defense Against Bioweapons   117
   Robert P. Kadlec
4. The Threat of Bioweapons Justifies Restrictions on Liberties 125
   Thomas May
5. The Bioweapons Threat Has Been Exaggerated   132
   Philip Alcabes

Chapter 5: Emerging Threats and Defenses
1. State-Aided Terrorists Pose a Serious Bioweapons Threat   142
   Elisa D. Harris
2. Engineering Deadly Germs   149
   Jon Cohen
3. Amateur "Biohackers" Could Pose a Serious Threat   158
   Chappell Brown
4. The United States Launches Project Bioshield   162
   Frank Gottron, as interviewed by Ira Flatow
5. Body Temperature Could Become an Early Warning System   168
   Robert Armstrong, Patricia Coomber, and Stephen Prior
6. America Should Lead a Global Biosecurity Effort   174
   Lauren T. Hickok and Reynolds M. Salerno

Glossary   178

Organizations to Contact   181

Bibliography   184

Index   187

FOREWORD

In the news, on the streets, and in neighborhoods, individuals are confronted with a variety of social problems. Such problems may affect people directly: A young woman may struggle with depression, suspect a friend of having bulimia, or watch a loved one battle cancer. And even the issues that do not directly affect her private life—such as religious cults, domestic violence, or legalized gambling—still impact the larger society in which she lives. Discovering and analyzing the complexities of issues that encompass communal and societal realms as well as the world of personal experience is a valuable educational goal in the modern world.

Effectively addressing social problems requires familiarity with a constantly changing stream of data. Becoming well informed about today's controversies is an intricate process that often involves reading myriad primary and secondary sources, analyzing political debates, weighing various experts' opinions—even listening to firsthand accounts of those directly affected by the issue. For students and general observers, this can be a daunting task because of the sheer volume of information available in books, periodicals, on the evening news, and on the Internet. Researching the consequences of legalized gambling, for example, might entail sifting through congressional testimony on gambling's societal effects, examining private studies on Indian gaming, perusing numerous websites devoted to Internet betting, and reading essays written by lottery winners as well as interviews with recovering compulsive gamblers. Obtaining valuable information can be time-consuming—since it often requires researchers to pore over numerous documents and commentaries before discovering a source relevant to their particular investigation.

Greenhaven's Contemporary Issues Companion series seeks to assist this process of research by providing readers with useful and pertinent information about today's complex issues. Each volume in this anthology series focuses on a topic of current interest, presenting informative and thought-provoking selections written from a wide variety of viewpoints. The readings selected by the editors include such diverse sources as personal accounts and case studies, pertinent factual and statistical articles, and relevant commentaries and overviews. This diversity of sources and views, found in every Contemporary Issues Companion, offers readers a broad perspective in one convenient volume.

In addition, each title in the Contemporary Issues Companion series is designed especially for young adults. The selections included in every volume are chosen for their accessibility and are expertly edited in consideration of both the reading and comprehension levels of the audience. The structure of the anthologies also enhances accessibility. An introductory essay places each issue in context and provides helpful facts such as historical background or current statistics and legislation that pertain to the topic. The chapters that follow organize the material and focus on specific aspects of the book's topic. Every essay is introduced by a brief summary of its main points and biographical information about the author. These summaries aid in comprehension and can also serve to direct readers to material of immediate interest and need. Finally, a comprehensive index allows readers to efficiently scan and locate content.

The Contemporary Issues Companion series is an ideal launching point for research on a particular topic. Each anthology in the series is composed of readings taken from an extensive gamut of resources, including periodicals, newspapers, books, government documents, the publications of private and public organizations, and Internet websites. In these volumes, readers will find factual support suitable for use in reports, debates, speeches, and research papers. The anthologies also facilitate further research, featuring a book and periodical bibliography and a list of organizations to contact for additional information.

A perfect resource for both students and the general reader, Greenhaven's Contemporary Issues Companion series is sure to be a valued source of current, readable information on social problems that interest young adults. It is the editors' hope that readers will find the Contemporary Issues Companion series useful as a starting point to formulate their own opinions about and answers to the complex issues of the present day.

INTRODUCTION

Biological weapons, or bioweapons for short, are devices that spread pathogens to sicken or kill an enemy. They can be as simple as a letter laced with anthrax or as complex as a missile-delivered aerosol of deadly smallpox viruses. Some of the pathogens used in bioweapons, such as tularemia bacteria, are not contagious and seldom prove fatal if victims receive prompt treatment with antibiotics. Other pathogens, such as anthrax spores, can be often deadly (especially if inhaled) but are also noncontagious, and victims can be treated successfully with antibiotics. The worst pathogens, notably smallpox, are lethal, contagious, and impossible to treat.

The threat of the worst pathogens has earned bioweapons a reputation as "the poor man's atom bomb." Recently, concerns have arisen that they could become the weapon of choice for terrorists. Biophysicist Steven Block explains:

> By any measure, the economic outlay required to develop offensive bioweapons capabilities is significantly less than that of a nuclear program. Less is needed in the way of equipment and infrastructure. The materials themselves are less rare. And less is required in the way of specialized knowledge for the biological aspects, since much of the information can be found in the public domain. Worldwide, trained microbiologists overwhelmingly outnumber nuclear physicists. All these aspects tempt not only nations of concern, but also non-state actors. In fact, it seems far more likely that biological agents will be used by terrorists than by warring nations.

The prospect of bioweapons in the hands of terrorists alarms governments, scientists, and citizens. However, as this anthology will illustrate, opinions on how great the present threat is vary. Not everyone is convinced that bioweapons are a threat equivalent to nuclear weapons. On the other hand, some experts believe that certain bioweapons may indeed come to rival atomic bombs in their destructive potential.

Attempts to assess the dangers of a catastrophic bioweapons attack have been controversial. To gauge the risks, the U.S. Centers for Disease Control conducted a simulation in June 2001 of a terrorist smallpox attack. Known as "Dark Winter," the simulation began with the discovery of one confirmed and twenty suspected cases of smallpox in Oklahoma City. The United States ended routine vaccination of children against smallpox in 1972. Therefore, experts say, most Americans, even those who were vaccinated before that date, would be highly susceptible to the virus. The exercise revealed that the health-care system, as it was then constituted, would be unable to cope. The simulation suggested that the rapidly spreading disease would overwhelm all attempts to contain it through vaccination and quarantine. Within a few months, according to Dark Winter's projections, nearly one in three Americans would be dead.

Not everyone considers the scenario realistic. Stephen Milloy, a science critic affiliated with the conservative Cato Institute, calls the projection of mass casualties "critically flawed." Critics like Milloy consider Dark Winter's assumption that smallpox would spread rapidly in modern-day America erroneous. Others think that it is wrong to assume that it would be relatively easy for terrorists to acquire such a devastating bioweapon. Indeed, many skeptics argue that bioweapons are anything but simple to develop. They point to the failed attempts by the Japanese doomsday cult Aum Shinrikyo to mount a bioweapons attack in the early 1990s. After repeated efforts to spread anthrax brought no results, the cult turned to development of chemical weapons, launching a sarin gas attack on the Tokyo subway system in 1995. In congressional testimony given in November 2001, bioweapons expert Elisa D. Harris argued,

> knowing what is needed to make a biological agent is not the same as knowing how to do it, as was demonstrated by the Aum Shinrikyo's experience in the early 1990s. Despite ample financial and technical resources, including a Ph.D. microbiologist, the Aum's repeated attempts to use biological agents, including anthrax and botulinum toxin, failed to produce a single casualty.

Notwithstanding such claims, in the fall of 2001, a person or group (who as of this writing remains unidentified) obtained weaponized anthrax and sent it through the U.S. mail to members of Congress and the media. Twenty-two people contracted anthrax disease from spores in the letters, and five of them died. Even so, critics contend that these incidents, terrifying and tragic though they were, hardly amount to evidence that bioweapons can cause mass casualties.

Skeptics of the bioweapons threat do not deny that certain diseases are capable of inflicting mass casualties; however, they have confidence that a major attack can be prevented. Indeed, the 2001 anthrax attacks highlighted a major difference between bioweapons and nuclear weapons: Effective defenses against the former exist. Once doctors identified anthrax as the bioagent in the letters, people who were thought to have been at risk of exposure were treated with the antibiotic ciprofloxacin, more widely known by its tradename, Cipro. Millions more bought it as a precaution. NBC news anchorman Tom Brokaw, who believed he had been exposed, closed his October 15, 2001, newscast with the observation, "In Cipro we trust."

Even if the current threat of a major bioweapons attack is relatively low, there remain reasons to believe that the peril will grow. Biosecurity experts worry about the increasing ability of geneticists to alter pathogens in ways that may overcome defenses. They are especially concerned that biowarfare scientists may have already succeeded in making a more virulent form of smallpox, and possibly even a variety that can evade the sole effective barrier to the disease: vaccination.

Ordinary smallpox is lethal. In the twentieth century alone, an estimated 300 million people died of the disease, more than triple the number who died in all the wars during the century. An international vaccination campaign eradicated the smallpox-causing variola virus in the wild in 1977. Remaining samples of variola were locked away at the U.S. Centers for Disease Control in Atlanta and the Soviet State Research Center for Virology and Biotechnology.

However, former Soviet bioweapons developer Ken Alibek alleges that starting in 1980, the Soviets began to produce large quantities of variola and to experiment with breeding more virulent and contagious strains. Such a stockpile would represent an attractive target for a terrorist organization seeking to cause mass casualties. "Scientists are particularly concerned about the possible theft of smallpox virus samples," notes journalist Kate Wong in *Scientific American*.

Scientists are also concerned about other genetically engineered bioagents created in Soviet labs. Among those bioagents are strains of anthrax and plague bacteria that are said to be resistant to antibiotics, as well as specialized pathogens developed to destroy an enemy's crops or livestock. There is little doubt about the dangers of the Soviet bioweapons program. The accidental leak of anthrax in 1979 from a Soviet base in Sverdlovsk, which killed at least sixty-four people, illustrates how little control the scientists have over their stockpile, many experts attest.

The temptation to cooperate with would-be bioterrorists may be strong for certain Russian scientists who have lost their prestige and livelihoods with the collapse of the Soviet Union. Bioweapons expert Jonathan Tucker notes that thousands of scientists and technicians have been laid off. "From the late 1980s to 1994, for example, the State Research Center for Virology and Biotechnology ("Vector") in Koltsovo lost an estimated 3,500 personnel," Tucker observes. "Similarly, between 1990 and 1996, the State Research Center for Applied Microbiology in Obolensk lost 54 percent of its staff, including 28 percent of its Ph.D. scientists." As a result, security experts are concerned that some Russian scientists will sell their bioweapons expertise and equipment in the underground market, possibly to terrorists.

To a lesser extent, there are also concerns about U.S. bioweapons getting into the wrong hands. The anthrax used in the U.S. mail attacks of 2001 was found to be genetically identical to a strain developed by the U.S. Army Medical Research Institute for Infectious Diseases, giving rise to suspicions that it had been stolen from U.S. stocks.

Cheap and Easy Bioengineering

Concerns about the legacy of past bioweapons programs is matched by concern about the emergence of new, genetically engineered pathogens. The number of people skilled in genetic engineering is rapidly growing. DNA experiments have become a regular feature of undergraduate biology labs. As biotechnology becomes simpler to use and more widely available, observers worry that tinkering with DNA will become as common as computer hacking is today. *Los Angeles Times* reporter Michael Schrage writes that the new biotechnologists "won't hack software bits or silicon chips; they'll hack E. coli, restriction enzymes and double helixes—life itself. Call them 'biohackers.' Instead of joy-riding computer networks, they'll get their kicks out of reprogramming DNA—for better and for worse."

The worldwide spread of relatively inexpensive and easy-to-use genetic technology raises the possibility that terrorist groups or countries that support them will be able to create increasingly virulent bioweapons. "Genetic engineering has already been used to enhance the potency of anthrax as a weapon and could be used to create designer germs for which there is no medical recourse," writes international studies scholar and DNA expert Laurie Vollen. "Such technology is not confined to secret laboratories. It is commercially available."

One of the most appalling scenarios involves a genetically altered smallpox virus that could defeat the immunity conferred by vaccination. The possibility of an unstoppable smallpox acquired new credibility in 2001 after Australian scientists working with a related virus called Mousepox accidentally discovered a way to make it vaccine-resistant. They inserted a gene into the virus that results in the destruction of its victim's immune system. No mouse infected with the genetically enhanced Mousepox survived.

Bioweapons Can Backfire

Extremely virulent bioweapons bring to mind a terrifying image of worldwide epidemics. However, the ability of some bioagents to spread may render them useless to anyone who wants to target a particular enemy. Indeed, one of the major restraining factors on the use of the worst bioweapons is their lack of predictability. No one deliberately releasing a highly contagious agent can be sure that it will remain in the vicinity of its intended target. A natural outbreak of viral SARS (Severe Acute Respiratory Syndrome) in November 2002 demonstrated the risk. The previously unknown virus struck first in rural southern China and spread rapidly to Hong Kong. From there, it leaped to Vietnam, Canada, the United States, and other countries. Before it peaked in June 2003, eight thousand people around the world had contracted the disease. At least seven hundred died. SARS showed that in an era of rapid, global transportation, once a contagious disease begins to spread, it can be quite difficult to contain. No one who would consider deploying a highly contagious bioweapon can be certain of staying safely beyond its reach.

The risk of bioweapons harming those who launch them is called "blowback." Unfortunately, the restraining influence of blowback may not last. Work has long been underway to create bioweapons that are free from the blowback risk. The white supremacist apartheid regime of South Africa spent decades researching bioweapons that would target specific racial groups. Jonathan Moreno, a biomedical ethicist at the University of Virginia in Charlottesville, told *Popular Mechanics*, "the South African Defense Force conducted research for the possible development of biological agents that could be used against the black population."

That ambition was not achieved, and many scientists ridicule the notion of racially discriminating bioweapons. However, another kind of approach may yet prove effective against blowback. Its aim is to engineer a bioagent that will self-destruct if it spreads to the people who launched it (or others they choose to protect). The key is "self-destruct" genes. Some researchers have been experimenting with such genes inserted into microbes for benign purposes, such as improved pesticides. Toxic bacteria used as pesticides are outfitted with genes that cause them to perish if they spread beyond their intended zone. A wide array of triggers to activate the self-destruct genes are being tested, including light, heat, and various chemicals.

To date, no bioweapons application of these agricultural experiments has come to light. However, experts warn that in principle this kind of technology could be used to design a bioagent that is lethal to most people but safe for those who know how to activate its self-destruct genes. Other genetic technologies now under development for medical or commercial uses may also have as-yet unrecognized bioweapons applications. "The repertoire over the coming decade is limitless," says George Poste, a bioterrorism expert and director of the Biodesign Institute at Arizona State University. "You'll never identify all the risks."

Since 2001, the United States has made efforts to strengthen its defenses against bioweapons. In thirty major cities, the government has installed air-sniffing devices capable of detecting key pathogens. It has more than tripled the supply of smallpox vaccines to 300 million doses, enough for everyone in the nation. In 2004 Congress passed a $5.6 billion bill known as BioShield, which authorizes the purchase of millions of doses of new vaccines, funds new research, and lays out new emergency medical response regulations in the event of a bio-weapons attack. To be sure, there is controversy over how effective these defenses would prove in the event of a biological attack. Months after the BioShield law was signed, Richard A. Falkenrath, former deputy homeland security adviser to President George W. Bush, summed up the uncertainty by remarking, "There's no area of homeland security in which the administration has made more progress than bioterrorism, and none where we have further to go." Still, many bioterrorism experts, including Steven Block and Christopher Chyba, believe that at present bioweapons amount to no more than "weapons of mass disruption." However, Block and Chyba are concerned that in the future, bioweapons production will become easier.

Room for Hope

The danger of bioweapons appears destined to grow, but this does not mean that their use is inevitable. It is worth remembering that although some nations possessed bioweapons throughout much of the twentieth century, very few were actually used. The rise of international terrorism adds a new dimension to the threat, but coordinated actions against terrorist organizations may prove effective. In the meantime, much international research is focused on finding new and more effective biodefenses. Novel antibiotics are being explored, as are new methods of targeting and destroying viruses.

Many experts point to existing treaties as evidence that nations can work together to mitigate the threat. However, biosecurity experts generally agree that in the face of emerging bioweapons threats, stronger international treaties must be ratified. For that to happen, they argue, the United States must lead the way.

CHAPTER 1

THE ORIGINS AND HISTORY OF BIOWEAPONS

Contemporary Issues
Companion

THE EARLY HISTORY OF BIOWEAPONS

British Medical Association

The use of infectious disease to attack enemies has a long history. According to the following selection by the British Medical Association (BMA), the Greeks, Romans, and Persians sometimes resorted to poisoning the wells of enemies with dead animals. Despite taboos and prohibitions, crude bioweapons continued to be used. During the Middle Ages, besieging armies sometimes catapulted the corpses of people who had died of disease over the walls of a city they were assaulting with the aim of spreading infection. The tactic frequently worked, even though those who used it had no idea of what caused disease or just how it spread. Indeed, it may have worked too well. Some historians suspect the deliberate spread of infection may have touched off one or more of the great plagues that periodically swept throughout Europe. However, the BMA notes that it was not until 1763 that anyone deployed a specific disease as a bioweapon. The British authorities, it says, distributed blankets infected with smallpox to American Indians in what the BMA calls attempted genocide. During World War I, when the major European powers first made extensive use of chemical warfare, bioweapons were relegated to attempts to destroy the enemy's food supply. The biological sabotage campaigns were comparatively small and ineffectual. Nevertheless, the BMA observes, following World War I, an international treaty was drawn up to ban the use of both chemical and biological agents in war. The British Medical Association represents Great Britain's physicians and medical students. It also carries out public education through a variety of means, including the publication of books such as the one from which this excerpt was selected.

In developing a proper concept of biological warfare, it is important that practice in antiquity is taken into account. The Greeks, Romans

British Medical Association, *Biotechnology, Weapons, and Humanity*. Amsterdam, Netherlands: Harwood Academic Publishers, 1999. Copyright © 1999 by British Medical Association. All rights reserved. Reproduced by permission of Taylor & Francis Books Ltd.

and Persians polluted the water supplies of their enemies with animal corpses. This was a calculated means of denying the essential water needed by all armies. There is also considerable evidence of the use of catapults, during the medieval period, to hurl diseased bodies into besieged cities in order to spread infection and force surrender.

A significant change took place in 1763, when there is documented use of a specific disease—smallpox—by the British against North American Indians. [Microbiologist Mark] Wheelis, who uses a stringent set of criteria in assessing the occurrence of biological warfare in the historical record, accepts this example as proven. The method used was the deliberate transfer of infected blankets to the Indians. The background to this incident, and other possible examples of the same kind, was the devastating impact of European diseases—particularly smallpox—on the native North American Indian populations. The European settlement of North America was thus a *re*settlement following, as contemporary European accounts record, widespread deaths amongst the original populations from natural infection. In short, the infected blankets incident is an example of attempted genocide/ethnic cleansing, using biological weapons. As the British Commander-in-Chief expressed it, in a letter of 1763 to his regional commander for the Pennsylvania frontier, "[Y]ou will do well to try to inoculate the Indians by means of blankets, as well as to try every other method that can serve to extirpate this execrable race".

Taboo on Poisons

Despite such examples, [historian John] van Courtland Moon, in an extended historical review of legal restraints, has argued that there has long been a strong prohibition against the use of biological weapons because of their relationship to chemical weapons and the general abhorrence of the use of poison. This prohibition had become a principal of customary international law by the end of the classical Greek and Roman period and, following better definition of the prohibition from the seventeenth century, it was beginning to become codified in the latter half of the nineteenth century. Thus Article 70 of the Lieber code, drafted to regulate warfare during the US Civil War, states that:

> *"The use of poison in any manner, be it to poison wells, or food, or arms, is wholly excluded from modern warfare. He that uses it puts himself out of the pale of law and usages of war."*

This code influenced thinking subsequently in Europe, and was reflected in the International Declaration concerning the Laws and Customs of War signed in Brussels in 1874 which, although never ratified, fed directly into the First and Second International Peace Conferences in The Hague in 1899 and 1907 respectively. Boserup, in the 1970s Stockholm International Peace Research Institute (SIPRI) study of "CBW [Chemical and Biological Warfare] and the Law of War", pointed out that the records of the Brussels Conference demonstrated that the reference to poison and poison weapons clearly included the spreading of disease.

Use in First World War

The development of the science of microbiology in the late nineteenth century had considerably extended the potential scope of biological warfare, as the specific agents and mechanisms of disease and disease prevention became better known. Thus German use of biological warfare in the First World War was directed at a number of countries with the aim of sabotaging valuable allied horse stocks and also grain shipments, an example of anti-animal and anti-plant biological warfare.

Despite most of the German records having been destroyed or lost there is no doubt that biological sabotage was directed by the General Staff. It must also have been preceded by a dedicated research and development programme devoted to determining how the agents could be transported and used effectively.

Table 2.1: German offensive anti-animal and anti-plant biological warfare in the First World War

Date	Place	Target	Agents
1915–16	Eastern seaboard of US	Horse shipments to Europe	Anthrax and glanders
1915–16	Romania	Horses and livestock	Anthrax and glanders
1916	Norway	Reindeer draft animals	Anthrax
1917	Western Front	Horses	Anthrax
1917–18	Argentina	Horse shipments to Europe	Anthrax and glanders
		Stored grain	Fungus

We know most about the German biological campaign against the United States because it was part of a much larger general sabotage campaign that was later the subject of legal proceedings. The adjudication of the US claims for losses in the sabotage campaign was not finally resolved until just before the Second World War, but the records allow an account to be given of the biological aspect of the overall sabotage campaign. Anthrax and glanders agents (an infectious disease of horses) were cultured from seed stocks by the principal German operative in the US, packaged and then distributed to local personnel, who jabbed the horses with infected needles. The campaign in South America against both animal and grain shipments was again, of course, at extremely long range and involved shipments of biological agents in part by U-boat. It is worth noting that British naval intelligence was following this operation through the decoding of German wireless telegraph transmissions and made attempts to interfere with its progress. The less well known German campaign in Romania was somewhat easier to carry out because material could be shipped overland through friendly countries.

French Biological Warfare

Most of the documentation on the French biological warfare programme before the Second World War was destroyed in 1940 to prevent it falling into German hands. The account we currently have is therefore incomplete. It is known, however, that at a meeting of a Bacteriological Commission in the War Ministry in December 1923, Veterinary Inspector Valleé stated:

> "... that he had had the opportunity during the Great War to prepare a virus that was inoffensive to man but easily inoculable in the horse, and which caused an infectious anaemia. This virus had been used against the enemy cavalry..."

The word virus was not being used by Valleé in the modern sense, and the agent was probably glanders. The Germans certainly believed that they were attacked by the French with biological weapons.

Whatever the nature of French biological warfare during the First World War, there is no doubt that serious attention was paid to the subject immediately afterwards. Three phases of research can be detected between the wars: 1921–26; 1927–34; and 1935–40. The first and third phases of interest and activity were triggered by French perceptions of German interest in biological warfare, whilst the second phase, of low levels of activity, was triggered by French concern to be seen to be living up to the obligations embodied in the 1925 Geneva Protocol. The French work, up to 1927, seems to have foreshadowed much of what was to follow in later programmes. There was clearly careful selection of suitable agents, consideration of the most efficient means of military use and then effective weaponisation. Weaponisation was a significant step because military use requires a means of delivering large amounts of agent to a target. Given the fragility of microorganisms, developing an effective weapon to deliver agents was a complex task.

Ban on Germ Warfare

Following the widespread employment of deadly chemical weapons during the First World War, it is not surprising that strenuous efforts were made when the war ended, to prevent them ever being used again. Eventually, the 1925 Geneva Protocol was agreed.

The Protocol is, in effect, a no-first-use agreement between states which has now essentially become a part of customary international law. During the drafting of the Protocol the Polish delegate pointed out the omission of bacteriological warfare. This, he argued, had been included in the discussions and was important because the agents were simpler and cheaper to produce than chemicals and could have significant long-term effects. This argument was accepted and led to the inclusion of the reference to "bacteriological methods of warfare" in the prohibition. This is an extremely general ban that clearly includes anti-plant and anti-animal warfare, as well as attacks on human beings. The term 'bacteriological' is now of course, taken to cover all biological agents. The Protocol has a number of weaknesses; in particular, it did not prevent biological warfare being researched or preparations being made for its use—at least in retaliation. Thus the offensive biological research and development carried out by states in the middle years of this century was not banned by the 1925 Protocol.

Many military establishments took the possibility of biological warfare very seriously prior to the Second World War. For example, in Hungary there was a secret biological warfare programme running from 1936 to 1944 which has recently been described. The programme involved a central institute in Budapest with eight microbiological and one chemical laboratory. The Hungarian programme shows consideration of the most efficient means of military use and careful agent selection, as in the earlier first phase of the French programme.

In attempting to understand the potential dangers we face, it is necessary to confront the inhumanity of Japanese offensive biological warfare. . . . [T]he Geneva Protocol had the unintended effect of suggesting to a Japanese officer, Ishii Shiro, that if use of biological weapons was banned in an international agreement they must be effective. Ishii Shiro and his colleagues then launched "perhaps the most gruesome series of BW experiments in history" which involved the deliberate infection and certain death of large numbers of human captives within occupied China.

JAPAN'S UNIT 731 PROGRAM

Greg Goebel

The widespread use of chemical weapons in the trenches of Europe during World War I led to a movement during the 1920s to ban all unconventional weapons. The result was the 1925 Geneva Protocol, which outlawed both chemical and biological weapons. Japan refused to sign the treaty. In the following selection, writer Greg Goebel describes how a Japanese military doctor, Shiro Ishii, took the opportunity to develop a large-scale program of bioweapons research, development, and deployment. Japan's Imperial Army had taken over much of Northeastern China in 1932 and set up a puppet state called Manchukuo. Within a few years of the invasion, Goebel writes, Ishii had obtained permission to begin bioweapons research in Japanese-occupied China. By 1937 Ishii had received the green light for construction of a secret bioweapons facility at Pingfan, near the Chinese city of Harbin. It became known as Unit 731. As the Japanese Imperial Army sought to conquer the rest of China, Unit 731 carried out grisly and inhumane experiments on the local population with germ-laden bombs and other bioweapons. In 1940, the weapons it had developed were used against civilian populations in Chinese cities. Disease-bearing fleas were dropped from airplanes over at least one city, resulting in a deadly outbreak of plague. This "success," Goebel writes, led the Imperial Japanese Army to greatly expand Ishii's bioweapons program. Greg Goebel is a writer who served in the U.S. Army Signal Corps in the 1970s and later became an electronics engineer. Until turning his hand to writing in 2000, he worked for the Hewlett-Packard company.

The use of disease as a weapon is nothing new. Centuries ago, armies would occasionally catapult the bodies of people who had died of plagues into cities under siege in hopes of spreading disease, a tactic

Greg Goebel, "1932–1942: The Origins of Biological Warfare/Unit 731," www.vector site.net.

that often proved successful. English colonists in the New World on occasion gave blankets and other items that had belonged to people who had died of smallpox to local native tribes, and the results could be devastating as the natives had little resistance to the disease.

These were purely opportunistic schemes. Methodical development of pathogens and potent biological toxins as weapons of mass destruction had to wait until the development of modern medical theory and the discovery of pathogens, in the last part of the 19th century.

Although the knowledge to manufacture biological weapons or "bioweapons" was available in the First World War, there is no strong evidence that anyone did, although rumors of biological warfare (BW) were widespread at the time. The possibility of BW was certainly evident, and the Geneva Protocol of 1925 included clauses forbidding it.

Development of bioweapons did not actually begin in earnest until the 1930s, with Japan taking the lead. The effort was directed by a single domineering figure, an Imperial Japanese Army officer and medical doctor named Shiro Ishii.

Ishii returned from a European tour in 1932, bringing with him a conviction that BW was the way of the future. Ironically, the fact that the Geneva Protocol had banned BW helped draw his attention to it, since the ban implied that people found such weapons unusually dangerous and frightening.

Japan Invades Manchuria

The Japanese invaded the Chinese province of Manchuria in 1932, and set it up as the Japanese puppet state of "Manchukuo". In 1935, Ishii managed to convince his superiors of the potential usefulness of BW, and so they set him up in a hospital in Harbin, Manchuria, to conduct small-scale experiments with dangerous pathogens. By 1937, Ishii's work had proved promising enough for the Japanese War Ministry to approve the construction of a full-scale BW research and development complex, at a small town named Pingfan, about 65 kilometers (40 miles) south of Harbin.

The Imperial Japanese Army had attacked China proper in that year. The Japanese were able to win almost every battle they fought, but they were entirely outnumbered by the numerous Chinese. The Japanese turned to BW as a potential equalizer. It is also possible that they hoped to exterminate Chinese in areas Japan intended to colonize.

The Pingfan Institute was completed in 1939. Ishii, now a general, was in charge of the research organization, which was given the cover designation "Water Purification Unit 731". The Pingfan complex covered over three square kilometers (1.16 square miles) and included an airfield, barracks, and laboratories.

Japanese recruits arriving there found it an odd place. For example, none of the vehicles carried any identifying marks. They quickly found out that it had other strange and much more unpleasant features. One

Japanese veteran who was a technician at the Pingfan site recalled there were many doctors and professors there, giving it something of the air of a university medical research facility, but noted that it was in fact the opposite: "Here, they were trying to find ways to kill people."

There was a certain scientific challenge in this effort. The understanding of pathogens and their actions in causing disease and epidemics was crude, and there was, and is, still much to learn. There were also the practical problems of developing bioweapons, such as selecting the appropriate pathogen, determining the lethal dosage, and engineering the right techniques for production, storage, transport, and dispersal. Unit 731 also worked on defensive measures, primarily the large-scale production of vaccines.

Various Agents Studied

Unit 731 studied almost every major known pathogen for its utility as a BW agent or "bioagent". Some of the more significant included:

• "Anthrax", a highly lethal disease of livestock and humans. Anthrax is a bacterial infection that can be acquired by contact with infected victims, eating of tainted meat, or by inhalation of anthrax spores. When anthrax is acquired by contact, it can create hideous sores that may lead to death by blood poisoning, though the mortality is relatively low, no more than about 20%. The sores tend to be shiny black with dried blood, which gives the disease its name, since the word "anthracis" is Greek for "coal".

Mortality is about 50% if the bacteria is ingested by eating tainted meat, though this form of anthrax is very rare. However, when inhaled, it leads to a lung infection that is over 90% lethal, killing in a few days.

The action of inhalation anthrax is dangerously deceptive, since the victim suffers an initial bout of what feels like the flu, which then seems to fade out. In fact, all that has happened is that the anthrax spores have been scavenged up by the body's lymphatic system, where they then proceed to multiply, bringing on a second and murderous bout of the disease. The bacteria actually kill by secreting a deadly toxin that results in toxic shock. The purified toxin itself can be in principle used as a deadly bioagent.

The only good thing about anthrax is that it is not contagious, though as a victim's corpse is full of spores, cremation is usually advisable. The lack of contagiousness is actually an advantage when using it for BW. In fact, anthrax would become the lethal bioagent of choice for future BW development programs. It forms spores that are very hardy and easy to store for long periods of time, and can be conveniently packed into munitions. Anthrax spores are so hardy, in fact, that they will persist in an area over which they have been spread for decades, though they are somewhat sensitive to bright sunlight.

• "Plague", the "Black Death" of Medieval times, is caused by infection from a bacterium named *Yersinia Pestis*. It has three forms: "bubonic plague", when spread by fleas or other parasites; "pneumonic plague", when spread by inhaling the bacteria; and "septicemic plague", when spread by contact.

Pneumonic plague has a lethality of 95% or more. Although bubonic plague is somewhat less lethal, its spreads more easily and is more useful for BW. However, bubonic plague still isn't all that good a bioagent, as it requires cultivation, storage, and distribution of live fleas.

• "Gas gangrene", a condition caused by the infection of wounds by the *Clostridium perfringens* bacterium, characterized by stinking putrefaction of the flesh.

• "Brucellosis", a bacterial disease caused by various pathogens of the genus *Brucella* that infects livestock and humans. It is not very lethal, but it is highly contagious and can incapacitate a victim for a week or more.

• "Tularemia", a bacterial disease caused by the bacterium *Francisella tularensis* that infects rabbits as well as humans, and so is known as "rabbit fever". Like brucellosis, tularemia is rarely fatal in humans but can make a victim wretchedly sick for a while.

• "Glanders", a disease of horses and humans that eats away the mucous linings of nose and respiratory tract, and attacks the lymphatic system. It is caused by the bacterium *Pseudomonas mallei*. It is uncertain if the Japanese were interested in glanders for killing horses and mules, or humans, or, most likely, both.

• Bacteria related to food poisoning, including the *Salmonella* and *Clostridium botulinum* bacteria, which secrete extremely deadly biotoxins. The toxins were potential bioagents in themselves, particularly botulism toxin. The lethal dose of botulism toxin is very small, and the toxin is easily produced in quantity and stored for long periods of time.

Toxins Considered

Other pathogens investigated included typhus, typhoid, cholera, tetanus, smallpox, and tuberculosis, but these agents proved difficult to "weaponize". The Japanese also experimented with exotic biotoxins, such as blowfish poison. They were traditionally familiar with this toxin, since blowfish is regarded as a delicacy in Japan but has to be prepared by a specially-qualified chef so that it may be eaten without fatal results.

Incidentally, as with chemical agents and chemical weapons, a "bioagent" only refers to a pathogen or toxin itself, while a "bioweapon" was a delivery system loaded with bioagents.

Production and Live Experiments

The Japanese had to produce pathogens in quantity for tests and, if they proved worthy, production. Unit 731 researchers devised a scheme using trays of meat and broth as cultures. The trays were kept in incubators and the scum of bacteria produced was skimmed off every few days. The stink of rotten meat was almost overpowering. Eventually, Pingfan was believed to have been capable of producing tonnes of pathogens every month.

Having obtained pathogens, the next step was to determine their effectiveness. There were plenty of Chinese available for use as involuntary test subjects. The Japanese would put up posters warning the Chinese that epidemics of the appropriate diseases had broken out, and then a squad of soldiers would go out and dump pathogens discreetly into the well of a village. Three or four days later, they would return to inspect the ill. The soldiers would anesthetize them, cut them open and take samples, and sew them back up again. "Then we threw the bodies down the well," as a veteran of the program recalled. The soldiers torched the village and left.

The tests were very successful. General Ishii then decided to perform more controlled tests in deep secrecy on Chinese prisoners taken to the compound at Pingfan. Many of these people were simply rounded up off the streets of Harbin to meet quotas set by Unit 731 officers. At least 3,000 were taken there, and few, if any, ever came back. The cover story for the compound was that it was a lumberyard, and so Unit 731 personnel referred to the prisoners as "maruta (logs)".

Prisoners were assigned serial numbers 1 through 200. Once that block had all been killed, the serial number count started over again through the next 200, and so on. Japanese veterans of Unit 731 recollect the place as a kind of hell on Earth, but the Imperial Japanese Army demanded unhesitating obedience, and a failure to deliver it was immediately and severely punished.

Chinese prisoners were tied to poles out in the open and forced to look into the sky as airplanes flew over and sprayed bacteria on them. The prisoners were carefully observed and their condition recorded with colored drawings as they sickened and died. Others were tied to stakes or panels and arranged around fragmentation bombs containing *Clostridium perfringens* bacteria. The bomb was detonated, and the test subjects were studied as they developed gas gangrene from their wounds. When test subjects died, their corpses were burned in a crematorium.

Flea Bombs

By 1940, Unit 731 had developed a ceramic anthrax bomb and built 4,000 of them. They were also considering ways of delivering bubonic plague. Researchers at Pingfan bred plague-infested rats in quantity and then gathered the fleas from the rats. The fleas could then be distributed as a bioagent vector, using tubular baskets strapped to the bomb pylons of aircraft.

In October 1940, a Japanese aircraft flew low over the city of Ningpo, which was still held by the Nationalist Chinese, and dispersed a spray containing plague-infested fleas. The results were appalling. Roughly 500 people died and the city was panic-stricken.

"There were so many people and not enough coffins," one survivor recalled. "So two people would share a coffin." It is thought that more attacks may have taken place in China, but records of such activities were destroyed by the Japanese at the end of the war and nobody knows for sure.

The researchers at Unit 731 went on to even more imaginative BW studies. They decided to use Chinese prisoners not merely to test pathogens, but to actually act as production incubators to breed them. The researchers believed that pathogens that managed to overcome the body's defenses were likely more virulent.

The prisoners were injected with pathogens. When the victims reached their limit, the prisoners were chloroformed and all the blood was drained from their bodies. When the blood flow from a prisoner slowed down, a soldier would jump on the man's chest to force out the last drops. "They did not leave even one drop of blood in the body!" one Japanese veteran recollected.

With such extensive handling of pathogens there were likely to be accidents, and it is believed that hundreds of Japanese staff of Unit 731 died from the pathogens they handled. Despite this problem, Ishii's BW research empire spread, establishing 18 satellite stations in China and in other locations ranging from Hokkaido to the Dutch East Indies.

British, U.S., and Canadian Bioweapons Collaborations

Wendy Barnaby

The advent of World War II prompted Britain, Canada, and the United States to cooperate on developing bioweapons capacity. In the selection that follows, author Wendy Barnaby describes how Britain began research in 1936 at its chemical and biological research site called Porton Down. Canada launched its official bioweapons research program in 1940, after war had engulfed Europe, and the United States soon followed. Before long, Barnaby notes, the Canadians were outpacing the British. They focused on mixing infectious bacteria into sawdust, which could then be dropped by airplane over a target. In the same year, discussions about a bioweapons program had begun in the United States. American scientists considered many different approaches to biowarfare, including using disease to destroy the enemy's agriculture and livestock. After the United States entered the war in 1941, Canada offered it the use of an island on the Saint Lawrence Seaway, near Quebec City. Soon, all three allies were collaborating to produce anthrax bombs. This became the major focus of joint efforts, and by late 1944 U.S. facilities were preparing to turn out thousands of anthrax weapons a month. However, before a decision to deploy them could be made, the war came to an end. Even so, Barnaby notes, the bioweapons programs of all three nations continued for years afterward. Wendy Barnaby is a science writer and broadcaster based in the United Kingdom, where she regularly appears on the BBC.

Biological weapons research in the UK, US and Canada was intimately connected until well after the Second World War. The British were the first to start thinking about it. They were alarmed in 1943 by reports that the Germans were conducting their own BW research, and began to discuss the possibilities. Colonel Sir Maurice Hankey, Secretary of

Wendy Barnaby, *The Plague Makers: The Secret World of Biological Warfare*. New York, NY: Continuum, 2002. Copyright © 1999 by Wendy Barnaby. Reproduced by permission of The Continuum International Publishing Group.

the Committee for Imperial Defence (CID), was the moving force behind the initiative; and on 12 February 1934 he told a meeting of the Chiefs of Staff that he 'was wondering whether it might not be right to consider the possibilities and potentialities of this form of war'. Hankey was a humourless bureaucrat who was prepared to become deeply involved in promoting research into various forms of biological warfare even though he was convinced 'that we should under no circumstances initiate these forms of frightfulness.' He added: 'although the possibility of retaliation, e.g., under pressure of public demand, could not be excluded'. In November 1936 he chaired a new sub-committee of the CID, which was to 'report on the practicability of the introduction of biological warfare and to make recommendations as to the countermeasures which should be taken to deal with such an eventuality'.

Canada Gets Involved

Meanwhile, the Canadians' interest was awakening. John Bryden, whose book *Deadly Allies* traces the development of the Canadian biological and chemical programmes, speculates that they may have been stirred into action in 1936 by fascist Italy's use of mustard gas on civilians in its war in Abyssinia. This was chemical, rather than biological, warfare, but it would have had special resonance for the president of Canada's National Research Council, General Andrew McNaughton, who had seen gas attacks when he fought at Ypres in the First World War. In September 1937, he had a conversation with Sir Frederick Banting, the Nobel Prize-winning co-discoverer of insulin, in which they discussed the possibilities of BW. Banting had been a medical officer in the War, and was no stranger to the effects of gas. He pointed out that the development of the aeroplane had opened up new opportunities for spreading infection over open reservoirs. They started lobbying for Canada to begin its own research. In November 1939, Banting and a colleague were terrified during a wartime crossing of the Atlantic, on a visit designed to see what research the British were doing. Afraid of being sunk by submarines, Banting promised to tow his colleague, who could not swim, if they found themselves in the water. Their planned defence against their fear and the elements was deep talking to each other. The two men arrived safely, and went on to Porton Down.

Porton Down was the official site of the UK's research into chemical and biological warfare. These days its official remit restricts its energies to defensive research. Established in 1916, it covers 7,000 acres on the southern edge of Salisbury Plain, and boasts 'more species of butterflies than anywhere else in the United Kingdom' on its chalk grasslands. At the time of Banting's visit, the British, in spite of the aggressive-sounding remit of the official deliberations, felt no urgency about the sort of BW research he proposed. Their main worry reflected the concept, prevalent up to the War, that disease would most likely be caused by conventional bombing and its disruption of public health infrastructures. It may have been for this reason that the British had not considered much more than how vaccines could be made available to the population. Their sub-committee had meta-morphosed into the Emergency Public Health Laboratory Service (EPHLS): a title chosen especially by one of its members, Sir Edward Mellanby, as not being 'disturbing to the public mind'. Although war had been declared, Mellanby, who was then Secretary of the Medical Research Council, did not think the Germans would use biological weapons—except possibly foot and mouth disease against cattle—and told Banting that the Council would never do research in the area. Banting was so annoyed by the laid-back attitude of the British that when he was back home again, he described Hankey in his diary as 'a superb example of the servile, all-important complacent superior ass that runs the British government'.

First Experiments

In 1940 Banting applied for and was granted $25,000 for Canada's first officially-funded BW research. Based at the University of Toronto's Connaught Laboratories, it aimed to mix infectious bacteria with saw-dust and deliver them from an aeroplane. The project did get as far as a trial of dispersing different grades of sawdust from a plane over Balsam Lake, north-east of Toronto—chosen because one of the scientists involved had a cottage there. Banting was very enthusiastic about the experiment, but John Bryden sums it up by saying that it 'proved little more than that gravity works'. Nevertheless, in the months that fol-lowed, the government gave the go-ahead for a group to be created to produce bacteria, and so Banting had a series of consultations with Canadian scientists about how best to develop a capacity for biological warfare. Dr Donald Fraser at the Connaught experimented with typhoid but found it unsatisfactory, as although it could be dried on sawdust, it lost its virulence when reactivated. Fraser evidently found the agent that causes salmonella poisoning to be a better bet, and Bry-den describes his work as appearing to be 'the first-ever attempt among English-speaking nations to cultivate a bacterial agent specifically for use against humans'. At this stage, the Canadians were working on BW more aggressively than the British.

As far as the British effort went, Banting had been more persuasive than he realised. In 1940, Hankey agitated for the UK to begin practi-cal BW tests. The official history of Porton Down cites 'comnmnica-tions with Sir Frederick Banting of Canada' as one of the reasons for the UK's renewed vigour. Banting himself would have found that deeply satisfying, had he ever found out. In February 1941, wanting to see what progress the UK was making, he hitched a lift on a bomber flying to England. It crashed in Newfoundland and he was killed.

Hankey's efforts resulted in a secret group being set up at Porton in October 1940 to discover whether BW was feasible and how the country could retaliate. Mellanby found this development disturbing to his own mind and left the work to others: specifically to another Medical Research Council scientist, the eminent bacteriologist Dr Paul Fildes. From then on, the British BW effort intensified. The British were to make extensive use of Canadian help, especially with space for testing. In 1941, the Canadians made nearly one thousand square miles of semi-arid grassland in Alberta available for agent trials. . . .

Experiments in Britain

By the end of 1940, [British Scientist Paul Fildes] had determined the most effective way to wage [biological warfare]: to manufacture something like a bomb that would burst, spewing out an aerosol consisting of particles of just the right size to be taken up and held in the lung. The aerosol would contain bacteria. Anyone in the target area would inhale them in sufficient numbers to cause disease.

The two agents that interested Fildes most were anthrax bacteria and botulinum toxin. He and his small group—there were never more than about 45 of them—went on to expose laboratory animals to anthrax spores, and to determine how many spores they needed to inhale to kill them. They also did field tests to see what concentration of spores could be suspended in aerosol dispersed from bomblets and how far the resulting cloud would waft downwind. The Porton area was too small for them to use anthrax spores for these field tests—they could not risk killing the inhabitants of the surrounding villages—so they used a harmless sporing bacterium they isolated from hay at Porton, instead. This work occupied the group during 1941. And in December of that year, they asked Prime Minister Winston Churchill for permission to produce the West's first biological weapon.

Operation Vegetarian

Lord Hankey, who wrote the request to Churchill, decided that the only weapon that was technically feasible was one to kill cattle. It was a crude affair, and it was not meant to initiate biological warfare; but it would have provided an effective retaliation against Germany if the Germans had used BW against the British. Not that there was much reason, except mistrust, to think they would. However, the Chiefs of Staff gave the go-ahead for the project, and production began at Porton in the autumn of 1942.

'Operation Vegetarian' took the form of cattle cakes filled with anthrax. The idea was to drop them from planes over German agricultural districts, so that the cattle would die and the food supply would be disrupted. The cakes were made from finely ground linseed meal by a Bond Street soap maker and perfumer. They had a hollow well in the centre which, once they were delivered to Porton, was filled with anthrax spores before being sealed. The official accounts of this episode suggest its quaintness, its unlikeliness as a weapon of war; the whole process, once established, 'was essentially run by one technician . . .', ladies from a Bristol soap factory who were employed at Porton during the war for ad hoc small production jobs, one laboratory assistant, two labourers and 'one boy to assist'. And yet it was a large project. It is hard to see how, in view of it, the British representative could have told the 1969 United Nations General Assembly that '. . . as successive British governments have made very clear, we have never had any biological weapons . . .' Porton produced five million cakes, which were ready for use by April 1943.

They were never used. The stockpile was destroyed soon after the War except for a few kept until 1972 as memorabilia, when they were also destroyed. . . .

The US Program

Even before the US officially entered the War, the subject of biological warfare had been discussed. As early as September, 1940, the President of the Carnegie Institute—Dr Vannevar Bush—had suggested to Dr Weed of the medical committee of the US Council of National Defense that this committee was the proper place to consider 'offensive and defensive measures in the field of human, animal and plant diseases'. At a meeting between Canadian bacteriologists Professor E.G.D. Murray and Dr Guilford Reed, and US scientists, army and navy personnel in December 1941, in the Lord Baltimore Hotel, Baltimore, the scientists outlined the areas they were interested in pursuing. The list was long: botulinus toxin which could perhaps be used to poison water supplies; malaria, yellow fever, psittacosis, diphtheria, tetanus, salmonella and plague. The Americans had looked into the possibility of killing crop plants—potatoes, soybeans, rice, wheat—and had (like the Canadians) started experiments with toxic plant hormones. Against animals the group considered foot-and-mouth disease, pleuropneumonia, African horse sickness, glanders and anthrax. But it was rinderpest that was most worrying. It was seen as a real threat to North American cattle. It killed up to 80 per cent of the herds it infected, and at the time there was not much defence against it. The meeting agreed that research to combat it should have priority. A month later, Murray offered the Americans the perfect place to carry out rinderpest experiments. It was Grosse Ile, a small island in the St Lawrence, near Quebec City.

Grosse Ile had been used as a quarantine station for immigrants to Canada in the nineteenth century. Many of them had been Irish; twelve thousand had died there, of cholera. When the Canadians and Americans inspected the island in July 1942, they found the school house complete with desks and the Catholic and Protestant churches still with hymn books in the pews. The island, only two miles long and one mile wide, had other buildings which could easily be adapted for the scientists' purposes. Here they worked with their germs. The vaccine against rinderpest was achieved in 1945, but long before then the scientists became side-tracked into the allies' greatest collaborative project of the War: to produce anthrax bombs. In this, the British were the prime movers.

Joint Anthrax Bomb Effort

While the Canadians and Americans had been getting together, the British had been busy producing anthrax both for their cattle cakes and as the preferred option in an anti-personnel weapon. Not satisfied with dummy trials at Porton, they wanted to experiment with the real thing; and by the summer of 1942 they were ready. The site they chose was Gruinard Island, in Gruinard Bay on the West Coast of Scotland. The trials proved that biological warfare worked, and left the island so contaminated that it was not pronounced fit for habitation by man or beast until 1990.

Commentators on these events have presented the Gruinard trials as dangerous lunacy, on the one hand, or an example of the sober efficiency of government, on the other. What is clear is that Fildes and his team, having chosen anthrax partly because of the longevity of its virulence, had no idea, when they undertook the tests, how to clean up after them. in May 1943, Fildes told the Canadians and the Americans about the Gruinard trials and their results. Ten months later, Churchill, realising that the UK could not develop an anthrax bomb capability on its own, ordered half a million anthrax bombs 'as a first instalment' from the Americans. Designed by the British, made by the Americans and tested by the Canadians, the so-called 'N-bomb' project was meant to deliver cluster bombs containing 4-lb sub-munitions filled with anthrax spores. The three countries put their energies into an anthrax weapon that could be used against people. . . .

In fact, anthrax bombs were tested at Suffield, the huge Canadian testing ground in Alberta, before the end of the War. Grosse Ile did produce anthrax, but not in sufficient quantities to satisfy demand; and the Americans took over production in August 1944.

The Americans set up their own BW programme at Camp (later Fort) Detrick in Maryland, in April 1943. The previous May, President Roosevelt had approved research along the lines discussed at the Baltimore meeting in December, 1941, into offensive and defensive measures in the categories of botulinus toxin and diseases of man, animals, plants and food supplies. Work began at Camp Detrick on the cloud chamber project, which studied how animals became infected through breathing in germs. At the time, the mechanics of infection by inhalation had not been studied; and the project showed that this route could be used to spread disease. This in turn led on to the practicalities of how this could be done: studies of aerosols and how munitions could produce them.

Mass Production

The American BW programme was the largest. By the end of the War it employed nearly 4,000 military personnel and civilians. As well as Camp Detrick, work was carried out at the Granite Peak Installation in Utah, which from 1944 was used for field studies of living pathogens. Agents were produced at the Vigo plant at Terre Haute, Indiana. By November 1944, the Americans had produced the agents causing brucellosis, psittacosis, tularemia and glanders—as well as five anti-crop agents which were actually chemicals rather than biological weapons. But most work went into anthrax and botulism. By May 1944, the programme could produce 50,000 bombs a month—up to a quarter of a million by the end of that year—that could be filled with anthrax once it was itself produced. The bombs were to be shipped to Britain in case they were needed for use. In fact, the weapon was not ready before the end of the War.

It was just as well. The British had drawn up contingency plans to use anthrax bombs in reprisal on six German cities: Berlin, Hamburg, Stuttgart, Frankfurt, Wilhelmshafen and Aachen. They estimated that '50 per cent of the inhabitants who were exposed to the cloud of anthrax without respirators would be killed by inhalation, while many more might die through subsequent contamination of the skin . . . The terrain will be contaminated for years, and danger from skin infection should be great enough to enforce evacuation'. In a BBC television interview in 1981, the then Director of CDE Porton, Dr R.G.H. Watson, said that if those German cities had been bombed, they would very probably still be uninhabitable because of contamination. And he knew: it was CDE that was responsible for monitoring contamination on Gruinard.

As the War turned out, the Germans did not attack the British with biological weapons and the British did not retaliate with them. The fact that there was no biological warfare between these two countries, however, may have been more a matter of their state of preparedness than their unwillingness to use BW. Germany's V-bomb attacks on Britain in June 1944 enraged Churchill, who considered using both chemical and biological weapons in retaliation. . . .

Deployment Averted

With Churchill in aggressive mode and ethical considerations explicitly being ignored, the Chiefs of Staff recommended against anthrax—evidently because it was not available.

Had it been, would their decision have been different? Robert Kupperman, senior advisor to the Washington Center for Strategic and International Studies, and David Smith, a scientist at Los Alamos (where the atomic bomb was developed), are unequivocal: '. . . had World War Two not ended when it did, biological weapons would undoubtedly have been used.' Such judgements must be influenced by the way the Allies acted in similar situations. When, a year later, they saw another way of shortening the War, ethical considerations did not stop them dropping atomic bombs on Japan.

The 'frightfulness' of biological warfare that Lord Hankey abhorred had, by the end of the War, been thoroughly prepared for. Malcolm Dando, Professor of International Security at the University of Bradford, summarises Britain's BW programme by saying that it 'confirms high-level interest, the allocation of large-scale resources, a perception of biological warfare as a real possibility, the perceived vulnerability of Britain to strategic attack and, finally, the production of offensive biological weapons'. These factors apply equally to Canada and the United States. In all three countries, work continued after the War.

The BW programmes of the UK, Canada and the US followed different courses after the War. The UK abandoned its offensive research in 1957; by 1970, Canada was denying its wartime activities; and the US developed a large offensive programme before halting it in 1969.

COLD WAR BIOWEAPONS PROGRAMS AND THEIR LEGACY

Alexandra M. Lord

Widespread revulsion at the use of chemical weapons during World War I led to an international treaty in 1925 banning their use, along with the use of biological weapons. However, the Geneva Protocol, as the treaty was known, had an ironic effect, as historian Alexandra M. Lord describes in the next selection. It alerted governments and scientists in various countries to the potential uses of biological agents as weapons. Japan became the first country to make extensive use of bioweapons during World War II. In the Cold War that followed, the United States and the Soviet Union each acquired fearsome bioweapons capabilities. Lord notes that the 1949 Soviet test of a nuclear bomb convinced American planners that bioweapons were an essential part of U.S. defense. Both sides engaged in a rapid buildup of bioweapons capabilities. In 1969, President Nixon announced that the United States would end its bioweapons programs and dispose of existing stocks. In 1972 the international community developed a treaty banning chemical and biological weapons. Most nations, including the Soviet Union, signed the accord. However, the Soviets continued to build up their program, Lord writes, creating ever more deadly forms of anthrax, smallpox, and other agents, some of which may be in unknown hands today. Alexandra M. Lord is staff historian for the United States Public Health Service. She received her Ph.D. from the University of Wisconsin-Madison in 1995. That same year, she won an award from the American Association for the History of Medicine for an essay on menstruation in eighteenth-century British medical thought. She has since published numerous papers on the history of medicine and health.

Alexandra M. Lord, "A Brief History of Biowarfare," http://lhncbc.nlm.hih.gov, January 2002.

The Geneva Protocol of 1925 *did* prohibit the development and use of biological weapons—but no concentrated attempt to enforce or expand the treaty followed its ratification. As a result, nations continued to push the boundaries of biology.

While politicians dismissed the threat of bioweapons, scientists came to view this issue quite differently—as Shiro Ishii, the head of Japan's program, put it, those engaged in bioweapons research had the opportunity not only to search "for the truth in natural science" but also "to successfully build a powerful military weapon against" their nation's enemies. Not surprisingly, this dual appeal—both to patriotism and the scientist's desire to understand and control nature—meant that governments in the United Kingdom, Canada, France, Germany, the Soviet Union, Japan and the United States were able to recruit top-notch biologists for their bioweapons programs.

Among the most successful in creating and *using* bioweapons were the Japanese. Throughout the 1920s and 30s, Japan's program grew in both the number of its employees and the scope of its mission—while their success in weaponizing disease remained limited, the program's *potential* was unlimited. Few industrialized superpowers, however, saw the Japanese program as a threat—a response which enabled the Japanese to be surprisingly indiscreet. As late as 1939, the Japanese government openly attempted to buy yellow fever from the American government. The Americans refused the request. But even without yellow fever, scholars suspect that the Japanese killed thousands of Chinese using bioweapons; direct evidence indicates that hundreds of Chinese prisoners of war were killed in secret germ warfare tests. Although the United States did indict and convict Japanese doctors and nurses who performed medical experiments on American flyers, there was no attempt to try or even indict the scientists who lead Japan's biowarfare program.

Cold War Fuels U.S. Interest

This reluctance to prosecute the creators of the Japanese biowarfare program stemmed from two contradictory factors. First, although France, Canada, Great Britain and Japan had what one journalist calls "substantial [bioweapons] programs during World War II," the United States was not very enamored of bioweapons. True, an American biological weapons program had been launched in 1943 and American scientists had created and stockpiled thousands of anthrax bombs but success in weaponizing biological agents had been limited. Consequently, most American politicians and military personnel continued to regard biological weapons as highly impractical. Second, the few officials and scientists who believed that these weapons could pose a threat were reluctant to pursue Japanese scientists—because they themselves were actively and secretly engaged in expanding America's biological weapons program.

This expansion was linked to the emergence of the Cold War. The Soviet's detonation of a nuclear bomb in 1949 had heated tensions between the East and West and leveled the playing field between the USSR and America. As a result, American officials turned to even less conventional weapons—defense experts, scientists and top government officials now came to believe that biowarfare was, if not crucial to America's survival, central to its defense. And there was some rationale for these fears. Although few Americans knew it at the time Russians had launched a bioweapons program in 1928 and the program had grown substantially during World War II.

Soviets Gain Japanese Know-How

The Soviet program had benefitted tremendously from the capture of a Japanese germ unit during the war. When grafted onto the Soviet program, Japanese technology significantly advanced the Russians' understanding of biowarfare. In 1946, at Sverdlovsk, the first factory specializing in anthrax was built; a year later, a factory specializing in smallpox was also built. By 1956, biological warfare was seen as not only a necessity for the defense of the USSR but also an inevitable price for progress; that same year, [Soviet General] Georgi Zhukov told a Communist Party Congress that future wars would undoubtedly include the use of biological weapons.

Zhukov's views were shared by defense officials in America. In 1956, American spy planes took a series of revealing photographs. Deciphering and interpreting these photos proved to be extraordinarily simple. The "dense clusters of buildings and odd geometric grids" which CIA analysts saw on photos taken of a Russian island were eerily similar to aerial photographs of the Utah desert—where America had set up its own biowarfare unit.

Like the Soviets, the Americans had launched their program in the wake of World War II and like the Soviets, the Americans had myriad reasons for embracing biowarfare. As viewed from the perspective of 1945, biological warfare, had several benefits. To begin with, it was incredibly cheap. Unlike the Manhattan Project [the secret program to develop the atom bomb], biowarfare programs required little or no investment in exotic or expensive equipment or ingredients. Additionally, biowarfare programs could be easily created and maintained in secrecy (buying pathogens on the open market has always been very easy to do). And finally, for most defense experts reviewing the history of the twentieth century, biological warfare may have seemed to be the wave of the future. Certainly, if one was to judge by the past and to think in the context of what was rapidly coming to be characterized as the ABCs of war (atomic, biological and chemical), then it was clear that World War III would be a biological war (World War I was a chemical war and World War II an atomic war). Indeed, many scientists and defense analysts argued, the threat posed by biological warfare was such that America should begin to prepare itself—both by creating a system of defense against these weapons as well as by building a program which could compete with America's enemies.

America's biowarfare program emerged, then, as a reaction to the excesses of World War II and the implicit threat posed by the Cold War. In 1944, an extensive base was built at Fort Detrick, Maryland—although testing and experiments would always be done at a variety of different locations. Fort Detrick boasted the program's "Special Projects School" which sought to provide students with "an understanding of the known technical facts and potentialities of germ warfare." Under the direction of Ira Baldwin, Fort Detrick grew rapidly between 1943 and 1945. The end of the war caused only a slight hiccup in this expansion, with programs and funding being temporarily cut. By 1946, American officials were prepared not only to continue the nation's biowarfare program but also to increase its budget and expand its range.

Korean War Adds Impetus

The start of the Korean War in 1950 further hastened this expansion with several buildings being constructed at Fort Detrick. The first of these—a massive metal sphere four stories high—was "a captive atmosphere" which could be adjusted to replicate anything from a tropical region to a desert. The "8 Ball" as it was called allowed scientists to test biological agents on animal subjects while minimizing the scientist's exposure to the agent. While the "8-Ball" was central to the program, the construction of an anthrax factory at Fort Detrick was also regarded as crucial. Along with this building program, scientists also assessed the nation's vulnerability to biowarfare attacks—they sprayed germs in San Francisco, shattered lightbulbs filled with biological agents in the New York City subway and even sprayed bacteria into the vents of the Pentagon air-conditioning system. Although Fort Detrick's experts believed that the germs which they used were harmless, later critics claimed that their actions released hidden epidemics and resulted in at least one death.

Not all was doom and gloom for the biowarriors, however. A new agency, the CDC (or Communicable Diseases Center as it was called then) became a prime beneficiary of the biological warfare program. In 1950, Alexander Langmuir, a member of the United States Public Health Service who had been assigned to the CDC, "developed a three point-plan for guarding [the nation's] health during the Cold War: research on airborne infections, development of an epidemic intelligence service and training in biological-warfare defense" [according to scholar Elizabeth Etheridge]. The primary task of the Epidemic Intelligence Service was the "detect[ion] of masked biological-warfare attacks," [writes Etheridge]; and under Langmuir's guidance, the CDC aggressively moved to create "more effective sampling methods to detect biological warfare agents . . . [to] employ faster reporting of disease incidence, upgrade laboratory facilities, and [provide] more extensive immunization programs and better investigations of all outbreaks of disease" [note scholars Elizabeth Fee and Theodore M. Brown]. In short, Langmuir's blueprint for biodefense became the blueprint for the CDC itself. But the CDC's emphasis on biopreparedness was, some historians have argued, short-sighted—"at the same time that funding for [and concern about] biological warfare research was increasing . . . funds for local health departments were cut sharply" [state Fee and Brown]. In other words, the nation's emphasis on "induced" epidemics may have lead epidemiolgists and scientists to ignore "natural" epidemics and existing public health problems.

For American biowarrriors, the Korean War provided a payoff. Accusations that America used bioweapons during the Korean War were made in 1952 and although the United States successfully refuted these accusations, "a cloud of suspicion" lingered. There is still some question today as to whether the United States did or did not use bioweapons during the war. During the 1960s, however, the CIA and the US military *did* attempt to use bioweapons against specific dictators; the most well-known of these attempts were staged against [Cuban dictator] Fidel Castro but attempts were also made against Patrice Lumumba, the Congo's first prime minister after independence. Tests were also run in Utah, Alaska, and the South Pacific— some of these tests used human subjects but most did not. By the end of the decade, bioweapons had become an established aspect of the American defense program and scientists at Fort Detrick had stockpiled an astonishing array of biological agents.

Nixon Halts Bioweapons Programs

In 1969, as the nation's stockpile continued to rise and as scientists pushed the boundaries of biology even further, then-president Richard Nixon suddenly announced that he had "ordered the Defense Department to make recommendations about the disposal . . . of bacteriological weapons." Arguing that "mankind already carries in its hands too many of the seeds of its own destruction," Nixon called for an end to research on biological weapons. It is unclear why Nixon decided to end the nation's bioweapons program but end the program did—over a period of three years, "death came to the nation's supplies of offensive weapons."

As the American bioweapons program was dismantled, the Soviet Union, Britain, Canada and the United States signed a new biological weapons treaty. The BWC (Biological Weapons Convention) of 1972 was ultimately signed by seventy-nine nations—the treaty called for the destruction of existing stocks of bioweapons as well as an end to biological weapons research. On paper, it looked as though the world would now be safe from biological weapons.

But this was true only on paper. Despite signing the treaty, the Russians continued their program. In fact, some scientists and historians have alleged that the USSR saw the BWC treaty as an opportunity to advance their program secretly—as the United States pulled out of the bioweapons game. And there would seem to be evidence to support this claim. In 1973, only a year after signing the BWC, the Soviets created a massive bioweapons program controlled by two entities, the Ministry of Defense and an agency called "Biopreparat" which was in the Ministry of Medical and Microbiological Industry. Officially, Biopreparat was a state-owned pharmaceutical company but "in reality it was an elaborate front for a military-funded program . . . which aimed to develop a new generation of super lethal biological weapons." Throughout the 1970s and 1980s, Biopreparat was one of the USSR's most closely guarded secrets—only a handful of top Soviet officials knew of its existence and it would not be until the break-up of the Soviet Union that American defense experts would discover the program.

Soviet Program Swells

At its peak, the Soviet bioweapons program employed 60,000 people at more than a hundred facilities in eight different Soviet cities; it stockpiled thousands of anthrax, plague and smallpox bombs, and it had an annual budget of close to a billion dollars. The most chilling aspect of this massive program was not its reliance on traditional bioweapons—but rather its development of "improved" biological agents. Using gene manipulation, the Soviets created both a highly lethal form of anthrax (against which vaccines were ineffective) as well as "improvements" on smallpox.

The latter "supergerm" was—and still is—an issue of great concern. Smallpox is a viral infection with no known treatment or cure. There are two forms of the disease—*variola major* and *variola minor*. Both forms can be fatal and throughout history, smallpox has been one of the greatest killers. The disease is highly infectious, with most of its victims becoming infected by inhaling the virus when in close contact with an infected person. The disease can also be acquired through contact with the corpse of a smallpox victim or even articles belonging to a smallpox patient. In the seventeenth century, smallpox was endemic in Asia, Africa and Europe—in other words, smallpox was omnipresent in these regions, passing from one person to another and erupting into a full-blown epidemic every ten or so years. To become an epidemic, smallpox needed a large population which was susceptible. However, once a person contracted smallpox, he or she became immune to the disease. So in Europe, Africa and Asia, significant proportions of the population were exposed to the disease as children; if they survived (which was more likely than not), they were then immune. The greater the immune population, the more difficult it was for the disease to spread.

Before 1750, medical practitioners had two methods for dealing with smallpox. The first of these was quarantining—this was fairly effective as a method of containment but obviously it was not perfect. The second of these techniques was variolation—here a healthy person was deliberately infected with smallpox—the case which developed was usually mild and the person generally recovered and was then immune. Variolation occasionally resulted in the death of the patient and, for this reason, it was regarded as problematic. In 1796, an English physician, Edward Jenner, discovered that sufferers of cowpox became immune to smallpox. Vaccination—or the deliberate infection of a patient with cowpox—then replaced variolation—the deliberate infection of an individual with smallpox—as the preferred method of dealing with smallpox. Throughout the nineteenth century, growing numbers of people were vaccinated against smallpox and the disease become less common. By the 1950s, smallpox was to be found in only a few regions of the world. The growth of airline travel as well as other global networks meant, however, that smallpox could easily spread from Africa to New York—as a result, public health officials saw smallpox as an issue of concern, regardless of where they lived. In 1958, a Soviet Minister of Health, Viktor Zhdanov began to advocate a world-wide campaign to eradicate smallpox through a massive vaccination campaign. In 1967, the campaign was officially launched; ten years later the last case of naturally occurring smallpox was recorded in Somalia. Officially, smallpox had been eradicated.

Greater Vulnerability to Smallpox

But the eradication of smallpox has raised new problems. If we build on the supposition that "the more diseased a community the less destructive its epidemics become" then the opposite is true—the less diseased a community is the more dangerous its epidemics become. And this is true with smallpox. Lacking the immunity of our ancestors and the immunity conferred by vaccination, we are now highly susceptible. But smallpox has been eradicated so we are all safe. Or are we? In 1980, the World Health Organization ordered "all institutions maintaining stocks of variola virus to destroy or transfer these stocks to WHO . . . centers." Officially, there were to be only two repositories for smallpox: the CDC in Atlanta and Russian State Research Center of Virology and Biotechnology in Koltsovo. In 1992, however, a high-ranking Soviet biologist, Kanatjan Alibekov defected to the United States. Over the course of a year-long debriefing, Alibekov informed horrified CIA officers that the USSR had grown and stored twenty tons of variola virus. It has been suggested that this stockpile was destroyed in the late 1980s but as a former Russian scientist told an American weapons inspector, "there were plenty of opportunities for staff members to walk away with an ampule [of virus and] although we think we know where our formerly employed scientists are we can't account for all of them." Although the Soviet Union and its bioweapons program no longer exist, their legacy in the form of smallpox bioweapons may have been sold to another nation or terrorist organization.

Soviet Anthrax

But this is not the only legacy of the Soviet bioweapons program. Although smallpox is the ideal biological weapon, the Soviets also developed anthrax. This work with anthrax became evident early on when an anthrax outbreak occurred in Sverdlovsk in 1979. Soviet officials at first denied the outbreak and, then, when forced to concede its existence, maintained that the outbreak had been caused by tainted meat and that the death toll was limited to 100. Soviet dissidents claimed otherwise, insisting that the outbreak resulted in about a thousand deaths and that the source of the infection was the release of agent from a secret military complex. American intelligence analysts agreed. The number of dead as well as the exact cause of the outbreak continue to be disputed (all records relating to this incident were destroyed in 1990). However, there is clear evidence that the Soviets were working with anthrax and that they stockpiled the anthrax bacillus. Again, the exact amounts of bacillus which were stockpiled is unknown as is the exact whereabouts of this agent.

The break-up of the Soviet Union has meant the break-up of the Soviet bioweapons program. Today, the Soviet's elaborate program and the buildings which harbored it are in decay. Soviet biowarriors, the former elite of Russian society are unemployed and stocks of bioweapons are poorly guarded and poorly stored. In the late 1990s as the Clinton Administration became aware of these problems, the United States moved to secure the program by providing money to salvage and convert its facilities as well as discourage the sale of bioweapons knowledge to rogue states. However, this program has received only sporadic funding and the fate of the Russian program is still uncertain.

CHAPTER 2

TYPES OF BIOWEAPONS

An Overview of Weapons-Ready Pathogens

Colleen M. Davenport

Many kinds of living agents are used to create bioweapons. In the selection that follows, Colleen M. Davenport offers a brief overview of the major plants, bacteria, and viruses that have been or potentially may be used as bioweapons. Davenport observes that bioweapons, whether deployed by a nation or a rogue group, have the potential to devastate both human populations and agriculture. She notes that the Centers for Disease Control have classified biological agents according to their level of threat and offers a thumbnail description of the most threatening instances of Class A and B agents. In response to the 2001 anthrax attacks, the U.S. Food and Drug Administration and the pharmaceutical industry have agreed to work together to address the threat of future bioweapons attacks by developing new vaccines and treatments. Colleen M. Davenport is a researcher for the pharmaceutical firm GlaxoSmithKline. She is based at its facility in King of Prussia, Pennsylvania.

We will all remember the events of September 11th [2001] with extreme clarity and emotion. The horror of the actual events and the uncertainty of further terrorist acts altered the way Americans and others worldwide view public safety. FDA [Food and Drug Administration] is responsible for the protection of the nation's food supply, blood supply, medical devices, safety and efficacy of drugs, vaccines, cosmetics, veterinary food and drug supplies, radiological diagnostic devices, and microwaves. FDA, as well as other government, academic, and industrial organizations, will play a critical role in dealing with the increasing threat of bioterrorism and/or biowarfare.

Regardless of whether the assault is state-sponsored (biowarfare) or nonstate sponsored (bioterrorism), deliberate transmission of naturally occurring or bioengineered pathogens has the potential to kill or disable the human population, as well as agricultural plants and ani-

Colleen M. Davenport, "A Primer on Bioterrorism: Potential Pathogens, Roles of United States Governmental Agencies, and Regulatory Models for Product Development," *Drug Information Journal*, vol. 37, January 1, 2003. Copyright © 2003 by Drug Information Association. Reproduced by permission.

mals. Unlike more traditional military assault with conventional weapons, chemical weapons, or nuclear weapons, bioterrorism may go undetected and eventually infect many more individuals than those exposed in the initial attack. Globalization and ease of travel put the entire population at risk until more effective surveillance, detection, and treatment measures can be put into place. Success will require the cooperation of many types of professions and groups to ensure the development of emergency response plans; increased scientific expertise for effective monitoring, treatment, and decontamination procedures; and development of drugs and devices that diagnose or treat pathogens used in bioterrorist attacks.

This review will focus on the types of organisms that can potentially be used in bioterrorism, the current government agencies and initiatives in the United States that focus on bioterrorism, and the specific role that FDA and the regulatory affairs professional can play in developing effective policy and the necessary medical technology required to protect the population.

Categories of Threats

The Centers for Disease Control and Prevention (CDC) has classified 'Select agents' by risk as defined by the individual hazard and potential exposure in a bioterrorist attack. Category A agents are believed to be of the greatest risk due to the severity of disease (they cause high mortality) and because such agents are easily transmitted through the population. Category B agents are believed to have a reduced risk due to lower mortality rates and moderate morbidity. Agents in category B are still easy to transmit from person to person. Category C agents include emerging threats that may be further engineered for mass dissemination and have the potential for both high mortality and morbidity rates. Current research efforts are focused on the category A agents while governmental policy restricts the transport of all 'select agents.'

Class A: Anthrax. Anthrax is caused by the spore forming organism *Bacillus anthracis*, which tends to mostly infect hoofed mammals but may also be transmitted to humans. Symptoms of inhalational anthrax occur within seven days after exposure, and may initially resemble the common cold but if untreated can quickly result in severe difficulty of breathing and shock. Fortunately, early initiation of penicillin, doxycycline, or fluoroquinolones is usually effective in preventing postexposure inhalational anthrax. Treatment of established inhalational anthrax is more challenging and the infection has a high mortality rate. Controlled trials have obviously not been conducted in humans, but data from guinea pigs and monkeys suggest that [antibiotics] doxycycline and ciprofloxacin have both prophylactic and curative effects if treatment is promptly administered. . . .

Class A: Botulism. Botulism results from either inhalation or ingestion of the toxin produced by *Clostridium bolulinum* and thus, is not treatable with antibiotics. An equine antitoxin containing antibodies specific for the A, B, and E toxin types has been useful in reducing the severity of symptoms if administered soon after development of symptoms. Luckily, most patients recover on their own with several weeks to months of supportive care because the supply of antitoxin is limited.

Class A: Bubonic Plague. Yersinia pestis is found in rodents and fleas throughout the world. Pneumonic plague results when the organism infects the lungs, resulting in fever, headache, weakness, cough, and potential shock. *Yersinia pestis* is a communicable disease in which face-to-face contact can result in transmission of disease with a one-to-four-day incubation period. Fortunately, pneumonic plague is treatable with streptomycin, tetracycline, and chloramphenicol. Published clinical trials evaluating the safety and efficacy of various treatments do not exist and animal data are also limited. Genetic engineering could result in the development of mutidrug resistant strains, leaving the population at even greater risk to possible terrorist acts.

Class A: Smallpox. Smallpox infection is caused by *Variola major* [virus] and has been eliminated from the world as a naturally occurring disease since 1977. Because of this, most of the world population is either immunologically naive or has reduced protection from vaccines given decades ago. It is known that the smallpox virus was mass produced in the Soviet Union in the 1970s for use as a bioweapon and it is possible that some of this stock could fall into the hands of bioterrorists.

The incubation period is between 7 and 17 days and onset of disease is characterized by high fever, fatigue, headache, and backache. Disease progresses into a rash initially with flat lesions that eventually become pus filled. By the second week the lesions crust over. Death can occur in up to 30% of cases. . . .

Class A: Tularemia. Tularemia is a respiratory infection caused by *Francisella tularensis.* Person-to-person contact has not been documented, but as few as 10 to 50 organisms can result in disease after a one- to five-day incubation period. Symptoms of inhalation Tularemia include fever, weakness, weight loss, and respiratory complications. Streptomycin, gentamicin, tetracyclines, and chloramphenicol have all successfully been used to treat Tularemia. Tetracyclines and chloramphenicol are associated with a higher relapse rate than Streptomycin or gentamicin. Unfortunately, each of these drugs has significant safety limitation and cannot be used in the full range of patient populations (eg. pediatric patients, pregnant women).

Class A: Viral Hemorrhagic Fever. Four different families of viruses can lead to development of viral hemorrhagic fever (VHF) including arena viruses (Lassa fever, Argentine hemorrhagic fever), filoviruses (Ebola and Marburg), bunya-viruses (Crimean-Congo, hantavirus), and flaviviruses (dengue). Both Lassa fever and Crimean-Congo Hemorrhagic fever are communicable and present with fever, myalagia, exhaustion, shock, and systemic bleeding at the mucus membranes. Ribavirin, an anti-viral drug, has met with some success in treating these two types of VHF.

Class B Agents

Class B: Q Fever. Q fever is caused by *Coxiella burnetti,* which normally infects animals but can be transmitted to humans. Exposure leads to symptoms typically occurring within 2 to 14 days and including headache, malaise, fever, night sweats, cough, and pneumonia. Up to 50% of people may be asymptomatic. Other patients may not show signs of disease for an extended time and then present with a chronic form of disease which may manifest as endocarditis. As a biologic weapon, it is thought that Q fever would result in low mortality but high morbidity. Doxycycline, erythromycin, clarithromycin, quinolones, and chloramphenicol have all been used to treat Q fever.

Class B: Glanders and Melioidosis. Glanders is caused by *Burkholderia mallei* and Melioidosis is caused by *Burkholderia pseudomallei.* The most likely route of exposure in the case of biologic warfare is believed to be via inhalation and it is thought that the risk of person-to-person transmission would be low. After an incubation period of 10 to 14 days, patients develop acute pneumonia and sepsis and may die without treatment. Ceftazidime, imipenem, meropenem, and doxycycline are believed to be effective based on in vitro data. . . .

Industry's Role

The pharmaceutical industry will play a key role in countering bioterrorism. FDA and pharmaceutical companies have stated their desire to work in a constructive manner with a sense of urgency to facilitate discovery, development, and registration of products for bioterrorism indications. For example, [anthrax vaccine producer] BioPort provided FDA with license supplements, which were quickly reviewed. FDA determined that the renovated facilities at BioPort were able to produce Anthrax Vaccine Adsorbed (AVA) meeting FDA standards of safety and efficacy and thus, approved the application for AVA in January 2002.

The development of new drugs and vaccines is scientifically challenging, time-consuming, and expensive. An orphan drug program was initiated in the 1980s to provide financial incentives for development of drugs, biologies, or antibiotics that treat rare diseases. Certain agents of bioterrorism might fall within this orphan grants program. Alternatively, the government could contract with pharmaceutical companies to provide a certain quantity of drug to be stockpiled as part of the National Phramaceutical Stockpile. Collaborations between academia and industry might also lead to development of new pharmaceuticals for the treatment of bioterrorist agents. Increased funding is available to support reasearch related to increasing the understanding of the pathogenesis of such bioterrorist agents. Academics might be able to work together with government agencies and industry, which have the actual drug development experience, to come up with some solutions. The Bioterrorism Bill that was passed in December 2001 provides incentives for government and industry to collaborate on the development of new approved counterterrorism products. . . .

Government, academic, industrial, and medical groups have worked quickly to respond to the horrific events of September 11th and the increased risk of bioterrorism. Numerous agencies and plans currently exist that will be called upon in the event of an attack. State and local medical resources have been bolstered and additional federal resources have been developed that would deal with the unique demands associated with a bioterrorist attack.

However, much remains to be done. FDA is working with industry so that additional vaccines and drugs will be available to counter bioterrorism, without compromising FDA's standards for safety and efficacy. New regulatory models will need to be constructed that can deal with some of the unique aspects of developing pharmaceuticals to combat bioterrorist agents. Such models can be built upon some existing strategies including the IND,[1] "animal rule," and orphan drug program. Together, the nation will fight what has been long recognized as one of the deadliest enemies of people—disease—which is now potentially in the hands of terrorists.

1. "Investigational New Drugs" which the FDA can make available without the usual rigorous safety and efficacy testing

ANTHRAX

Sallie Baliunas

Before September 2001, for many Americans "Anthrax" was just the name of a heavy metal band. By the end of that month it had gained a fearsome reputation as a deadly bioweapon. A spate of letters containing anthrax powder sickened more than twenty people and killed five. According to Sallie Baliunas, whose article is reproduced below, anthrax has been sowing terror throughout human history. The durable and deadly bacterium may have been responsible, she says, for two of the biblical plagues on Egypt. The symptoms described in the Book of Exodus, she asserts, match up with cutaneous anthrax infection. This skin-invasive form of the disease is just one of the several ways that anthrax attacks. The deadliest is pulmonary, or inhalational, infection. When powder containing anthrax spores reaches the lungs, the spores—a hardened version of the bacterium—revert to active form, releasing a deadly toxin. Because the spores are very difficult to kill, anthrax makes a stable bioweapon. Fortunately, Baliunas writes, the disease is not contagious. It can be prevented by vaccine and cured by antibiotics if the infection is caught early. Nevertheless, anthrax remains a serious threat because the vaccine is not yet available for general administration to the public and rapid diagnosis of anthrax infection can be tricky. Sallie Baliunas is an astrophysicist at the Harvard-Smithsonian Center for Astrophysics and serves as senior scientist at the George C. Marshall Institute in Washington, DC. In 1991 *Discover* magazine profiled her as one of America's outstanding women scientists. She has written more than 200 scientific research articles.

On June 8, 2001, President George W. Bush called for remediation of the threat of biological warfare because it is one of the "true threats of the 21st century." His words proved prescient, as by September [2001]

Sallie Baliunas, "Anthrax: A Threat Nearly as Old as Mankind," www.objective science.com, December 1, 2001. Copyright © 2001 by Tech Central Station. Reproduced by permission.

this nation suffered the world's first bioattack of the 21st century with anthrax.[1]

As investigators scratch for leads as to the source of strains of anthrax and the perpetrators of bioassaults taking the lives of people as divergent as a Florida reporter, Washington postal workers and a grandmother in Connecticut, they are dealing with a threat nearly as old as mankind.

Anthrax as a weapon of terror may have roots reaching back to two plagues that visited Biblical Egypt. In Exodus Chapter 9, one of those plagues was described as a "very rare pestilence" on sheep, cattle, camels and oxen. For the next plague, Moses was directed to toss ashes on the wind, which "will become fine dust" that attacks both "man and beast" with boils and pustules. The stated rarity, association with grazing animals, dissemination by motes of dust or ashes and appearance of boils suggest anthrax, a bacterial disease.

The symptom of skin lesions described in Exodus may have been the less deadly cutaneous form of anthrax. It infects the body through the skin, one of three forms since identified by science for anthrax disease. Inhalation, or pulmonary, anthrax that enters through the lungs, is the cause of the six deaths in this country since Sept. 11. Its lethality and difficulty to cure make it a potent bioweapon.

A Rod-Shaped Bacterium

The source for all anthrax infections is a common bacterium, Bacillus anthracis. Bacteria fall generally among one of three classes by shape: sphere (coccus), spiral (spirillum) and rod (bacillus). So, anthrax is rod shaped. It is relatively large as bacterial sizes go—as big as 2 by 10 microns, or roughly one by five ten-thousandths of an inch.

Not all bacteria are deadly. They often survive by living off host organisms, even benefiting their hosts. Of the rod-shaped species, many are harmless; in contrast, anthracis is lethal, especially when inhaled. And because it causes disease, that makes anthracis a pathogen.

Pathogens that kill their host often survive because they can move to other hosts as they come in contact with them. Spores need to directly invade each victim. Anthrax bacilli normally attack herbivores such as sheep, horses, goats and cattle, and when an infected animals dies, the bacilli escape the carcass to form spores that guard their genetic code or DNA with an exceptionally durable capsule. Effectively protected against deterioration in the environment, the spores of anthrax bacilli can persist decades. They can contaminate soil and infect new hosts, primarily the herbivores. Insects that feed on live infected animals or vultures that consume carcasses also can spread the spores.

But while anthrax is not contagious from person to person, its pulmonary form is particularly virulent. Once inhaled, spores move fast

1. As of mid 2005, the mail-borne anthrax attacks remained unsolved.

from the lungs to the lymph nodes near the heart and major blood vessels. The entering spores, viewed by the host as an invasion by a foreign body, trigger a counterattack by one of the human body's remarkable defense systems, the white blood cells. They ingest and attempt to digest the spores to destroy them. But encased in their protective coats, the tough spores may survive, and then scavenge metabolic material from the white blood cells in order to reproduce. Within a day or days, newly made anthrax bacilli burst from the white blood cells, hungering for more host cells and discharging toxins. Those toxins are extremely potent, destroying surrounding body tissue and rapidly overwhelming the host with blood poisoning, organ failure and death.

Invention of Anthrax Vaccine

Ironically, for all the devastation anthrax can sow, the study of anthrax itself led to a tremendous advance in conquering many horrific infectious diseases.

The great chemist Louis Pasteur in the mid-19th century founded the theory that microorganisms, or "germs" were microscopic agents of infectious disease. Other of Pasteur's great accomplishments include the development of the pasteurization process to keep milk supplies safe, discovery of the agent of silk worm disease, and creation of a vaccine successful in preventing hydrophobia, or rabies.

With germ theory gaining consideration as a cause of infectious disease, Robert Koch in 1876 proved that bacillus anthracis is the bacterium that produces anthrax. Pasteur then not only confirmed the bacillus as the germ responsible for anthrax, but also worked to reduce the bacteria to a less potent state. The weakened, or "attenuated" form of the bacillus was employed as a vaccine that, when injected into potential animal hosts, tries to stimulate the body's immune system to recognize and defend against a future invasion by the bacillus. The early anthrax vaccinations were of limited success, in part because of anthrax's virulence. Yet, astonishing success against other diseases derived from Pasteur's study of the technique of vaccination and germ theory.

Vaccination has vanquished many infectious diseases and so lengthened the human life span. But even as the anthrax vaccine to prevent infection has improved, it is not yet ready for widespread inoculation of the population. That leaves treatment after exposure, when antibiotics are given to attack the bacilli created in the host. Because the bacilli reproduce rapidly, antibiotic therapy must ideally begin just after exposure—often a fact difficult to assess. The race to kill the bacilli before they massively reproduce is crucial in surviving anthrax because of the toxin's lethality.

The Allure of Bioterror

The lethality—coupled with the hardiness and persistence—of bioterror agents such as anthrax that has prompted governments to fear for civilian safety and establish something of a breakwater against their widespread use.

President Lincoln, during the Civil War, was among the first leaders to direct troops to spare or protect civilians and civilian institutions when possible. His "General Orders 100" for Federal Troops became a building block for codes of conduct developed at international conferences at The Hague in the Netherlands in 1899 and 1907. Among atrocities prohibited by codes written there were the use of poison gas or other poison during warfare.

Yet, just as General William Tecumseh Sherman destroyed civilian property in his race to the sea during the Civil War, combatants in World War I, including the United States, used murderous chemical agents like chlorine, mustard gas or phosgene despite international pressure.

And subsequent agreements, such as the 1975 Biological and Toxin Weapons Convention, signed by almost every nation and forbidding developing or stockpiling biological agents for other than peaceful purposes, have not eliminated bio or chemical weapons as a threat.

Soviet Anthrax Catastrophe

The Soviet Union, despite signing the 1975 convention, appears to have disobeyed it with tragic consequences for their own people. Tantalized by its potential to provide a strategic advantage, the Soviet escalated bio-weapon development, leading in 1979 to the accidental release of anthrax from a lab in Yekaterinburg at Sverdlovsk. The plume of vapor released in that accident killed at least 66 people.

It was from that event that the incubation period for the disease was estimated to be as long as 43 days after exposure, leading to current prophylactic treatment by antibiotics for 60 days.

As America has learned, though, the anthrax threat must be fought at many levels. One way is to try to prevent terrorists from getting the spores. Equally important is to enhance protection and survival should anthracis's deadly spores be criminally dispersed. That includes techniques to sterilize, e.g., by irradiation, contaminated environments. As biology enters the post-genome era, hope brims from scientists' drawing boards sketched with ideas of futuristic vaccines and antibiotics to diminish anthrax's lethality.

But because it is the toxin that causes death, technological efforts to weaken the toxin would improve chances for survival as antibiotics work to eradicate the invading bacillus from the host. Researchers at Harvard, for example, are developing a synthetic chemical that may decrease the virulence of the toxin. Other researchers are studying the toxin through genetic modification.

The struggle with biological agents is nearly as old as civilization itself. And in the hands of terrorists or rogue states, as President Bush noted, bioweapons pose a threat to civilization.

SMALLPOX

Donald A. Henderson et al.

Smallpox is among the world's most feared diseases. Before its eradication in 1977, it had caused some 300 million deaths in the twentieth century alone. The following selection presents excerpts from a report by a "working group" of expert physicians and researchers. The American Medical Association convened the group to assess the threat of smallpox as a bioweapon. Despite eradication in the wild, the possibility of smallpox reemerging in weaponized form remains, the authors write, because two stocks of smallpox were preserved—one in Atlanta, the other in Moscow. They discuss concerns that weaponized Russian smallpox could be acquired by terrorists. A single case of smallpox, the authors state, would be an international emergency, because vaccination ceased decades ago and the disease is highly contagious. Since there is no effective treatment for smallpox, they recommend preparing large stocks of vaccine. Since the publication of this report in 1999, the United States has built up its smallpox vaccine reserves. Donald A. Henderson, leader of the global smallpox eradication campaign, is recognized as one of the world's chief authorities on the disease. In 2001, he became the first director of the U.S. Office of Public Health Preparedness. Fourteen other experts joined him in writing this report.

If used as a biological weapon, smallpox represents a serious threat to civilian populations because of its case-fatality rate of 30% or more among unvaccinated persons and the absence of specific therapy. Although smallpox has long been feared as the most devastating of all infectious diseases, its potential for devastation today is far greater than at any previous time. Routine vaccination throughout the United States ceased more than 25 years ago. In a now highly susceptible, mobile population, smallpox would be able to spread widely and rapidly throughout this country and the world.

Smallpox probably was first used as biological weapon during the

Donald A. Henderson et al., "Smallpox as a Biological Weapon," *Journal of the American Medical Association*, vol. 281, June 9, 1999, pp. 2,127–2,137. Copyright © 1999 by The American Medical Association. All rights reserved. Reproduced by permission.

French and Indian Wars (1754–1767) by British forces in North America. Soldiers distributed blankets that had been used by smallpox patients with the intent of initiating outbreaks among American Indians. Epidemics occurred, killing more than 50% of many affected tribes. With Edward Jenner's demonstration in 1796 that an infection caused by cowpox protected against smallpox and the rapid diffusion worldwide of the practice of cowpox inoculation (ie, vaccination), the potential threat of smallpox as a bioweapon was greatly diminished.

A global campaign, begun in 1967 under the aegis of the World Health Organization (WHO), succeeded in eradicating smallpox in 1977. In 1980, the World Health Assembly recommended that all countries cease vaccinations. A WHO expert committee recommended that all laboratories destroy their stocks of variola virus or transfer them to 1 of 2 WHO reference laboratories—the Institute of Virus Preparations in Moscow, Russia, or the Centers for Disease Control and Prevention (CDC) in Atlanta, Ga. All countries reported compliance. . . .

Recent allegations from Ken Alibek, a former deputy director of the Soviet Union's civilian bioweapons program, have heightened concern that smallpox might be used as a bioweapon. Alibek reported that beginning in 1980, the Soviet government embarked on a successful program to produce the smallpox virus in large quantities and adapt it for use in bombs and intercontinental ballistic missiles; the program had an industrial capacity capable of producing many tons of smallpox virus annually. Furthermore, Alibek reports that Russia even now has a research program that seeks to produce more virulent and contagious recombinant strains. Because financial support for laboratories in Russia has sharply declined in recent years, there are increasing concerns that existing expertise and equipment might fall into non-Russian hands.

Horrifying Potential

The deliberate reintroduction of smallpox as an epidemic disease would be an international crime of unprecedented proportions, but it is now regarded as a possibility. An aerosol release of variola virus would disseminate widely, given the considerable stability of the orthopoxviruses in aerosol form and the likelihood that the infectious dose is very small. Moreover, during the 1960s and 1970s in Europe, when smallpox was imported during the December to April period of high transmission, as many as 10 to 20 second-generation cases were often infected from a single case. Widespread concern and, sometimes, panic occurred, even with outbreaks of fewer than 100 cases, resulting in extensive emergency control measures.

Smallpox was once worldwide in scope, and before vaccination was practiced, almost everyone eventually contracted the disease. There were 2 principal forms of the disease, variola major and a much milder form, variola minor (or alastrim). . . . Typical variola major epidemics such as those that occurred in Asia resulted in case-fatality rates of 30% or higher among the unvaccinated, whereas variola minor case-fatality rates were customarily 1% or less.

Smallpox spreads from person to person, primarily by droplet nuclei or aerosols expelled from the oropharynx of infected persons and by direct contact. Contaminated clothing or bed linens can also spread the virus. There are no known animal or insect reservoirs or vectors.

Historically, the rapidity of smallpox transmission throughout the population was generally slower than for such diseases as measles or chickenpox. Patients spread smallpox primarily to household members and friends; large outbreaks in schools, for example, were uncommon. This finding was accounted for in part by the fact that transmission of smallpox virus did not occur until onset of rash. By then, many patients had been confined to bed because of the high fever and malaise of the prodromal illness. Secondary cases were thus usually restricted to those who came into contact with patients, usually in the household or hospital. . . .

Response to an Outbreak

The discovery of a single suspected case of smallpox must be treated as an international health emergency and be brought immediately to the attention of national officials through local and state health authorities.

The majority of smallpox cases present with a characteristic rash that is centrifugal in distribution, ie, most dense on the face and extremities. The lesions appear during a 1- to 2-day period and evolve at the same rate. On any given part of the body, they are generally at the same stage of development. In varicella (chickenpox), the disease most frequently confused with smallpox, new lesions appear in crops every few days and lesions at very different stages of maturation (ie, vesicles, pustules, and scabs) are found in adjacent areas of skin. Varicella lesions are much more superficial and are almost never found on the palms and soles. The distribution of varicella lesions is centripetal, with a greater concentration of lesions on the trunk than on the face and extremities. . . .

Laboratory confirmation of the diagnosis in a smallpox outbreak is important. Specimens should be collected by someone who has recently been vaccinated (or is vaccinated that day) and who wears gloves and a mask. To obtain vesicular or pustular fluid, it is often necessary to open lesions with the blunt edge of a scalpel. The fluid can then be harvested on a cotton swab. Scabs can be picked off with forceps. Specimens should be deposited in a vacutainer tube that should be sealed with adhesive tape at the juncture of stopper and tube. This tube, in turn, should be enclosed in a second durable, watertight container. State or local health department laboratories should immediately be contacted regarding the shipping of specimens. Laboratory examination requires high-containment facilities and should be undertaken only in designated laboratories with the appropriate training and equipment. Once it is established that the epidemic is caused by smallpox virus, clinically typical cases would not require further laboratory confirmation.

Smallpox infection can be rapidly confirmed in the laboratory by electron microscopic examination of vesicular or pustular fluid or scabs. Although all orthopoxviruses exhibit identically appearing brick-shaped virions, history taking and clinical picture readily identify cowpox and vaccinia. Although smallpox and monkeypox virions may be indistinguishable, naturally occurring monkeypox is found only in tropical rain forest areas of Africa. Definitive laboratory identification and characterization of the virus involves growth of the virus in cell culture or on chorioallantoic egg membrane and characterization of strains by use of various biologic assays, including polymerase chain reaction techniques and restriction fragment-length polymorphisms. The latter studies can be completed within a few hours.

Preventive Action

Before 1972, smallpox vaccination was recommended for all US children at age 1 year. Most states required that each child be vaccinated before school entry. The only other requirement for vaccination was for military recruits and tourists visiting foreign countries. Most countries required that the individual be successfully vaccinated within a 3-year period prior to entering the country. Routine vaccination in the United States stopped in 1972 and since then, few persons younger than 27 years have been vaccinated. The US Census Bureau reported that in 1998, approximately 114 million persons, or 42% of the US population, were aged 29 years or younger.

In addition, the immune status of those who were vaccinated more than 27 years ago is not clear. The duration of immunity, based on the experience of naturally exposed susceptible persons, has never been satisfactorily measured. Neutralizing antibodies are reported to reflect levels of protection, although this has not been validated in the field. These antibodies have been shown to decline substantially during a 5- to 10-year period. Thus, even those who received the recommended single-dose vaccination as children do not have lifelong immunity. However, among a group who had been vaccinated at birth and at ages 8 and 18 years as part of a study, neutralizing antibody levels remained stable during a 30-year period. Because comparatively few persons today have been successfully vaccinated on more than 1 occasion, it must be assumed that the population at large is highly susceptible to infection.

In the United States, a limited reserve supply of vaccine that was produced by Wyeth Laboratories, Lancaster, Pa, in the 1970s is in storage. This supply is believed to be sufficient to vaccinate between 6 and 7 million persons. This vaccine, now under the control of the CDC, consists of vaccine virus (New York Board of Health strain) grown on scarified calves. After purification, it was freeze-dried in rubber-stoppered vials that contain sufficient vaccine for at least 50 doses when a bifurcated needle is used. It is stored at –20°C. Although quantities of vaccine have also been retained by a number of other countries, none have reserves large enough to meet more than their own potential emergency needs. WHO has 500,000 doses.

There are no manufacturers now equipped to produce smallpox vaccine in large quantities. The development and licensure of a tissue cell culture vaccine and the establishment of a new vaccine production facility is estimated to require at least 36 months.

Because of the small amounts of vaccine available, a preventive vaccination program to protect individuals such as emergency and health care personnel is not an option at this time. When additional supplies of vaccine are procured, a decision to undertake preventive vaccination of some portion of the population will have to weigh the relative risk of vaccination complications against the threat of contracting smallpox.

Risk of Adverse Reactions

A further deterrent to extensive vaccination is the fact that presently available supplies of vaccinia immune globulin (VIG), also maintained by the CDC, are very limited in quantity. The working group recommends VIG for the treatment of severe cutaneous reactions occurring as a complication of vaccination. Vaccinia immune globulin has also been given along with vaccination to protect those who needed vaccination but who were at risk of experiencing vaccine-related complications. It has been estimated that if 1 million persons were vaccinated, as many as 250 persons would experience adverse reactions of a type that would require administration of VIG. How much VIG would be needed to administer with vaccine to those at risk is unknown.

At this time, the best that can be offered to the patient infected with smallpox is supportive therapy plus antibiotics as indicated for treatment of occasional secondary bacterial infections. No antiviral substances have yet proved effective for the treatment of smallpox, and the working group is not aware of any reports that suggest any antiviral product is therapeutic. Encouraging initial reports in the 1960s describing the therapeutic benefits of the thiosemicarbazones, cytosine arabinoside, and adenine arabinoside proved questionable on further study.

Recent studies on tissue culture, mice, and a small number of monkeys have suggested the possibility that cidofovir, a nucleoside, analog DNA polymerase inhibitor, might prove useful in preventing smallpox infection if administered within 1 or 2 days after exposure. At this time, there is no evidence that cidofovir is more effective than vaccination in this early period. Moreover, the potential utility of this drug is limited, given the fact that it must be administered intravenously and its use is often accompanied by serious renal [kidney] toxicity.

Stopping an Outbreak

A smallpox outbreak poses difficult public health problems because of the ability of the virus to continue to spread throughout the population unless checked by vaccination and/or isolation of patients and their close contacts.

A clandestine aerosol release of smallpox, even if it infected only 50 to 100 persons to produce the first generation of cases, would rapidly spread in a now highly susceptible population, expanding by a factor of 10 to 20 times or more with each generation of cases. Between the time of an aerosol release of smallpox virus and diagnosis of the first cases, an interval as long as 2 weeks or more is apt to occur because of the average incubation period of 12 to 14 days and the lapse of several additional days before a rash was sufficiently distinct to suggest the diagnosis of smallpox. By that time, there would be no risk of further environmental exposure from the original aerosol release because the virus is fully inactivated within 2 days.

As soon as the diagnosis of smallpox is made, all individuals in whom smallpox is suspected should be isolated immediately and all household and other face-to-face contacts should be vaccinated and placed under surveillance. Because the widespread dissemination of smallpox virus by aerosol poses a serious threat in hospitals, patients should be isolated in the home or other nonhospital facility whenever possible. Home care for most patients is a reasonable approach, given the fact that little can be done for a patient other than to offer supportive therapy.

In the event of an aerosol release of smallpox and a subsequent outbreak, the rationale for vaccinating patients suspected to have smallpox at this time is to ensure that some with a mistaken diagnosis are not placed at risk of acquiring smallpox. Vaccination administered within the first few days after exposure and perhaps as late as 4 days may prevent or significantly ameliorate subsequent illness. An emergency vaccination program is also indicated that would include all health care workers at clinics or hospitals that might receive patients; all other essential disaster response personnel, such as police, firefighters, transit workers, public health staff, and emergency management staff; and mortuary staff who might have to handle bodies. The working group recommends that all such personnel for who vaccination is not contraindicated should be vaccinated immediately irrespective of prior vaccination status.

Vaccination administered within 4 days of first exposure has been shown to offer some protection against acquiring infection and significant protection against a fatal outcome. Those who have been vaccinated at some time in the past will normally exhibit an accelerated immune response. Thus, it would be prudent, when possible, to assign those who had been previously vaccinated to duties involving close patient contact.

It is important that discretion be used in identifying contacts of patients to ensure, to the extent that is possible, that vaccination and adequate surveillance measures are focused on those at greatest risk. Specifically, it is recommended that contacts be defined as persons who have been in the same household as the infected individual or who have been in face-to-face contact with the patient after the onset of fever. Experience during the smallpox global eradication program showed that patients did not transmit infection until after the prodromal fever had given way to the rash stage of illness.

Isolating the Infected

Isolation of all contacts of exposed patients would be logistically difficult and, in practice, should not be necessary. Because contacts, even if infected, are not contagious until onset of rash, a practical strategy calls for all contacts to have temperatures checked at least once each day, preferably in the evening. Any increase in temperature higher than 38°C (101°F) during the 17-day period following last exposure to the case would suggest the possible development of smallpox and be cause for isolating the patient immediately, preferably at home, until it could be determined clinically and/or by laboratory examination whether the contact had smallpox. All close contacts of the patients should be promptly vaccinated.

Although cooperation by most patients and contacts in observing isolation could be ensured through counseling and persuasion, there may be some for whom forcible quarantine will be required. Some states and cities in the United States, but not all, confer broad discretionary powers on health authorities to ensure the safety of the public's health and, at one time, this included powers to quarantine. Under epidemic circumstances, this could be an important power to have. Thus, each state and city should review its statutes as part of its preparedness activities. . . .

Building Up Vaccine Stocks

The working group recommends that an emergency stockpile of at least 40 million doses of vaccine and a standby manufacturing capacity to produce more is a critical need. At a minimum, this quantity of vaccine would be needed in the control of an epidemic during the first 4 to 8 weeks after an attack. Smallpox vaccine, contained in glass-sealed ampoules and stored at −20°C, retains its potency almost indefinitely. However, several steps are necessary before manufacturing can begin. The traditional method for producing vaccine on the scarified flank of a calf is no longer acceptable because the product inevitably contains some microbial contaminants, however stringent the purification measures. Contemporary vaccines require the use of tissue cell cultures. Thus, as a first step, the traditional New York Board of Health strain needs to be grown in a suitable tissue cell culture and comparative studies performed of the reactogenicity and immunogenicity of calf-derived and tissue cell culture vaccines. This should be a comparatively straightforward exercise. The cost of such a stockpile should be comparatively modest because the vaccine would be packaged in 50-dose rather than costly single-dose containers. In the mid-1970s, 40 million doses would have cost less than $5 million.

The frequency of vaccine complications is sufficiently great to recommend development, if possible, of a more attenuated strain that, hopefully, would retain full efficacy. Development of an entirely new, genetically engineered strain would be both costly and time consuming. Moreover, it would be difficult at this time to justify its use in large numbers of human subjects to evaluate safety. There is, however, a candidate attenuated strain that was developed and field tested in Japan in the mid-1970s (a Lister strain–derived vaccine that has been produced in volume in rabbit kidney cell culture and has been given to more than 100,000 persons in Japan). Research showed no severe complications among the first 30,000 vaccinees. The cutaneous responses to vaccination were much less severe and far fewer vaccinees developed fever. . . .

Vaccinia immune globulin has been used for the treatment of vaccine complications and for administration with vaccine to those for whom vaccine is otherwise contraindicated. Production of VIG should be a high priority for research. An alternative to VIG is also needed because VIG is difficult to produce and cumbersome to administer. Immunotheraphy using humanized monoclonal antibodies is an alternative that should be explored. Studies of antiviral agents or drugs, already approved or near approval for marketing for use in other viral diseases, have suggested that 1 or more such products might prove useful.

Finally, a simple, rapid diagnostic test to identify variola virus in the oropharynx during the . . . early . . . phase of illness would be of considerable help in triage of suspected patients during the course of an outbreak.

The specter of resurgent smallpox is ominous, especially given the enormous efforts that have been made to eradicate what has been characterized as the most devastating of all the pestilential diseases. Unfortunately, the threat of an aerosol release of smallpox is real and the potential for a catastrophic scenario is great unless effective control measures can quickly be brought to bear.

Early detection, isolation of infected individuals, surveillance of contacts, and a focused selective vaccination program are the essential items of a control program. Educating health care professionals about the diagnostic features of smallpox should permit early detection; advance regionwide planning for isolation and care of infected individuals in their homes as appropriate and in hospitals when home care is not an option will be critical to deter spread. Ultimately, success in controlling a burgeoning epidemic will depend on the availability of adequate supplies of vaccine and VIG. An adequate stockpile of those commodities would offer a relatively inexpensive safeguard against tragedy.

Ricin

Doug Hanson

Ricin, according to scientist Doug Hanson, is a highly toxic and easily extracted poison. It comes from the castor bean plant, prized by many gardeners for its foliage and flowers, and by the pharmaceutical industry for the oil of its beans. Unlike most bioweapons, Hanson explains in the following selection, ricin contains no living agents. But it can kill. Indeed, Hanson describes it as a thousand times more potent than the famous poison cyanide. Ricin has already been used in attacks on the U.S. government. In 2003 and 2004, letters containing particles of the deadly substance were sent to the White House and the U.S. Senate. Fortunately, security officials intercepted them before they could do any harm. In view of the grave threat to life that ricin poses, Hanson advises law enforcement authorities to be prepared to recognize a clandestine ricin production operation. He describes what a ricin-producing lab looks like, and how an attack might be launched. The good news about ricin, he writes, is that unlike bacterial agents it is difficult to distribute over a wide area. Additionally, there are several devices available for detection of ricin, and heat treatment or bleach can destroy the toxin. However, once a person has inhaled or ingested ricin particles, there is no antidote. All that can be done is to treat the symptoms and hope that the person recovers. Doug Hanson is a biochemist who has headed toxicology and analytical chemistry laboratories for many years. Formerly, he participated in bioweapons testing for the U.S. Army Medical R&D Command.

In Washington, DC, on February 3, 2004, laboratory tests confirmed that "white powder" found in the mailroom of Senate Majority Leader Bill Frist's office was the deadly plant toxin, ricin. That same day, it was disclosed that, in November 2003, a letter containing ricin was sent to the White House, but it was intercepted at an "off-site mail facility." On October 15, 2003, Greensville, SC, postal authorities discovered an

Doug Hanson, "Ricin Toxin: Law Enforcement's New Challenge," *Police and Security News*, vol. 20, March/April 2004. Copyright © 2004 by *Police and Security News*. Reproduced by permission.

envelope containing a metal canister with ricin in it. On January 13, 2004, French police broke up an Islamic terrorist cell which was said to be planning ricin attacks in France and Britain. Why was ricin toxin used in all of these cases? It is cheap, relatively easy to produce, and does not have to be highly purified or weaponized to be effective.

Ricin is a protein material which is extracted from the beans of the common castor bean, *ricinus communis*. The protein toxin is composed of two polypeptide chains. When the toxin enters a cell, it rapidly inactivates protein synthesis by inactivating the ribosomes, a key component of the cell's synthetic machinery.

Made from Castor Beans

Castor beans are grown for their oil which is used in various industries, including paints, cosmetics, textiles, and others. The main countries producing castor beans are India, China and Brazil. Ricin can be extracted directly from the castor bean or from the "wet mash" byproduct produced by crushing and extracting the castor oil. The annual world production of castor oil is 460,000 tons, requiring over 1.1 million tons of seeds and producing 550,000 tons of wet mash. Thus, a tremendous amount of raw material exists at a cheap price for terrorists to use for ricin production. Only five percent by weight of the wet mash is ricin. However, from 100 pounds of this material, you can extract up to five pounds of ricin. Ricin is over a thousand times more poisonous than cyanide and 30 times more potent than the chemical warfare nerve gas agent, VX. In its pure form, an amount no bigger than a grain of table salt can kill an adult. Ricin can be either a white powder or a colorless, tasteless solution. It is soluble in water, can be aerosolized, and is stable in soil or in the environment for approximately three days.

The US Army called ricin toxin "Agent W." Ricin is considered a biological agent because it is prepared from a biological source. However, unlike most biological agents, such as anthrax, it is not a living organism and can't reproduce and increase its presence after an attack. It is also considered a chemical agent because it is a chemical, a protein, and is much like sarin or other nerve agents. It is probably best to consider ricin a biochemical agent, like the botulism toxin which is extracted from the bacteria, *clostridium botulinum*. Ricin is listed as a "Category B Bioterrorism Agent," and a "Schedule 1 Chemical Warfare Agent."

Clandestine Laboratories

It is important for law enforcement personnel to be able to recognize a clandestine toxin production operation. For the most part, such an operation will look very similar to any other illegal drug lab. Flasks, beakers and other standard laboratory glassware would be present, but the more complicated glass stills and distillation glassware would be absent. What would be present are large containers (glass or metal pots) where the mash could be made into a slurry with water. There would also be some type of large filter devices; these could be standard laboratory funnel filters or something as simple as large kitchen spaghetti strainers into which filter paper is placed. The basic procedure for ricin production could be carried out in a garage, basement or even a bathroom. The oil is removed from the castor bean by crushing it and then running the material through rollers which squeeze the oil out of the solid material. The remaining wet "cake" of solid material is the starting material for toxin production. This process involves the following steps: 1) slurring the cake in water at an acidic pH—the toxin is water soluble; 2) filtering the slurry; 3) precipitating the toxin from the water solution with sodium sulfate; 4) filter again, then resuspend and precipitate the material several additional times . . . and 5) finally, the resulting cake is dried and then ground to a fine powder. Grinding would be done in a ball mill apparatus. Alternatively, a more finely powdered material can be produced by passing a water solution of toxin through a spray drying machine. This type of equipment is widely used in the pharmaceutical and food industries. Used equipment is available for pennies on the dollar from used equipment sales companies. To produce highly purified material requires someone with a greater degree of skill than the average terrorist; although, this skill could be easily learned by working in a pharmaceutical plant or in a food plant which makes candy or instant drinks, like powdered hot chocolate. However, ricin can be effectively used in an impure form which could be developed as a "home brew" by unskilled people. The toxicity of this material will be lower, but greater quantities can be produced and more material delivered to an attack site; this would achieve the same result as using a highly purified agent. . . .

Sarin, a chemical nerve agent, is a highly volatile chemical and very hard to produce and handle in large volumes. Botulinum toxin requires growth of a highly infectious microorganism, *clostridium botulinum*, under sterile conditions, then a complex extraction. Ricin, on the other hand, isn't volatile, so handling it and transporting it is relatively safe. It is very stable, so long-term storage is not a problem. Protective equipment for the individuals preparing ricin would consist of a good quality gas mask, protective eye gear and vinyl gloves. No special protective clothing would necessarily be required, as long as the clothing worn was washed immediately after use. The chemicals one would expect to find in a ricin production lab would include sodium sulfate; sodium carbonate; sulfuric acid (concentrated and as a 5% solution); and solvents like hexane, acetone and, possibly, DMSO (dimethylsulfoxide).

Detailed procedures for ricin extraction and use were found in Al-Qaeda's military manuals seized in safe houses and caves in Afghanistan, according to a recent Monterey Institute of International Studies

(MIIS) report. Procedures are available in militant publications like *The Poisoner's Handbook* (1988), an underground publication by a militant, antigovernment group here in the US. . . .

It is just as important for law enforcement professionals to realize that the threat from ricin may come as easily from within our borders as from abroad. In such cases, law enforcement may have initial primary responsibility for any incidents. A case in April of 1991 demonstrated that as members of a domestic extremist group called the "Patriot's Council of Minnesota" set up a lab to manufacture ricin. Their apparent target was federal law enforcement officers. The National Infrastructure Protection Center (NIPC) reported that the lab had produced enough ricin to kill 100 people.

Unsuitable for Large-Scale Attacks

Ricin is not a living bioagent and, therefore, is not contagious, so the likelihood of it being spread too far beyond the initial attack site is small. It is not volatile so, in an aerosol attack, the chance of a secondary aerosolization [airborne] event is unlikely. Other people could be exposed through contact with the clothing of an exposed person or exposed articles from the target site. Wind and rain could also spread ricin from the initial target.

Ricin has not been effectively weaponized like anthrax or smallpox. The weaponization process is very involved, requiring pure material and, in the final steps, the agent is bound to microporous silica particles called "fumed smoke." The material is so small that it literally floats in the air on release. That is how the weaponized anthrax powder used in the post 9/11 events was able to spread throughout the postal facility. But, ricin toxin is a protein, not a bacteria; binding to the silica particles changes the shape of the toxin protein and renders it inactive (detoxified). The US Army gave up trying to develop a large-scale, weaponized aerosol preparation of ricin; in 1991, Iraq admitted to producing large quantities of toxin, but was unsuccessful at weaponizing it.

Thus, ricin would most likely be used in small-scale events: contamination of an office building or shopping mall by introducing aerosolized material into the ventilation system or release of aerosol into a subway or train station. Relatively simple pressurized sprayers could be used in these areas to deliver a mist of ricin which could be both inhaled and ingested by breathing through the nose and mouth. The aerosol produced would not need to be highly refined in this instance to be effective. Ricin could also be sprayed on foods like fruit or vegetables; or mixed into prepared food at a restaurant, a large catered event, or a food processing plant. However, the toxin is a protein and is destroyed by heating so it would only be effective on uncooked or improperly cooked food products. It is possible that it could be used to contaminate a drinking water well or water supply system. However, this is not practical because the water reservoir for an average-sized city contains about 50 billion gallons of water; this would require addition of several tons of ricin before a toxic concentration would be achieved. Ricin will primarily be used by terrorists to cause chaos, confusion and fear in the target population. This is much like what is accomplished by a suicide bomber who puts on a vest loaded with explosives and nails, then blows up a deli full of people at lunch hour. The relative number of people killed or injured is small, maybe 15 or 25, but the fear generated by such an attack can have a disabling affect on a whole city.

Effects of Exposure

An attack with sarin or other chemical nerve agents produces immediate effects—death and serious injury to people in the target area, just like the suicide bomber. With biological agents like anthrax or plague, or biochemical agents like ricin, the exposed individual does not necessarily know they are exposed for several hours or up to two to three days. Only then does serious illness present itself and the progression to death may take days or weeks. The standard measure of toxicity, LD50 (the "Lethal Dose" which causes death in 50% of the animals tested), for inhalation or aerosol exposure is three micrograms/kilogram. So, for an average-sized man (200 pounds or 91 kilograms), it only takes 0.27 milligrams or an amount the size of a grain of salt to cause death. For the ingestion route of exposure, the LD50 is higher at 30 micrograms/kilograms because some of the toxin is destroyed by the action of the stomach. Skin or dermal exposure to ricin toxin is insignificant, although toxin dissolved in the solvent DMSO will penetrate the skin to a small degree.

With ricin exposure by inhalation, general symptoms first appear eight to 12 hours after exposure. Initial symptoms are weakness, fever, cough, and pulmonary edema (water in the lungs). Death occurs within two to three days from severe respiratory distress. Exposure by ingestion (eating or drinking) requires a higher dose of ricin to produce death because, as previously mentioned, some of the ricin is destroyed in the stomach. Symptoms generally occur about six hours after exposure. Initial symptoms are abdominal pain; vomiting and diarrhea; followed in several days by severe dehydration, decreased urine production, and a significant decrease in blood pressure. Death may not occur for up to ten days. Ricin is a cytotoxic agent capable of destroying any human cells; once in the cell, it shuts down the cell's protein making capability.

There is no effective treatment for ricin poisoning. Medical treatment is generally supportive, aimed at easing the symptoms and simply making the patient comfortable. Not all exposures result in death and some patients do recover. At present, there is no antidote or vaccine for ricin; however, research at a variety of laboratories is encouraging. Researchers at the University of Texas, Southwestern Medical Center, in Dallas, have reported production of a vaccine which protects mice from ricin. The FDA may approve the start of human clinical trials by the end of the summer. Other studies are being carried out at the US Army Medical Research Institute for Infectious Diseases and by Canada's Military Research Agency. . . .

Ricin Detection Methods

There are several on-site devices available for ricin detection. The on-site kits are designed to provide a "first test" assessment. These tests may produce false positives in the field and, later, more sophisticated analysis may rule out ricin's presence. However, in these situations, it is better to get a false positive in the field than a false negative and then find out later that the material was present and all the necessary precautionary steps were not taken. These test kits should only be used to establish whether a reasonable threat of ricin exposure has occurred in an incident, thus allowing first responders to take appropriate decontamination and cleanup activity until definitive test results are obtained from a certified laboratory. In the case of ricin, a "reasonable threat" would be the presence of toxin in sufficient quantity to represent a threat to unprotected people in the area.

Handheld detection devices are quite sensitive at detecting low levels of agent. However, the problem is exactly "where to test" in an attack situation. Thus, these devices may be most reliable in situations where a relatively high level of agent is present, i.e., vials of powder; agent spills on a lab bench or in a subway car; suspect visible material released from an air ventilation system; or material in an envelope or package, etc. . . .

Assessing the Ricin Threat

For law enforcement, the question is, "How real is the threat of a ricin attack in my jurisdiction?" What then do we know about ricin? We know it is a highly toxic poison capable of killing exposed people in three to five days. We know that the raw materials for its production are readily available. We know it can be used as an aerosol or to contaminate food suppliers. We know it is not a weapon of mass destruction, but rather a weapon to be used for small events (more like the suicide bombers). We know that Al-Qaeda, Hamass, and other international terrorist groups all have manuals outlining ricin production and use, and that militant groups here in the US also have this know-how and have considered using ricin. We know that the US Government put out a classified intelligence bulletin to be on the lookout for the biological toxin ricin.

However, to date there have been no real episodes when ricin has been used in a real large-scale terrorist incident. Thus, law enforcement groups are left to decide if ricin is high on their list of security concerns. If there are suspected sleeper cells of Al-Qaeda or militant groups in your area, or individual suspects who might be capable of a domestic attack, then the handheld detection kits should probably be considered among [the tools law enforcers need]. In any event, the information on ricin provided in this article should be general knowledge for all law enforcement personnel as part of their overall education in this growing issue of bioterrorism.

TULAREMIA

Gretchen Vogel

Tularemia is a virulent bacterium that can rapidly debilitate a person with flulike symptoms and worse. As author Gretchen Vogel writes in the following selection tularemia has been known to medicine since 1911, yet many questions about it remain unanswered. For example, no one knows how the disease is spread, though doctors speculate that mosquitoes and small mammals may play a role in transmission. Fortunately, the disease is relatively rare, which led some researchers to speculate that a 1999 outbreak in Kosovo during the Balkan civil war may have been deliberate. Certainly tularemia had previously attracted the attention of bioweapons researchers. Japan tested it as a bioweapon during World War II, and the United States and the former Soviet Union stockpiled it in their bioweapons armories. Vogel writes that the bacterium attracts weapons designers because it is both virulent and highly infectious. It is not, however, especially deadly. Recent genetic research into the bacterium's genome has raised hopes for an effective vaccine against the disease. At present, however, tularemia continues to pose a threat as a bioweapon. Gretchen Vogel is a science writer whose work focuses largely on biology and biotechnology.

In the winter of 1999 in war-torn Kosovo, scores of people started coming down with headaches and sore throats that hung on much longer than a normal flu. In many cases, the patients' lymph nodes swelled to gigantic proportions and sometimes broke through the skin to form hideous open sores. It took half a year for scientists from the World Health Organization to make a surprising diagnosis: tularemia, a rare bacterial infection most often seen in North American rabbit hunters, villagers in central Sweden, and farmers in southern Russia. Tularemia succumbs readily to antibiotics, and by May the outbreak had subsided after 327 cases, none of which were fatal.

But although the bug was vanquished, a disconcerting question

Gretchen Vogel, "Infectious Diseases: An Obscure Weapon of the Cold War Edges Into the Limelight," *Science*, October 10, 2003, p. 222. Copyright © 2003 by American Association for the Advancement of Science. Reproduced by permission.

remained. Tularemia had never been spotted before in Kosovo. Had someone deliberately spread the bacterium?

This was not an idle fear. Japan tested the bacterium Francisella tularensis as a potential weapon during World War II, and the United States and the Soviet Union stockpiled it during the Cold War. Although those munitions are supposedly long gone, experts argue that tularemia remains a bioterror threat. It is one of the most infectious organisms known: Inhaling as few as 10 of the microbes can cause debilitating illness. A few grams of a virulent strain of F. tularensis dispersed in a city could quickly sicken thousands, says Anders [Sjöstedt] of the University of [Umeå], in Sweden.

For rogue governments and terrorists, tularemia's allure is that of a weapon of mass disruption, not mass murder. This possibility, combined with the bug's checkered past, has made it one of the latest targets of the U.S. government's massive R&D [research and development] effort to defend against bioweapon attacks. Civilian tularemia research, once a backwater, is now flush with cash, and new researchers are rushing in. The fourth International Conference on Tularemia, held here from 15 to 18 September [2003], drew nearly 200 participants, more than twice as many as previous gatherings.

There are plenty of puzzles for the recent converts to tackle. It's still unknown where the bacterium lives in the wild, how exactly it is transmitted, or even how it makes people sick. At the meeting, however, scientists reported tantalizing clues to the bug's virulence from its nearly finished genome sequence as well as new leads to track it in the environment and after it infects people.

Carried by Rabbits

Tularemia was first identified in California in 1911 and was soon recognized as the cause of epidemics in Russia and Scandinavia. In North America, the disease was associated primarily with hunters who skinned and ate infected animals; as hunting has declined, so has the disease. There are still several dozen cases of tularemia in the United States each year, however. One of the highest risk factors—blamed for recurrent outbreaks on Martha's Vineyard island in Massachusetts and for a cluster of cases this summer [2003] in Nebraska—is lawn mowing. Unsuspecting yard workers who run over a sick or dead rabbit can unleash tularemia-laden droplets into the air. Two of Germany's three reported cases in 2001 were a father and daughter who had eaten a rabbit the father had hit with his car.

Fortunately, the bacterium does not spread from person to person, but it has a wide repertoire of ways into the body. In some cases, doctors have attributed infections to tick or mosquito bites, although it is unclear whether the bacterium thrives in such insects. Tainted milk was blamed for an outbreak in Moscow in 1995; other outbreaks have been traced to contaminated wells. Epidemiologists have yet to pinpoint the source of the Martha's Vineyard cases. As for Kosovo, epidemiologists say a terror attack is an unlikely explanation. They now believe that a runaway population of rats and mice gorging on unharvested crops and contaminating human food and water supplies triggered the outbreak.

Outbreak in Russia

One of the largest known epidemics sickened tens of thousands of soldiers and civilians during the battle of Stalingrad in the winter of 1942 to 1943. In his 1999 book *Biohazard*, Ken Alibek, a former top official in the Soviet bioweapons program, alleges that the Soviet army unleashed airborne tularemia bacteria on German troops during the battle, which was a turning point of World War II. But many medical historians doubt that claim, arguing that miserable conditions for the besieged German soldiers, rampant rodents, and contaminated water and food combined for an unprecedented but natural outbreak. "To my knowledge, there is no hard proof for the deliberate spread of these organisms," says [Sjöstedt]. The Stalingrad outbreak followed the epidemiological pattern of previous outbreaks in the region, he says: "People were relying on water sources from rivers or lakes, and there were huge numbers of dead rodents."

[Sjöstedt] and his colleague Mats Forsman of the Swedish Defense Research Agency in [Umeå] are hoping to track down the source of the perennial outbreaks in central Sweden; nearly 500 people have fallen ill this year alone. Few Swedish patients report recent contact with rabbits or other small mammals, leading doctors to speculate that mosquitoes may be transmitting the bacterium. In Bath, Forsman noted progress in flushing out Francisella's Swedish retreat. It has been cultured from streams and lakes, but researchers suspect that its reservoir is a water-dwelling host, perhaps a protozoan. Forsman says that F. tularensis indeed grows in lab cultures of amoebae as well as several freshwater species of flagellates and ciliates common in central Sweden. But the team has yet to detect the bacterium in wild microorganisms.

Genetic Insights

Researchers have made a bit more progress unraveling Francisella's genetic secrets. A consortium from Sweden, the United States, and the United Kingdom is nearly finished sequencing the genome of two strains: a weakened strain used in an experimental vaccine from the 1960s and a virulent one. Complementing that effort are new techniques for making mutant versions of the finicky organism to assess the importance of various genes. "Having tools to generate mutants makes a huge difference," says Karen Elkins of the U.S. Food and Drug Administration (FDA) in Rockville, Maryland. "You can knock something out and test whether it still makes an animal sick."

Researchers are especially intrigued by a possible "pathogenicity island," a DNA region that looks like it might have found its way into the genome relatively recently. The island includes several genes that appear to have something to do with the bacterium's ability to enter and grow inside other cells, Francis Nano of the University of Victoria in British Columbia, Canada, told those attending the meeting. And Igor Golovliov of [Umeå], University reported that he and his colleagues at the State Research Center for Applied Microbiology in Obolensk, a former bioweapons lab near Moscow, have modified a version of the live vaccine strain, stripping it of a protein in the region called iglC. The knockout bacteria are not as good at multiplying in cell lines, and they make mice only mildly ill. (For some reason, mice readily succumb to the [1960s] vaccine strain, which doesn't sicken humans.)

Working on a Better Vaccine

One aim of such work is a smarter tularemia vaccine. Several strains that prompt immunity but don't cause disease were isolated in Russia in the 1930s. A mixture of those strains was brought out of the Soviet Union by a researcher with the U.S. Army Medical Research Institute of Infectious Diseases (USAMRIID) in the 1950s. Scientists at USAMRIID cultured the mixture in the lab and in mice, eventually recovering a single effective vaccine strain that was used to inoculate lab workers and military personnel for decades. But in 2001 the FDA halted use of the vaccine because of concerns about the stability and potency of the vaccine strain; there is currently no vaccine available outside Russia. Knowing how the bacterium causes severe disease would allow researchers to design a more reliable vaccine, says Elkins. "You need to know if the crippled bacteria are going to revert to wild type." If manufacturers could test a strain for the absence of specific virulence genes, they could reasonably assure a vaccine's safety.

Mining the bacterium's genome should also help speed the development of diagnostic tests. Because tularemia is so rare, it often goes undiagnosed for weeks. "No one thinks Francisella unless you're in central Sweden," says Elkins. Standard tests involve culturing the bacterium or checking whether a patient has antibodies. But antibody tests work reliably only several weeks into an infection, and because the bacterium is so infectious, few labs are willing or able to handle it. Such tests "are 20 years out of date and are only applied very late in the disease—after doctors have tested for everything else they can think of," Elkins says. "We now have genomics information that can be used within a day or two" in polymerase chain reaction tests for the bacterium.

Some tularemia experts confess that a disease causing fewer than 50 deaths a year worldwide may not merit all the money and attention it's getting. Nonetheless, the effort to understand tularemia won't go unrewarded, argues Elkins: "There's new biology lurking everywhere"—not to mention a once and possibly future bioweapon threat.

PLAGUE

Institute for Biosecurity

The word plague connotes any widespread and calamitous illness. In the medical context, however, it refers to a specific bacterial disease. In the following selection, the Institute for Biosecurity at Saint Louis University's School of Public Health describes the disease, its symptoms, and its threat as a bioweapon. Plague killed many millions throughout history, the report notes, and as a weapon it could kill millions more unless effective countermeasures are taken. *Yersinia pestis*, the plague bacterium, normally infects people via fleabites. Most people infected this way develop bubonic plague, marked by large, dark swellings of the lymph nodes. However, some victims develop the pneumonic plague, which centers on the lungs. In either case, the disease starts with flulike symptoms, that if left untreated can quickly kill. Unfortunately, the report notes, no tests for rapid diagnosis of plague are available. Treatment of the disease relies mainly on antibiotics, which are usually effective. However, the report raises a concern that bioweapons makers could engineer a strain of plague able to put up resistance to antibiotics. Moreover, it notes, a previously available vaccine has been withdrawn from the market. Thus, the need for careful monitoring of those who may be infected remains.

The Institute for Biosecurity is part of the Centers for the Study of Bioterrorism and Emerging Infections at Saint Louis University School of Public Health. Their mission is to provide health professionals, other response organizations, and the public with the readiness education needed for preparedness, response, recovery, and mitigation of emerging public health threats.

Plague is an ancient disease that is thought to be responsible for over 200 million deaths, many of which occurred during three pandemics, including the infamous Black Death of 14th century Europe. Populations were decimated by up to 50% during these pandemics. *Yersinia*

Institute for Biosecurity, "Plague," www.bioterrorism.slu.edu, September 2003.

pestis [the bacterium that causes plague] is one of the agents that the Japanese attempted to use as a biological weapon in World War II at the Unit 731 camp in Manchuria, and it is thought to have been produced in large quantities by the former Soviet Union bioweapons program.

Plague remains endemic in many areas of the world, including the southwestern United States, where up to 10 cases per year are reported. Globally, there are approximately 1700 cases each year. Plague is primarily a disease of rodents, but can be transmitted to humans through the bite of infected fleas, the most common route, or through direct contact with infected animals. Additionally, plague can be transmitted via inhalation of infectious droplets from persons with pneumonic plague or from infected animals, particularly cats. Experiments with primates have confirmed that an infectious aerosol of *Y. pestis* can be created, and this would likely be the form encountered in a bioterrorist event.

Disease Takes Various Forms

There are 3 predominant forms of human plague: pneumonic, bubonic and septicemic. Pneumonic plague can be either primary, which is the development of pneumonia from direct inhalation of organisms, or secondary through the hematogenous [blood-borne] spread of organisms from any primary site to the lungs. Two percent of United States plague cases are primary pneumonic, while 12% of bubonic and septicemic cases spread to secondary pneumonic. Presentation and clinical course are similar for both with an overall case fatality of 50–70%, which nears 100% when treatment is delayed by 18–24 hours or after onset of symptoms. In the United States, 84% of cases are bubonic, caused by flea bites or handling infected animals, and characterized by buboes, or tender and markedly swollen regional lymph nodes. Mortality is less than 5% in treated cases, but can reach 40–60% in cases that go untreated or where treatment is significantly delayed. Bubonic plague would not likely be the initial form of disease in a bioterrorism-related outbreak, but could occur after development of an epidemic and subsequent widespread rodent infection. Septicemic plague accounts for 13% of cases in the United States and consists of a severe systemic illness without preceding lymphadenopathy or pneumonia. Any route of exposure can lead to septicemic plague, and this form of disease might be seen after aerosol exposure in rare individuals who did not develop a substantial pneumonia. Mortality is 30–50% despite treatment and greater than 90% when treatment is delayed.

Yersinia pestis is one of the three pathogenic *Yersinia* species within the family Enterobacteriaceae. The other two, less virulent species, are *Y. enterocolitica* and *Y. pseudotuberculosis*. It is a nonmotile, intracellular, aerobic Gram-negative coccobacillus that has a characteristic bipolar appearance on Wright, Giemsa and Wayson's stains. It is among the most virulent human pathogens, with an antiphagocytic [anti-immune] capsule, lipopolysaccharide endotoxin [a toxin released when the bacterium dies] and other virulence factors. . . .

Symptoms of Infection

Primary pneumonic plague ensues after live organisms are inhaled. . . . The incubation period is typically 1–4 days, but can be as long as 6 days. Disease starts suddenly with non-specific symptoms resembling an acute flu-like illness, including fevers, chills, myalgias, malaise and headache. There are often prominent gastrointestinal symptoms including nausea, vomiting, diarrhea and abdominal pain, before more specific symptoms of pneumonia appear. Patients typically progress from feeling well to having severe pneumonia with severe dyspnea [breathing trouble], cough, chest pain, and stridor [harsh wheezing] within 24 hours. . . .

Bubonic plague also begins with flu-like symptoms 2–8 days after exposure, but is accompanied by painful, enlarged, and sometimes draining lymph nodes called "buboes" proximal to the inoculation site, generally in the groin or axilla [armpit]. Lymph node destruction and hi-grade bacteremia with systemic disease and sepsis occur in severe cases. Septicemic plague presents only as the severe systemic disease after nonspecific flu-like symptoms and without preceding lymphadenopathy or pneumonia, making initial diagnosis extremely difficult.

Timely diagnosis is difficult as there are no tests available that are rapid, specific and confirmatory, making a high index of suspicion necessary. . . .

Treating the Disease

Treatment of *Yersinia pestis* consists primarily of antibiotic therapy that must be initiated rapidly upon first suspicion and prior to confirmation. Historically, monotherapy with an appropriate antibiotic results in rapid improvement. Aminoglycosides are first line therapy, particularly streptomycin, which is approved by the Food and Drug Administration (FDA) for this purpose . . . for adults. Gentamicin is also recommended and is easier to administer, because it can be given intravenously and can be dosed once daily. . . . Tetracyclines can be used, such as doxycycline . . . for adults, which is also the first choice if oral therapy is required, for example in the setting of mass casualties. Other alternatives include ciprofloxacin . . . for adults, which is effective versus *Y. pestis* in vitro, although there are no human data. Other fluoroquinolones may be effective as well, but have not been studied. Chloramphenicol is the first choice for plague meningitis as it penetrates the blood-brain barrier. . . . Children under 2 years old should not be treated with chloramphenicol if at all possible to avoid the "grey baby" syndrome.

Antibiotics that are generally ineffective and should not be used for *Yersinia pestis* include beta-lactams such as penicillins and cephalosporins, rifampin, aztreonam and macrolides. Natural antibiotic resistance to the drugs of choice is rare, but it should be anticipated that genetically-engineered antibiotic resistance may be encountered in a bioterrorism scenario. Intravenous antibiotics can be switched to oral therapy if available for the drug being used after clinical improvement occurs. Duration of therapy should be for 10–14 days, or at least 3 days after becoming afebrile with clinical improvement. Post-exposure prophylaxis with oral doxycycline or ciprofloxacin should be administered for 7 days to anyone who may have had inhalational exposure to *Yersinia pestis* within the prior 6 days, either as an aerosol or as droplets from a patient with pneumonic plague. Significant exposure is defined as a household or hospital contact, or being within 2 meters of the infected patient. Contacts who refuse prophylaxis should be observed closely for 7 days and started on full treatment regimens for the development of any cough or fever.

Vaccine Unavailable

A vaccine produced from a killed virulent strain was used in the United States in the past, but has not been commercially available since 1999. It was effective against bubonic plague only and did have some adverse effects.

It is thought that pneumonic plague is transferred person-to-person via respiratory droplets. Thus, any suspected pneumonic plague patients should be placed in respiratory droplet isolation, where a surgical mask is required. These precautions should be maintained until the patient has received at least 48 hours of appropriate antibiotics and is clinically improving.

CHAPTER 3

ENCOUNTERS WITH BIOWEAPONS

JAPAN'S EXPERIMENTS ON PRISONERS

Yoshio Shinozuka

Japan's occupation of a large portion of China began in 1931 with a bombing along the Manchurian Railway. The Japanese Imperial Army, acting on its own initiative, took over much of the province of Manchuria. Within a few years, a medical officer in the army set up a biological weapons unit. Over the years, Unit 731, as it was known, developed a wide variety of bioweapons. Many of them were tested on Chinese prisoners. In the selection that follows, one of the low-level members of Unit 731 testifies about his role in some of those experiments. At the age of fifteen, Yoshio Shinozuka was recruited to be a member of the unit's Junior Youth Corps. He thought he was joining a water purification program, but soon discovered that the unit's secret mission was bioweapons development. He describes the manufacture of germ bombs, the mass cultivation of germs, and the breeding of fleas as a vector to spread disease. Among the many diseases he helped to produce were plague, typhoid, cholera and anthrax. In 1942, Shinozuka says, he began to take part in deadly experiments on Chinese prisoners. According to his testimony, the victims were not only subjected to horrible diseases, but when they grew ill, doctors on the staff of Unit 731 would dissect them alive to gain knowledge about the course of the disease. To dehumanize the people they were killing, members of Unit 731 referred to them as "logs." Afterward, their corpses were incinerated. Following the war, Shinozuka was captured by the People's Liberation Army of communist China. In 1956, after serving a sentence in a Chinese "re-education camp," he was repatriated to Japan, where for many years he led a quiet life as a local government official. Following his retirement, however, he began to speak about Japanese atrocities in China during the war. In recent years, Yoshio Shinozuka has become one of the few Japanese Imperial Army veterans willing to testify in court on behalf of victims and to speak candidly about his experiences in public.

Yoshio Shinozuka, "Testimony," *Harper's*, April 1, 2003. Copyright © 2003 by Harper's Magazine Foundation. Reproduced by permission.

From testimony by Yoshio Shinozuka concerning atrocities committed by the Japanese army in China during World War II. Shinozuka
was a member of Unit 731, which conducted human experiments on
more than 250,000 Chinese civilians and prisoners of war. Shinozuka
testified on behalf of a group of victims' families who sued the Japanese government, which has refused to issue an apology or to provide
any compensation. In August [2002] a Tokyo district court dismissed
the lawsuit and said that it had no legal basis. Translated from the
Japanese by Mihoko Tokoro.

Please state how you joined Unit 731, the so-called Ishii Unit.
It was March 1939. Recruiters came to junior high schools, voca-
tional schools, and agricultural schools, and I volunteered to join the
unit. We were ordered to report to the Epidemic Prevention Labora-
tory of the Imperial Japanese Army's School of Military Medicine in
Tokyo. When I arrived I was told, "You are a member of the Junior
Youth Corps of the Ishii Unit. You will soon be transferred to Harbin,
China. It is a wonderful place."

When were you transferred to Harbin?
We arrived on May 12, 1939, and I was sent to Ping Fan. The first
thing I noticed in Ping Fan was that there were moats and barbed wire
around the buildings. At the time, I wondered why the security was so
tight, since the head of the unit and many others there were just
army doctors. The next day we were told that this area was designated
as a special military area, and that even Japanese military planes were
forbidden to fly over. Also, we were bound by a strict law to see nothing, hear nothing, and say nothing. We were told that if we ran away,
we would be punished as runaway soldiers from the front lines.

Testing Germ Bombs
*After you arrived in Ping Fan, what were you told about the duties of Unit
731?*
We were told to accompany frontline units and supply them with
purified water. But in reality, starting in 1940, the division that provided purified water was located outside of Harbin.

Would you please explain the structure of Unit 731?
Each division was named after its chief. I was sent to the Yam-
aguchi division, which manufactured and tested germ bombs.

What else did you do as a Junior Youth Corps member?
We were sent wherever help was needed. That was our duty. There
was mass production of germs for the Nomonhan Incident [border
clashes with Soviet troops] and again in 1940, and also flea breeding
in 1940.

What was the state of Unit 731 at the time of the Nomonhan Incident?
Many of the Unit 731 members went to Nomonhan. I figured their
duty was to purify water. But those who were left behind started making germs. My assignment was to prepare culturing cans for germ

growth. I was also in charge of transporting the microbes we called "stumps." Other members of the Junior Youth Corps who knew how to drive participated in the incident directly.

What did they do?

They said they flung the germs into the Horustein River.

What types of germs were thrown into the river?

I think they were typhoid, paratyphoid, and dysentery bacilli.

Plague-Spreading Fleas

Did you ever participate in the breeding of fleas?

Yes. We were ordered to report to a dark room on the third floor. There were oil drums lined up on a platform. There were grains of wheat in them, and rats in small cages were placed in the wheat. Our assignment was to check them once a day and if we found the rats dead to replace them with live ones. The room was humid and hot. There was a Western-style white porcelain bathtub placed on the platform. The wheat chaff and fleas were mixed in it, and as we used a hair dryer and stirred them we noticed that the fleas were multiplying. Then the fleas were collected in glass containers.

What were those fleas used for?

Rats and humans are the most sensitive to the plague bacillus. Fleas are carriers. If you release fleas from an airplane, the fleas scatter everywhere. They settle on rats, and as the rats die the fleas settle on humans. Before a plague epidemic breaks out, you see many dead rats around. We learned this in plague class.

The Junior Youth Corps was disbanded. Was that around July 1941?

Yes, and then I was assigned to the Karasawa Unit and ordered to handle chemical warfare.

What was the function of the Karasawa Unit?

Mass production of pathogenic germs.

What kinds of pathogenic germs did you produce?

We cultured dysentery, typhoid, paratyphoid, cholera, plague, and anthrax. Especially after 1941, anthrax, plague, and cholera were produced in quantity. We were never told what kinds of germs we were producing. We just figured it out by the smells and shapes. Dysentery bacillus smelled like cucumber. Typhoid bacillus was rather beautiful: a colony of the bacilli reminded me of a group of pearls. Anthrax bacillus was muddy, and cholera bacillus was rough in texture. Plague bacillus was rather stringy, like if you stir up fermented soybeans and pull off the stringy material.

Human Vivisections

In the Karasawa Unit where you worked, did you ever participate in live human dissections?

Yes. It started in December 1942. Before that, we used mice. But in 1942 the experiments I attended were on Chinese people. There were special-unit members who wore lab coats and carried guns in the treatment room. They had boots and field caps on. They brought the human specimens to the treatment room, and I drew their blood. We would draw blood and then test for antibodies. Then we would inject the plague vaccine that had been developed by Unit 731. After that, blood would be drawn and tested again. The live plague bacteria would be injected. Then, after they got critically sick, the doctors would start a dissection.

The people who were brought in by the special-unit staff looked sick and black. I was ordered to wash these people with a deck brush. I was somehow hesitant to use a deck brush on their faces. I remember now that I closed my eyes and washed the faces with the deck brush. My legs were shaking. As soon as the medic checked the specimen with the stethoscope, the chief pathologist started to dissect him. I put the pieces of organs in the culturing medium, which was placed in the culture dish. This was done, we were told, to verify the toxicity of the pathogenic germs we had produced, as well as to check the efficacy of vaccinations. Also it enabled us to obtain stumps for future germ production.

How many times did you participate in such vivisections?

I remember participating four times.

Burning "Logs"

How were those people's cadavers disposed of?

There was a tall chimney in the building; it was a very big chimney. The special security squad burned the cadavers in there.

Did you ever talk about the human vivisections among yourselves at night?

We would go back to our quarters later than usual when we performed such atrocities. During our baths, other members who had similar duties would join us. Our usual conversations went like this: "How many logs did you take down today?" "We took down two today," or, "We didn't take down any logs today."

You left the Karasawa Unit in June 1943. Please explain briefly what you did after that.

I worked in a physics research lab. Then I became a technical worker in the neurology department of the Manchuria Medical School and spent a few months there before I got drafted and served as an infantryman in a division of Shen Wu Tun, near the Russian border. In 1944, I was transferred to the hygiene department and then to the medical department of Division 125 in Tong Hua, Liaoning Province. The war ended when I was there. When I was called to headquarters for the disarmament, I ran away. A year later, on February 3, 1946, I was arrested for starting a riot. When I was released in June 1946, the local police asked us if we wanted to join the Chinese army. They said there was probably no other way to stay alive. So I joined the People's Liberation Army. In the army, I was treated as one of the members. There was no discrimination. Then I started to think about what I had done before, and it made me feel very bad. In 1952, I was sent to Fushun War Criminal Penitentiary as an ex-member of Unit 731.

A Perpetrator's Guilt

Please explain how you were treated in Fushun War Criminal Penitentiary and how your beliefs changed.

In the penitentiary, we were fed three times a day. In the People's Liberation Army, I had started to feel bad. Now, given the free time, I was able to rid my mind of the rationalizations with which I had been brainwashed ever since I was a primary-school student. With my own acts of atrocity dawning on me, I started to regret what I had done as something that no human should do. I started to wonder how I would feel if I got sick from germs dispensed without my consent. I wondered how not only the people who were experimented on but also their families must have felt about their being killed in experiments or vivisections. When I put myself in the victim's place, the atrocities I committed were unforgivable. I should face execution.

The Japanese government has consistently denied and concealed the existence of the germ warfare mentioned in this lawsuit. What is your opinion about the country's attitude?

All the war crimes I committed were performed under orders I received. They were carried out under the direction of my superiors. As for the head of the unit and other staff members, they also acted because they were part of a system. I still believe that Japan should be held responsible as a country. I hope that the nation will consider the feelings of the victims and consider their needs. The victims will never forget.

I sometimes think the atrocities I committed were so inhumane that I am unsure if I am human or inhuman. Because of what I did, sometimes I feel I am in between.

WORKING IN THE SOVIET BIOWEAPONS PROGRAM

Ken Alibek

Relatively few people have ever been inside the Russian bio-weapons laboratory, and fewer still have ever spoken up about the experience. Ken Alibek's memoir is extraordinary, because he actually helped develop deadly bioweapons for the Soviet Union. In the following selection from his book *Biohazard*, Alibek re-counts how, after graduating from a military medical school in 1975, he was assigned to Biopreparat, the Soviet Union's secret bioweapons development facility. Although warned of an inter-national treaty banning germ warfare, he quickly became one of the Soviet regime's top bioweapons developers. In 1987, under the leadership of Soviet premier Mikhail Gorbachev, Alibek was transferred to Moscow to work on even more deadly bioweapons. Among the many projects he worked on was a smallpox weapon-izing program. So secretive was the operation, Alibek says, that workers in the smallpox bioweapons program were given inocula-tions in a place where the scar was unlikely to show.

Ken Alibek was born in the Soviet republic of Kazakhstan in 1950. He graduated in 1975 from the military faculty of the Tomsk Medical Institute, where he majored in infectious diseases and epidemiology. From 1988 to 1992 Alibek served as first deputy chief of the Russian bioweapons program. In 1992, having suffered major disabilities from his decades of work with deadly microbes, Russia's leading bioweapons scientist defected to the United States. He now teaches and serves as executive director for education and science at George Mason University's National Center for Biodefense.

I have lost all sense of smell and have the broadest range of allergies of anyone I know. I can't eat butter, cheese, eggs, mayonnaise, sausages, chocolate, or candy. I swallow two or three pills of anti-

Ken Alibek, *Biohazard*. New York: Dell Publishing, 1999. Copyright © 1999 by Ken Alibek. All rights reserved. Reproduced by permission of Random House, Inc.

allergy medicine a day—more on bad days, when my sinuses start to drain. Every morning, I rub ointment over my face, neck, and hands to give my skin the natural lubricants it has lost. The countless vaccinations I received against anthrax, plague, and tularemia weakened my resistance to disease and probably shortened my life.

A bioweapons lab leaves its mark on a person forever. But this was all in the distant future when I stepped off the train in a desolate corner of western Russia on a wet midsummer's night in 1975.

The East European Scientific Branch of the Institute of Applied Biochemistry was tucked away in a forest carpeted with mushrooms just outside the old Russian city of Omutninsk. It was almost a city of its own. More than ten thousand people lived and worked there, nearly a third of the population of the nearby town. Some thirty weatherbeaten brick buildings, including dormitories, labs, schools, and a heating plant, dotted the grounds. The working area was surrounded by a concrete wall and an electric fence, but the entire complex could have been mistaken for any of the self-sufficient civilian industrial enterprises built by the dozens in equally remote areas of the country. Trucks lumbered in and out every day. Schoolchildren played in one section of the compound. The guards at the front gate never wore uniforms.

Omutninsk housed one of Russia's newest biological warfare facilities. A chemical plant that had been producing biopesticides in the compound since the 1960s was expanded by the Fifteenth Directorate to serve as a reserve "mobilization" plant for wartime production of biological weapons. In the 1970s, construction began on a new complex of buildings. When I arrived, two years after [Soviet Premier Leonid] Brezhnev's secret decree, Biopreparat was in the process of turning Omutninsk into a major center of biological weapons production.

In organizational charts the compound was designated as the "Omutninsk Scientific and Production Base," but we referred to it in our coded cables by its post office box number: B-8389. Officially, Omutninsk manufactured pesticides and other agricultural chemicals. Unofficially it served as a training ground for the next generation of Soviet bioweaponeers.

A Secret World

Some ten or fifteen of us, all in our twenties, arrived that summer. Freshly commissioned officers, we came from military graduate institutes around the Soviet Union. Several had been trained, as I had, in medicine, but our group also included engineers, chemists, and biologists—picked after mysterious interviews followed by long background checks to ascertain that no hint of subversion lurked in our families.

From the very first night when I arrived, soaking wet, to report to my new commanding officer only to be chastised for wearing my military uniform, I knew I had entered into a new world. There were no orientation lectures or seminars, but if we had any doubts as to the real purpose of our assignment, they were quickly dispelled. We were given a paper with a list of regulations for behavior at the plant. At the bottom we were made to sign off on a pledge never to reveal what we were told or what we did.

Our "instructors" came from the KGB. They handed us more forms explaining that we would be doing top-secret research in biotechnology and biochemistry for defensive purposes. Then we were called, one by one, for individual sessions.

"You are aware that this isn't normal work," the officer told me as I sat down. It was a declaration, not a question.

"Yes," I replied.

"I have to inform you that there exists an international treaty on biological warfare, which the Soviet Union has signed," he went on. "According to that treaty no one is allowed to make biological weapons. But the United States signed it too, and we believe that the Americans are lying."

I told him, earnestly, that I believed it too. We had been taught as schoolchildren and it was drummed into us as young military officers that the capitalist world was united in only one aim: to destroy the Soviet Union. It was not difficult for me to believe that the United States would use any conceivable weapon against us, and that our own survival depended on matching their duplicity.

"Good," he said with a satisfied nod. "You can go now—and good luck."

The five minutes I spent with him represented the first and last time any official would bring up a question of ethics for the rest of my career.

Learning to Make Bioweapons

Bacteria are cultivated identically whether they are intended for industrial application, weaponization, or vaccination. Working first with harmless microorganisms, we were taught how to make nutrient media, the broths in which they multiply. Making these potions is an art in itself. Bacteria require highly specialized mixtures of proteins, carbohydrates, and salts—often culled from plant or animal extracts—to achieve the most efficient growth rate.

We would take samples of the nutrient media and analyze their biochemical components, testing for pH and amino acids and calculating the concentration of carbohydrates and other compounds. Then we mixed in the seed material—the bacterial agent—to determine its quality, concentration, and viability. The process of seeding the agents was a delicate one and had to be performed under perfectly aseptic conditions. Next, we studied how temperature, oxygen concentration, differing components of nutrient media, and countless other factors affected bacterial growth.

Within months, I would move from the simple lab techniques of medical school to complicated industrial procedures in biochemistry and microbiology. For the first time in my life, I would work with pathogenic agents, learning how to infect lab animals and conduct autopsies. . . .

Transfer to Moscow

In December 1987, three months after I arrived in Moscow, [General Yuri] Kalinin presented me with my first big assignment: I was to supervise plans to create a new smallpox weapon.

I spent an afternoon inside the third-floor KGB archives at Samokatnaya Street reading my instructions, contained in a secret document setting out the goals of Soviet biological weapons development for the five-year period ending in 1990. Smallpox appeared as a "special item" among the list of diseases marked for weaponization.

The Five-Year Plan, signed in his characteristic scrawl by [Soviet Premier] Mikhail Gorbachev, outlined the most ambitious program for biological weapons development ever given to our agency. It included a three-hundred-million-ruble viral production plant (then equivalent to four hundred million dollars) at Yoshkar-Ola in the autonomous republic of Mordovia. The plan established a new military facility at Strizhi, near Kirov, for the production of viral and bacterial weapons and, most significantly, it funded the construction of a 630-liter viral reactor to produce smallpox at the Russian State Research Center of Virology and Biotechnology, a facility known within The System as Vector. Our military leaders had decided to concentrate on one of the toughest challenges of bioweaponeering—the transformation of viruses into weapons of war.

Gorbachev's Five-Year Plan—and his generous funding, which would amount to over $1 billion by the end of the decade—allowed us to catch up with and then surpass Western technology.

Churning Out Viruses

When I went to Vector in 1987, our new smallpox project was just getting off the ground. The facility, founded by Biopreparat in the early 1970s to specialize in viral research, was located in the small Siberian town of Koltsovo. It had been left to stagnate while we focused on improving our bacterial weapons, but Gorbachev's decree gave it a new lease on life.

Dozens of new lab and production buildings earmarked for research into viruses had been constructed by the time I arrived. More were on the drawing board. There was a large biocontainment structure designed especially for laboratory experiments with contagious viruses such as smallpox, Marburg, Lassa fever, and Machupo, as well as new explosive test chambers and facilities for breeding animals.

Vector's prize acquisition was the expensive new viral reactor authorized by Gorbachev's decree. Designed by one of our Moscow institutes and assembled at a special Biopreparat plant in western Russia, it was the first of its kind in the world. It stood about five feet high and was enclosed within thick stainless steel walls. An agitator at the bottom kept the mixture inside churning like clothes in a washing machine. Pipes led out in several directions, both for waste matter and weapons-ready material. A window on its convex roof allowed scientists to observe the viral culture at all times.

Lev Sandakchiev, Vector's director, was a garrulous Armenian biochemist who had been with Biopreparat since its inception in 1973. Sandakchiev was an expert in orthopoxviruses, the viral genus that includes smallpox. When I saw him he was at his wits' end.

New scientists and technicians were arriving at Vector every month as the program began to take shape. He had to arrange their housing and set up their work programs while keeping track of the construction projects. The scholarly virologist had been leading a backwater scientific research group of several hundred people; now he found himself supervising a work force of more than four thousand workers.

"Just tell me what you need, and I'll get it for you," I said, determined to meet what I regarded as the first test of my talents as a senior executive.

Sandakchiev gave me a haughty look, as if I were one of his lab assistants.

"Time," he replied. "Can you give me time?"

I may have impressed the military and the bureaucrats in Moscow, but there was widespread skepticism inside our elite scientific community about my qualifications for the job. I felt this implicit criticism in his pointed remark.

"I can't give you time," I said with a smile. "It's the one resource we're not permitted to exploit."

Safeguarding Employees

As the months progressed, Sandakchiev and I developed a respectful working relationship, and I was able to unsnarl some of the bureaucratic logjams that had been making his life impossible. At first our biggest concern was safety. If even a tiny amount of smallpox were to escape into the surrounding countryside, it would cause a horrific epidemic. It would be much harder to cover up than the anthrax outbreak in Sverdlovsk.[1]

Sandakchiev was determined to protect his employees. He repeated time and again that he would not sacrifice the health of a single worker to the pressure of a deadline. But running a biological weapons plant was not like managing a small research facility. New rules had to

---

1. On April 2, 1979, an accidental release of anthrax from a bioweapons facility near the Soviet city killed more than sixty people. The authorities blamed it on tainted meat.

be enforced, and there were higher expectations. To keep the country—and our program—safe from exposure, Moscow imposed quarantine conditions on all Vector employees engaged in smallpox research. The staff was confined to special dormitories near the compound and guarded around the clock by security police. In a compromise, we granted them periodic leave to visit their families.

Considering that outsiders might be suspicious if they saw hundreds of people with the distinctive marks of fresh smallpox inoculations on their arms years after the Soviet Union had discontinued all immunization, we decided, after some deliberation, to issue a directive that workers be inoculated on their buttocks. We assumed this part of their anatomy was safe from prying foreign eyes.

Despite his laboratory expertise, Sandakchiev knew little about the technological process required to mass-produce smallpox. We needed someone who was not only a smallpox expert but who could make our new equipment and production lines work efficiently. A search of Biopreparat's personnel records turned up no one in the country who satisfied both requirements. Without such a production manager, the project was sure to falter.

Bringing in an Expert

I was at my desk early one morning in Moscow when Sandakchiev's excited voice came through on the phone.

"I've found the man we need," he said. "But I'm going to need your help to get him here.". . .

"I'll do my best," I said cautiously. "Who is he?"

"His name is Yevgeny Lukin. He's a colonel, works for the Fifteenth Directorate at Zagorsk. No one in the country knows more about producing smallpox. I've already spoken with him and he wants to come. We need you to do the paperwork.". . .

Lukin's transfer was one of the best decisions Biopreparat ever made. Lukin was able to create a production line to manufacture smallpox on an industrial scale, and over the next year I watched with growing satisfaction as Vector blossomed under Sandakchiev's management into a formidable weapons development complex.

In December 1990, we tested a new smallpox weapon in aerosol form inside Vector's explosive chambers. It performed well. We calculated that the production line in the newly constructed Building 15 at Koltsovo was capable of manufacturing between eighty and one hundred tons of smallpox a year.

ANTHRAX ATTACK ON THE CAPITOL

Bill Frist

On October 15, 2001, Senator Bill Frist (R-Tennessee) the only physician in the Senate, learned with horror that his Democratic colleague, Majority Leader Tom Daschle, D-South Dakota, had been the target of an anthrax attack. In the following selection, Frist describes how events unfolded and how he responded to them. A week after the terrorist attacks of September 11, 2001, anthrax-filled letters were mailed to five national news organizations, including three major network news operations. The letters contained a weaponized form of anthrax spores that easily traveled through the paper of the envelopes containing them and became an airborne hazard. Public health authorities were unaware that such a finely milled form of anthrax existed outside military stocks. Senator Frist recounts how confusion prevailed on the first day of the Senate attack. The Hart Senate Building, where Senator Daschle's office was located, remained open, and only those in the immediate vicinity were given precautionary doses of antibiotics. However, Frist recalls, once preliminary tests showed that more than two dozen staff members had inhaled anthrax spores, fear gripped the federal government. Mail to Congress was put in quarantine, Senate offices were sealed off, and thousands of people on Capitol Hill were tested for the presence of anthrax. Then, a mail handler working in a U.S. postal facility miles from the Senate building came down with symptoms of anthrax illness. By the time the 2001 wave of anthrax mailings subsided, twenty-two people around the nation had been infected, and five of them had died. Frist argues that the attacks showed that the nation was unprepared to deal with bioterrorism. He emphasizes the need for the United States to protect itself by gathering scientifically accurate information about the threats from bioweapons and making plans to respond to them. Bill Frist was a transplant surgeon before being elected to the U.S. Senate

Bill Frist, *When Every Moment Counts*. Lanham, MD: Rowman & Littlefield, 2002. Copyright © 2002 by Rowman & Littlefield Publishers, Inc. Reproduced by permission.

in 1994. A graduate of Harvard Medical School, Frist was the first
practicing physician elected to the Senate since 1928. In December 2002 he became majority leader of the Senate.

For two hours that morning [Oct 15, 2001], we talked about bioterrorism in hypothetical terms. Now, suddenly, it was all too real.

An Associated Press reporter asked me to respond to the news that a letter containing anthrax had been delivered to the Washington office of my colleague, Senate Majority Leader Tom Daschle. An undetermined number of staffers in Senator Daschle's Hart Senate Office Building suite had apparently been exposed to the potentially lethal biological agent when the letter was opened. President George W. Bush just minutes before had told the nation about the letter during informal remarks following an event at the White House.

I was stunned. I had spent the morning hosting a roundtable on bioterrorism at the Tennessee Emergency Management Agency headquarters in Nashville. I listened carefully as about three dozen doctors, nurses, hospital administrators, firefighters, police, and other law enforcement, public health, and emergency personnel from all across the state talked about how unprepared they were for the growing threat of bioterrorism.

Little did I know at the time that this initial press question would be my initiation into seven days that would severely test much of what we thought we knew about bioterrorism. Seven days that would challenge our fundamental clinical understanding of anthrax—how to diagnose it, how to treat it, how to protect those who may have been exposed—and how to communicate with the press and the public about a public health emergency with shifting facts and a fluid, rapidly evolving scientific knowledge base.

The coming week also would bring sharply into focus the vital role our public health system plays in responding to such an attack. After all, this was part of the first biological attack on U.S. soil involving anthrax and was only the second known biological attack in the United States in at least a century (the first, in 1984, involved salmonella poisoning of restaurant salad bars by a cult in Oregon).

The lessons learned from the abstract discussions in Nashville on Monday morning, October 15, 2001, would come alive and be played out in vivid detail in Washington over the next seven days.

First Fatality

As I prepared to host the bioterrorism roundtable in Nashville, a Florida man already had died of inhalational anthrax, and an assistant to NBC News anchor Tom Brokaw had been diagnosed with skin, or cutaneous, anthrax. An additional case of each form of the infectious disease would be confirmed later in the day.

So everyone in that room knew that the threat we once considered remote was growing. Frontline responders, those who will answer that panicky phone call or first see a person with symptoms, lacked appropriate training and protective equipment. State and county public health laboratories lacked adequately trained epidemiologists and state-of-the-art facilities and equipment. Community hospitals had no system to share information with each other or with local public health facilities in a timely way.

Vanderbilt Hospital—one of Tennessee's premier teaching and referral hospitals, where I had worked for nine years as a transplant surgeon before coming to the U.S. Senate—acknowledged that it did not have a bioterrorism preparedness plan in place and had not done training exercises to deal with this emerging threat. Nor had any of the community hospitals.

From rural doctors to city police and firefighters to state public health officials, all the way up to the governor's office, the story was the same: They just weren't prepared to respond to what might happen.

Following the conference, I walked into an adjacent room for a press briefing, and the question was no longer about what might happen. It was about what had already happened. . . .

Business Continues

At this point, the Hart building remained open and people were still at work at their desks. In fact, the building would stay open for another day and a half. The risk of exposure was unknown at the time.

I returned to Washington that afternoon and was asked by Senate Republican leader Trent Lott to be the liaison for the Republican senators to the fledgling medical and law enforcement investigation into the anthrax exposure at the Hart building.

Already, those within Senator Daschle's suite had been given nasal swab tests along with a three-day course of antibiotics. And a public health command room had been set up by Majority Leader Daschle in the secretary of the Senate's office on the third floor of the Capitol. It was in this room that data were reported and shared and strategies to deal with the evolving public health and environmental issues were discussed and developed.

Officials representing many agencies—the Centers for Disease Control and Prevention (CDC), the Capitol physician's office, the Defense Advanced Research Projects Agency (DARPA), the Senate sergeant at arms, the Capitol police, Senate leadership, the deputy surgeon general representing the Department of Health and Human Services, and the director of the District of Columbia health department—were almost always in that room for the next several days, coordinating among themselves and then reporting back to their home agencies.

To provide information to the Senate staff and the public at large, we held two press conferences on the first full day and then scheduled daily press conferences for the next week. But many staffers were still confused and anxious about their potential health risk.

Just a few doors from Senator Daschle's suite, my own health sub-committee staff members were experiencing firsthand the difficulty in obtaining helpful information during a public health emergency. Although they knew about the letter, primarily from press reports, almost nothing else was reaching them. Like the rest of the nation outside the walls of the building, their principal source of information was TV.

Lack of Information

On that first day, staffers from Senator Daschle's offices turned to our health subcommittee staff with questions about anthrax and their own health risk, in part because they knew that my staff had been working on issues related to bioterrorism for a long time and in part because, as I am the Senate's only doctor, they knew that my staff and I are involved in most health-related issues. Is anthrax contagious? If I've been exposed, is my family at risk? However, no official word came from those conducting the investigation until later that after-noon, when a police officer visited my staff in the Hart building to confirm that a letter possibly laced with anthrax had been delivered to Senator Daschle's office.

In response, they were closing off a section of the Hart building. The officer would remain on duty outside my staff's door, but the pri-mary reason was to ensure that the press did not bother them as they continued to work. Staffers moved in and out of that wing of the Hart building, totally unaware of any health concerns.

The ventilation system had been shut down within an hour of the incident to avoid potential spread of anthrax, and the staff was told to expect the offices to be warmer than usual. At that time, there was no discussion about their own health risk, and previous experience would suggest that they were not in harm's way.

Nasal swabs to determine how widespread exposure to the anthrax spores had been were eventually obtained from everyone in the Hart building. On Monday, only those present in the vicinity of the Daschle suite when the letter was opened were given preventive antibiotics pending results of the nasal swab tests.

When nasal swab test results confirmed the direct exposure to anthrax of twenty-eight people inside or immediately adjacent to the Daschle suite, anxiety across Capitol Hill soared. The innocent open-ing of a letter, a routine task that is done millions of times every day in offices across the country, suddenly escalated into a public health crisis that truly frightened many people who work on the Hill. Congres-sional mail was quarantined, and a month later, on November 16, 2001, a second anthrax-laced letter—this one addressed to Sen. Patrick Leahy—was discovered by government investigators.

Few of the office workers on that first day really understood what a positive nasal swab meant. What about those whose tests came back negative? Did they have anything to worry about? Why did some of them still have to take antibiotics? It seemed so confusing to everyone involved, including members of the press who were trying to interpret it all.

Anxiety was high. People were not getting the answers they needed. And it was only just beginning. . . .

Utilizing the Web

With offices closing, the normal flow of information through e-mail was instantly cut off because people could no longer get to their office computers, and they couldn't access internal Senate information from their home computers. At the staff meeting, I announced that I would make my official personal Senate website available for the foreseeable future, posting all the information to which I had access. I gave them the website address (Frist.senate.gov) and instructed my staff to stay on it full-time to keep it current throughout the developing situation.

The website contained basic information about anthrax as well as particular ways to deal with this recent attack, including the protocol for opening mail, easy-to-access references, frequently asked questions, and updated information about the current test results, how to obtain your test results, and where additional individuals could be tested. It became a central repository for information for staffers and senators alike.

Everyone wanted to know more about skin and inhalational anthrax, and the initial TV news reports by political figures and health officials were confusing. What does the rash look like? Even as a physician familiar with infectious diseases because of my transplant experience, I'd never seen it. So I immediately called my colleagues around the country, found pictures of the rashes, and within a few hours posted them on the website for the world to see. As questions came throughout the next several days, we posted them with the best answers available. What about pregnant women who were exposed? Go to the website. What are the side effects of Cipro? Go to the website. You could not get that information from the family doctor because the doctor had never been taught about the symptoms and signs of anthrax disease. The answers generally are not in medical textbooks because anthrax is too rare. But we were able to get it all up quickly on a centralized website. Another lesson learned.

Because of my long-standing interest in bioterrorism and the work I had done putting together the Public Health Threats and Emergencies Act of 2000 a year previously, I already had a section on bioterrorism on my site. I was able to expand it quickly over a few hours and updated it twice a day as reports came out of the public health command room at the Senate. My staff made sure this site was linked to other reputable sites with useful information on bioterrorism, biological agents, and public health safety, including the CDC (the overall best site) and other government and university sites. Thousands of people in Washington began to visit our site. Indeed, because it provided current and accurate information, people from around the country began to use it as a primary site.

Testing for Victims

Thankfully, other than the initial twenty-eight staffers, no one else on the Hill tested positive for exposure to anthrax. So only individuals on the fifth and sixth floors of the southeast corridor of the Hart building were initially given the sixty-day course of antibiotics. (All the nasal swab tests reported for my staff were negative, although one individual's test result was lost.)

More than six thousand nasal swabs were tested through the Capitol attending physician's office alone. In addition, thousands of environmental cultures were taken over the next several days. The laboratories were stretched to their limits, and their capacity to handle a sudden rush of new test requests—their "surge capacity"—was surpassed. People were working around the clock. When test results confirmed that anthrax contamination had been detected in the Dirksen Senate Office Building mailroom and elsewhere in the Hart building, as well as in one of the House buildings, the decision was made to close all of the congressional buildings Thursday until further environmental tests could be completed.

This only added to the anxiety of several thousand staffers who were left to wonder whether they had been exposed and were at risk for anthrax infection. Paralysis began to set in. . . .

A patient a few miles away from Capitol Hill had presented with signs and symptoms that might possibly be consistent with the inhalation form of anthrax: shortness of breath, an abnormal chest X ray with enlarged lymph nodes but clear lung fields. But the symptoms were also consistent with the flu. No blood cultures or other tests had confirmed the presence of anthrax, but all the pertinent tests were pending. The results would not be back for another twenty-four hours.

When I heard the details, I was startled—truly alarmed. I realized then that what I'd thought would continue to be a relatively controlled situation on Capitol Hill, with all potential victims already identified and appropriately treated, might abruptly become a national emergency.

Old Truths Gone

According to everything we knew to be true about anthrax at the time, it would have been impossible for someone miles away from where the anthrax-laced envelope was opened to have been infected with the disease. We had relied on our current textbook understanding of the disease: Inhalational anthrax disease does not occur unless there is direct inhalation of more than ten thousand spores.

Given that numerous witnesses saw the letter opened in the suite of offices in the Hart building, it did not seem possible that enough spores could have escaped to infect someone who wasn't fairly close to where the letter was opened.

What we were discovering was that even the information from the best medical scientists and public health specialists in the United States was wrong. Dead wrong. We did not know enough. No one did. We as a nation were underprepared scientifically for bioterrorism.

Although the test results would not be back for another day and the clinical data were really not very clear, I believed the information could portend a national catastrophe. Was this part of a much bigger conspiracy or terrorist activity? Would we start seeing cases around the country now? Were postal workers safe? Would our mail system be shut down locally—or possibly nationally—just as the air transportation system had been paralyzed a month previously by the terrorist attacks on Washington and New York?

What was next?

With bioterrorism, the perpetrator doesn't have to be present, the weapon is invisible, and the victims may not become apparent until days after exposure. It is much different from any other type of crime.

Facing the Unknown

The one thing I knew was that all certainty had disappeared. We were seeing things happen that had never even been envisioned by scientific or health officials. Just as five weeks before, the September 11 terrorist attacks at the Pentagon and World Trade Centers were beyond what anyone had ever envisioned could happen.

I immediately got up, went across the room to the telephone, and called the White House. I asked to speak to Tom Ridge. Just a few weeks earlier, Ridge, the former governor of Pennsylvania, had been appointed homeland security director by President Bush. Governor Ridge called back immediately, and I told him that we no longer had a local public health situation but a potential national emergency, with disease appearing and behaving like we had never seen before. I said that this could explode as a national security issue and a national public health emergency.

If people could get infected by simple exposure to mail (not the opening of mail), would we see others presenting with symptoms around the country over the next several days? Would we be prepared if they did? I asked Governor Ridge to give us a bit more time to get more information, and we agreed to have a conference call one hour later with the nation's highest officials in charge of emergency preparedness and response. . . .

As with all areas of medicine, the body of knowledge is an ever changing enterprise, updated daily with more information from various studies. However, we had not updated our understanding of anthrax or other potential biological agents in years, primarily because of a lack of data.

In short, we weren't ready for what occurred. . . .

Our nation is on high alert. We're being faced with new challenges, in our places of work and in our homes. But our nation, our officials at all levels of government, and the American people are taking the steps necessary now to be prepared to meet whatever challenge comes our way.

Toward this end there are things that each and every one of us can do. One of the most powerful is to become knowledgeable and informed. An understanding of some of the basics on how to prepare for, and respond to, the use of microbes as weapons goes a long way to reduce anxiety and minimize any chance of paralysis in our lives.

In the war against bioterrorism, information is power.

An Anthrax Victim Struggles to Recover

Angela Rucker

In September and October of 2001, anthrax-laden letters entered the U.S. mail system. They were sent to news organizations in New York and Florida, and to two Democratic senators, Tom Daschle of South Dakota and Patrick Leahy of Vermont. The anthrax spores in the letters eventually sickened twenty-two people, of whom five died. One of the victims was Norma Wallace, a postal worker employed at a mail-sorting facility near Trenton, New Jersey, where some of the anthrax letters seem to have been posted. In the following selection, reporter Angela Rucker offers Wallace's reflections on her nearly fatal exposure to anthrax and on her struggle to recover from the disease. On October 9, 2001, an envelope containing powder jammed the sorting machine that Wallace was operating. Some of the powder, later identified as weaponized anthrax, spilled out, and Wallace breathed in enough of the tiny spores to contract inhalational anthrax, the deadliest form of the disease. The disease has left her with frequent aches, fatigue, and memory loss. Her nights alternate between sleeplessness and nightmares. Because there are few recorded cases of inhalation anthrax survivors, doctors are unable to offer much help. Wallace expresses some doubt about whether government officials are actually interested in helping rather than just studying, her. Nevertheless, Wallace expresses gratitude for the help of family, friends, and even strangers. Wallace, who was fifty-six at the time of the attack, is the mother of two grown children. She has been unable to return to her job and has been living on disability payments. Angela Rucker is a reporter for the The Courier-Post. She specializes in health and medical issues.

Uncertainty is Norma Wallace's constant companion. So is a lump in her back slightly larger than a music CD, a "souvenir," as she calls it,

Angela Rucker, "Life Is Still a Struggle for Anthrax Survivor," *The Courier-Post*, Cherry Hill, N.J., September 10, 2002. Copyright © 2002 by *The Courier-Post*. Reproduced by permission.

from the battle she won against the most lethal form of anthrax.

Today [Sept. 10, 2002] the 57-year-old postal worker is left with questions that don't have answers: When will she regain her energy? Her memory? A normal life?

"It's a very, very slow process," said Wallace, a resident of Willingboro. "I can go one day to therapy and go through treatment, and the next week I'm back to square one. I don't know why, but it just isn't catching."

Five Others Died

Hers is a familiar story among the six people who survived inhalation anthrax. The spores that cause the illness were spread through a spate of mailings to congressional leaders and journalists in October [2001], a month after the terrorist attacks on the World Trade Center and Pentagon.

Scientists have virtually no data on the long-term effects of surviving a bout with inhalation anthrax. The reason: In the past, more than 85 percent of victims would die, and the disease is rarely seen in the United States. In last year's acts of bioterrorism, five of 11 victims died, a 45 percent death rate.

Anthrax survivors like Wallace find themselves unwitting participants in a medical mystery. Only one of the six has returned to work. And, of the postal workers Wallace speaks with routinely, she is the only one not taking drugs to manage her pains and "souvenirs."

Not that she doesn't have any problems.

The woman who once took college correspondence courses while also holding down two jobs—substitute teaching in Willingboro during the day, working at the post office at night—must now nap in the afternoons.

She also suffers from unexplained pains in her joints, sleepless nights and memory loss.

"I can go for periods of time if I'm in conversation and be coherent, and then all of a sudden I've lost it. My mind has gone blank," Wallace said in her soft but confident voice.

She has not returned to either job, and receives disability pay from the post office.

A Deadly Powder

Wallace was working an evening shift at the Trenton Processing and Distribution Center in Hamilton, Mercer County, when investigators say an envelope containing a powder later identified as anthrax apparently whizzed through the sorting machine she was operating. Something twice jammed the machine on Oct. 9, and a mechanic removed dust to get it going again while Wallace was standing nearby.

The contents of that dust are believed to have sickened Wallace.

She spent 18 days at Virtua-Memorial Hospital, Burlington County in Mount Holly, where doctors gave her a 50–50 chance of survival when she showed up in the emergency room. Slowly, she recovered and left the hospital after a triumphant news conference where she became a symbol of hope to a nation shattered by the toll terrorists had taken.

Doctors had predicted a full recovery for Wallace and the five other inhalation anthrax survivors once they were sent home.

"I think they're waiting for death so they can do an autopsy," Wallace now says matter-of-factly. "They don't have an answer."

Wallace is regaining her health and her upbeat nature is apparent, but she also says hers is a daily struggle mentally and physically.

On good days, she pursues hobbies like sewing, walks 30 minutes in her neighborhood for exercise, studies for an English degree and acts as the family gofer.

She hasn't seen a physician since May, but continues with a therapist for post-traumatic stress disorder.

Bad days are filled with pain, bad nights with sleeplessness or nightmares. "I think that I'm there (at the post office) and I feel frozen, like I can't move," Wallace said. "I can't go past that threshold."

Initially she wanted to press federal health officials—she thinks they know more than they are telling—for answers to her medical maladies. As in her dreams, she felt like someone had wrested control away from her.

And now?

"I'm complacent at this point because I realize . . . there's not going to be a real resolution, not immediately anyway," Wallace said.

"They're not going to tell us. That's why I'm OK with that now. Every day has enough stuff in it, activities going on, events and circumstances. Why would you want to take on the whole United States government?"

Government Monitoring Survivors

Llelwyn Grant, a spokesman with the Centers for Disease Control and Prevention, said the agency is concerned about all of the estimated 10,000 people—including the inhalation anthrax survivors—who were or could have been exposed to anthrax and continue to experience medical problems. "We take very seriously any medical issues that have been brought to our attention," he said. "We're doing whatever we can to investigate.

"We're still learning a lot about this particular bacteria," Grant continued. "One of the things we had hoped to see was for the survivors to return to normal activities. In some cases that has not been the case."

The CDC anticipates it could spend two years following up with the anthrax survivors. In part, public health officials are looking to Wallace and the others for information that could help future victims.

Federal researchers have analyzed and dissected the cases of the inhalation anthrax victims—Wallace was "Case 8" in a 2001 report.

Unlike with illnesses such as heart conditions or diabetes, however, medical authorities are not able to provide advice to anthrax victims on how to manage their condition once the worst has passed.

No Arrests

On the legal end of the investigation, the FBI has not arrested anyone in connection with the anthrax attacks, though the government, the post office and a large direct mail company are offering a $2.5 million reward for information leading to the perpetrator's capture and conviction.

Wallace keeps tabs on the slow-moving investigations—people telephone her whenever anthrax is back in the news—but doesn't follow them intently.

She has found some positives to focus on instead.

Now she celebrates the chance to reconnect with family and friends. Before, they wouldn't have thought to include her in their activities because she was so busy with work and school. And her two children, both adults with their own lives to pursue, call or stop by at least once a day. "My kids hover over me," she said.

Strangers also come up to her and tell her to call if she needs anything.

All this lets Wallace know "that the world is not as cold a place as it's made out to be."

Wallace said her faith in God has sustained her even as she has grown skeptical about the government's commitment to helping the survivors.

In July, the CDC telephoned her to request another vial of her blood. The agency already has five. Wallace agreed, but thinks this will be her last donation.

"I said, 'Will it benefit me? Will anything I do . . . benefit me? Will I get better because I'm participating?' He said, 'No ma'am, it's not going to help you.'"

CHAPTER 4

DEFENDING AGAINST BIOWEAPONS ATTACKS

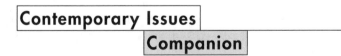

Contemporary Issues
Companion

Emergency Vaccine Programs

Mark B. McClellan and Anthony S. Fauci

A series of deadly anthrax attacks in 2001, which targeted government as well as news media facilities, led to numerous efforts to improve the nation's defenses against bioweapons. In his February 2003 State of the Union speech, President George W. Bush announced plans for Project BioShield, a comprehensive effort to protect U.S. citizens from bioterrorism. In the following selection, the directors of two key administration agencies testify before Congress in support of President Bush's BioShield bill. Mark B. McClellan and Anthony S. Fauci describe for members of the House Government Reform Committee the three major components of the bill. First, the bill would give the National Institute of Allergy and Infectious Diseases new authority to accelerate the research and development of new countermeasures to bioterrorism. Second, they state, BioShield would create a fund in the Department of Homeland Security for the purchase of new vaccines and other biomedical agents developed by private industry to guard against bioterrorism. Third, the bill would give the federal government the power in times of national emergency to use unlicensed remedies to protect the population. Congress passed the bill, and President Bush signed it into law on July 21, 2004. Mark B. McClellan was commissioner of the Food and Drug Administration at the time he gave this testimony on April 4, 2003. Anthony S. Fauci is director of the National Institute of Allergy and Infectious Diseases, which is part of the National Institutes of Health.

Chairman [Tom] Davis, Congressman [Henry] Waxman, and Members of the Committee, thank you for holding this hearing today to discuss the Administration bill, the Project BioShield Act of 2003. As you know, the Department of Health and Human Services has been heavily engaged in the Federal government's efforts to prevent, prepare for, and respond to acts of terrorism, particularly those involving

Mark B. McClellan and Anthony S. Fauci, testimony before the U.S. House Government Reform Committee, Washington, DC, April 4, 2003.

chemical, biological, radiological and nuclear threat agents. This bill is a continuation of such efforts. . . .

It is important to appreciate how each of the three components contained in this proposal interact to quickly and safely develop and make available lifesaving bioterrorism countermeasures. As such, we would like to take this opportunity to describe the three main components of Project BioShield.

Pharmaceutical research and development historically has focused on development of products likely to attract significant commercial interest. Many countermeasures for potential agents of terrorism realistically have no market other than the government and thus have not generated a great deal of manufacturer interest. Because the market for developing medical countermeasures against terrorism is speculative private companies have not invested and engaged in developing the medical countermeasures that the current situation warrants. However, in the vaccine development area, representatives of the pharmaceutical industry have stressed that, to the extent that the federal government can define its vaccine requirements and assure up front that the requisite funds will be available to purchase the vaccines, the industry will meet the challenge.

Unconventional Threats Are Looming

In these post-9/11 times of increased potential for chemical, biological, radiological, and nuclear and other terrorist attacks, it is important now more than ever for the United States to take all necessary steps to protect its citizens from these agents. The current security environment dictates the need for rapid acquisition of countermeasures. Armed with technology that only recently was the stuff of science fiction, the U. S. armed forces are better equipped than ever to take military actions against threats to our national security and defend U.S. citizens against missiles, aircraft, guns and other traditional weaponry. But other not-so-traditional threats are lurking. Our enemies seek, and in some cases have already obtained, biological, chemical, radiological and nuclear weapons that could penetrate our military defenses and civilian surveillance systems, and cause significant harm. We need your help to confront these threats to our homeland.

The possibility of the intentional use of chemical, biological, radiological, and nuclear agents presents a true threat to our society. You have heard about many of these threats: anthrax, smallpox, tularemia, botulinum toxin, hemorrhagic fevers and plague. We will fight these new weapons, not with bombs and guns, but with countermeasures such as vaccines, therapeutics, and early diagnosis. We may be called upon to provide mass inoculation or drug treatment. The personnel who will lead the efforts to develop, acquire, regulate, and administer these medical tools will not necessarily wear military uniforms or be headquartered at the Pentagon. They are civilian administrators and scientists of the Department of Health and Human Services located in such places as the Centers for Disease Control and Prevention (CDC), the Food and Drug Administration (FDA) and the National Institutes of Health (NIH), as well as State and local health officials.

New Vaccines Arriving

We are making rapid progress in acquiring countermeasures for the agents of greatest concern such as smallpox, anthrax, and botulism toxin and have made advances in development of new products. We have sufficient Aventis smallpox vaccine to vaccinate the country in an emergency and the new ACAM2000 cell culture [smallpox] vaccine is coming into the stockpile at a rapid rate. We expect to have 155 million doses by this summer [2003]. NIH initiated the industrial development of a safer next generation smallpox vaccine by signing two contracts with manufacturers last month. On the NIH campus, a new, potentially safer smallpox vaccine entered the first stage of human testing. We currently have a stockpile of antibiotics to deal with an attack with anthrax, plague, and tularemia. In addition, we have access to a stockpile of the current anthrax vaccine and are optimistic that an accelerated development program involving two manufacturers begun last October [2002] will result in production of a new recombinant anthrax vaccine sometime next year partially with BioShield funding. Tularemia and plague vaccines are in the research phase and expected to move into advanced development within 2 years. We also have acquired additional quantities of botulinum antoxins for the treatment of botulism.

Because of a relative lack of focused research on terrorist agents, the medical treatments available for some types of terrorist attacks have improved little in decades while there has been tremendous and rapid progress in the treatment of serious natural-occurring diseases. At a time when Americans must confront the realities of terrorism directed at the United States, it is imperative that the Federal government be prepared to protect our citizens from potential agents of bioterrorism.

Many of the available countermeasures have been made using traditional, older technologies, and some have significant side effects (e.g., the traditional "Dryvax" smallpox vaccine). Newer products produced using advanced technologies such as the production of recombinant anthrax or botulinum toxin proteins or more attenuated viral strains to protect against smallpox hold out hope of reducing adverse reactions while maintaining effective protection. Extensive studies must be performed to assure that these products are both safe and effective. Showing effectiveness when diseases do not occur naturally can be challenging and requires the use of appropriate animal models and careful studies of the critical immune responses to a vaccine. These studies are best planned with close interaction between government scientists and the countermeasure sponsors. Such early product development planning has been going on in partnership with FDA,

NIH, CDC, and others (e.g., the development and evaluation of new smallpox and anthrax vaccines). Other examples where older vaccines or other technologies have been employed (often effectively) include vaccines for plague and anthrax and immunoglobulins for treating smallpox vaccine complications and botulism. Also, the promise of rapid productions of large amounts of monoclonal antibodies that could be used to protect against a variety of bioterrorist pathogens or vaccine adverse events is becoming a reality.

Need for Partnerships

This must be a public and private partnership. The pathway from idea to final product is complex. The optimal scientific approach to identifying the best drug and vaccine candidates must be based on laboratory studies. Testing must be performed in appropriate animal models to document safety and appropriate protective or treatment response, and to help determine dosing. Human studies must be carefully initiated to assure the basic safety of the product, and then appropriate dosing and response must be determined based on measurements of levels of drug or antibody predicted to have a protective effect. Steps must be taken to assure that the materials used to make the countermeasures—and the final product itself—can be manufactured safely, free of contaminants, and with reproducible and predictable purity, potency, and composition. Careful trials in humans, or where not possible, animal models, must be performed to show that the product is safe and effective for the types of populations which might receive it and against the methods of infection or exposure that could be encountered. All of these steps require careful planning, experience, and ongoing management and scientific evaluation. Costs to develop and manufacture high quality biological products and perform and evaluate the needed animal and human studies are high. Grants and contract mechanisms may not always be sufficient or attract the most experienced manufacturers. Manufacturing capacity for biological products, for vaccines, is not substantial. For all these reasons, the best possible support and public-private partnerships and teamwork are essential.

The President announced BioShield in his 2003 State of the Union Address. This is a key legislative priority for this Administration. The BioShield bill is designed to speed the development and availability of medical countermeasures in response to the current threats our Nation faces. The goals of Project BioShield are: 1) to accelerate and streamline government research on countermeasures; 2) to create incentives for private companies to develop countermeasures for inclusion in the stockpile; and, 3) to give the government the ability to make these products widely available quickly in a public health emergency in order to protect our citizens from an attack using a select agent. This legislation is a critical component of our Nation's homeland security strategy.

The three major provisions of the Bill are described below.

Expediting Research and Development at NIH

First, the Department, working primarily through the National Institute of Allergy and Infectious Diseases at NIH, would be given new authorities to speed research and development in promising areas of medical countermeasures against potential bioterrorism agents. The increased authority will provide additional flexibility in awarding contracts, cooperative agreements, and grants for research and development of medical countermeasures including vaccines, drugs, biologics, and diagnostics, and streamlined authority to hire necessary technical experts. Funding awards would remain subject to rigorous scientific peer review, but expedited peer review procedures could be used when appropriate.

NIH is leading the Federal government's campaign to improve the Nation's public health through biomedical research. The major reason that NIH has been entrusted with this vital leadership role is its proven record in combating naturally occurring emerging and re-emerging diseases, which is fortified by its rigorous system for ensuring that only the best science is supported by Federal dollars. Underpinning NIH's research is a rigorous peer review system, which brings together top experts from the public and private sectors of scientific research, as well as patient representatives and other members of the public, to evaluate research grant applications. NIH applies stringent management controls over contracts, personnel, leasing, and construction to ensure careful and responsible use of taxpayer dollars. These safeguards have served the country well. Currently, NIH is leading us through the greatest era of discovery in the history of medical research.

The President's Project BioShield initiative is intended to speed up NIH research and advanced development in targeted areas by providing more flexible authorities for NIH including procurement and personnel recruitment for critical biodefense work. Our BioShield proposal would authorize the Secretary of Health and Human Services, acting through NIH, to simplify and expedite acquisition requirements for material and services through such mechanisms as raising the dollar threshold for simplified acquisitions and using noncompetitive procedures when necessary. The Act would allow the Secretary to expedite scientific peer review requirements in urgent circumstances, but still require a process of quality review.

Project BioShield is intended to strike a balance, during times of crisis, between the Federal government's need to guarantee that the best research is conducted effectively and efficiently, and the national need to have a quick turnaround in responding to biological, chemical, and nuclear weapons of terror. With the authorities contained in the Act, we can improve our ability to respond to chemical, biological, radiological or nuclear attacks against American citizens and soldiers.

It often takes many months to issue research grants, engage pharmaceutical companies to manufacture vaccines and other drug therapies, hire personnel and consultants, or acquire material and services. In times of emergency, we cannot afford the time that it currently takes to accomplish these goals and events. We need vaccines and drugs to fight bioweapons right now. We need expertise right now. We need to build biocontainment facilities to conduct research right now. Project BioShield gives us the tools to cut through red tape and accomplish our mission.

Procurement of Countermeasures

Second, and perhaps most important to this Committee, as it falls under your jurisdiction, the Administration's bill creates a new permanent, indefinite funding authority within the Department of Homeland Security (DHS) to procure medical countermeasures for inclusion in the DHS Strategic National Stockpile. This Department will play a major role along with DHS in identifying and evaluating critical biomedical countermeasures. Certain countermeasures, including antibiotics, are procured and distributed by the Department of Veterans Affairs' National Acquisition System. A great deal of work has been done to identify vaccines and antitoxins that would be needed to protect the U.S. population from dangerous pathogens, e.g. anthrax, smallpox, botulinum toxin, tularemia, Ebola, and plague. In the interest of national security and public health, it is essential that the Administration engage in the process as early as possible with sponsors and organizations that are developing the therapeutics, vaccines, and other countermeasures. This Department will maintain a proactive role to help ensure that the products are developed as efficiently as possible.

The Administration already has identified several products as promising countermeasures and is meeting with sponsors to help foster the successful development of these products. Such products include new generation smallpox and anthrax vaccines and therapies to treat botulism, plague, and Ebola and other hemorrhagic diseases. . . .

The Administration recognizes that no other significant commercial market exists for many of these products that will be needed to protect our military and civilian population. This authority will enable the government to purchase vaccines, therapies, and other interventions provided experts believe that the countermeasures can be made safe and effective. The Secretary of HHS and the Secretary of DHS will collaborate in identifying these critical medical countermeasures, by evaluating likely threats, new opportunities in biomedical research and development, and other public health considerations.

Emergency Use Authorization

The FDA approval process for drugs, devices, and biological products is the gold standard for the world. Sixty percent of the world's drugs are introduced first in the United States. Research and development pipelines hold the promise of dramatically advanced treatments, thanks to breakthroughs in genomics, proteomics, nanotechnologies, and other biomedical sciences. In the years ahead, we can look forward to more sophisticated, individualized, and effective treatments. Our policies and regulations help ensure that products that get to market are safe and effective. In addition to animal studies, sponsors of new drugs and vaccines typically conduct three phases of clinical trials in humans to demonstrate the safety and efficacy of a product. This process can take years, and is procedurally cumbersome.

In preparing for the challenges we face today, we may not always have a desirable amount of time to address the threat presented by agents of bioterrorism. The current FDA approval process is too long to be used during emergency situations. We have some mechanisms in place to get products to market faster, e.g. the accelerated approval mechanism, and expedited review. The animal efficacy rule provides a new avenue for approval for products whose efficacy cannot be tested in human clinical trials. The single patient IND [Investigational New Drug] process and the treatment IND process permit access to unapproved products. However, these mechanisms alone are not sufficient in an emergency.

This Bill will permit the Government to make new and promising treatments still under development available quickly, if needed, for use in emergency situations where no effective approved or licensed products are available, potentially saving many lives. This authorization will only be used when a national emergency has been declared. In the absence of FDA approval of a product for a specific countermeasure use, the BioShield Bill permits the HHS Secretary to issue an emergency authorization that would provide Americans with access to certain unlicensed countermeasures. The Secretary has discretion to facilitate the availability of these important products. Before issuing an emergency authorization, the HHS Secretary must make the following conclusions:

• the agent specified in the determination can cause serious or life-threatening disease;

• the product may reasonably be believed to be effective in detecting, diagnosing, treating, or preventing the disease;

• the benefits of the product may reasonably be believed to outweigh its risks;

• there is no adequate alternative to the product that is approved and available; and

• any other criteria prescribed in regulation are met.

This Bill would allow use of the best technology available at the time of a declared emergency. The emergency use authorization would remain in effect no more than one year, unless the specific terrorist threat justifies extension of the authorization.

FDA regulations are stringent when it comes to informed consent for investigational products. Because urgent situations may require mass inoculations and/or drug treatments, such informed consent requirements may prove impossible to implement within the necessary time frame when trying to achieve the public health goal of protecting Americans from the imminent danger. The legislation would provide for the Secretary to impose conditions on the authorization, either by regulation or on a case-by-case basis, where appropriate to protect public health. Specifically, the bill provides that such conditions shall include labeling and other requirements to ensure that health care professionals are informed of the special emergency nature of the authorization; of the benefits and risks (and the extent to which such benefits and risks are unknown); and of the alternatives to the product, and their benefits and risks. In addition, the conditions of authorization may include the following:

• labeling and other requirements to ensure that patients are informed of the special emergency nature of the authorization; of the benefits and risks (and the extent to which such benefits and risks are unknown); of any option to refuse the product; and of the alternatives to the product, and their benefits and risks;

• limitations on who may distribute the product and how distribution should be performed;

• limitations on who may administer the product, to whom it may be administered, and when it may be administered;

• requirements to perform further studies or clinical trials;

• record keeping and reporting requirements;

• requirements, or waiver of otherwise-applicable requirements, regarding good manufacturing practice; and,

• requirements for monitoring and reporting adverse events.

The language of this Bill is narrowly tailored to address the essential components for use of an emergency authorization. It provides specific conditions and criteria for issuance of such an authorization. It requires a declaration of emergency and provides for a limited duration of use. It gives the Secretary authority to require record keeping and access to records. Finally, it provides civil monetary penalties for violations.

Protecting the United States

The Department of Health and Human Services is committed to ensuring the health and medical care of our citizens. Project BioShield is another step towards enhancing our Nation's ability to respond to biological or chemical threats.

• Ensure that sufficient resources are available to procure the next generation of countermeasures;

• Accelerate NIH research and developing by providing more flexibility in the contracting process, procurement authorities, and grant making for critical biodefense work; and,

• Make promising treatments available more quickly for use in emergencies by establishing new emergency use authorization procedures at the FDA.

Mr. Chairman and members of the Committee, we seek your bipartisan support to move this issue forward and support this Bill. We look forward to working closely with this and other Committees to pass this important legislation and improve our nation's preparedness for and response capability to the threat of bioterrorism.

BIOWEAPONS DETECTORS

Margaret E. Kosal

Bioweapons are exceptionally stealthy. Unlike guns or bombs, bioweapons can be launched without their victims being aware that they have been attacked. Only when enough people fall ill with some unusual disease do suspicions of a bioweapon incident arise. In the selection that follows, researcher and entrepreneur Margaret E. Kosal describes a range of sensors and detection devices intended to alert authorities to the presence of biological agents before they can do harm. When a bioweapon is deployed in a spray or mist of deadly germs, the earliest warning system may be Doppler radar, similar to that used by forecasters to detect tornadoes. Lasers can also be useful in spotting a bioweapons mist. To single out particular germs, test strips that mimic human antibodies are available. However, Kosal notes, these tests frequently provide erroneous results. Genetic analysis offers greater accuracy in detection, and recent technological advances have speeded up the process to as little as ten minutes. However, such systems are delicate and require expert operators. Mass spectrometry, in which charged molecules are identified by their electrical signatures, can be useful detectors but have the drawbacks of bulk, expense, and complexity. In short, Kosal concludes, no one system meets all needs. Margaret E. Kosal is a science fellow at Stanford University's Center for International Security and Cooperation. She is currently leading a study of chemical and biological weapons detectors. In 2001, she co-founded a high-tech biological and chemical sensor company.

Like modern canaries in a coal mine, the goal of chemical and biological weapons detectors and sensors is to alert to an imminent danger. This article's intent is to provide an overview of the technologies underlying detectors and the type of sensing systems currently employed or under near-term consideration for detecting chemical and biological warfare or terrorist weapons. . . .

Margaret E. Kosal, "The Basics of Chemical and Biological Weapons Detectors," http://cns.miis.edu, November 24, 2003. Copyright © 2003 by Center for Nonproliferation Studies. Reproduced by permission.

Biological agents come in many flavors—from delicate RNA-based filoviruses to robust spores of the *Bacillus anthracis* bacterium to toxins bestriding the margins of biological and chemical agents. These differences make the creation of a single detector for all biological agents challenging.

The "gold standard" for identification of microbiological species remains culturing—literally growing a colony of microbes on a nutrient containing surface (Petri dish) and observing it with the eye or through a microscope. Culturing is inexpensive and highly sensitive but slow. Roughly a minimum of a million (10^6) bacteria are necessary to form a visible colony. Detection of single cells is possible but only after long incubation times, usually days. Typical evaluation times are twelve to twenty-four hours for many bacteria but can exceed a week for exotic, slow-growing or more difficult to culture agents.

Cloud-Spotting

The initial criterion for monitoring and surveillance of potential biological agent at a distance is the observation of aerosolized masses (clouds). Spotting and evaluating the contents of a cloud is referred to as "standoff" detection. At a rudimentary level, these detector types aim to alert to the presence of an (approaching) cloud. Depending on the situation the recipient of that alert may be military, civil authorities, public health personnel or an individual. From that basic awareness, a more refined assessment of the contents, such as water droplets, inert inorganic material, dead biotic particulates or non-pathogenic microbes is pursued. Ideally a standoff detector will also be able to provide some information as to the nature of an aerosolized agent.

One technique which is familiar from weather reporting is the use of Doppler radio detecting and reanging (radar). Using reflected radio waves, the shape, size, directionality and speed of a cloud can be monitored. The elapsed time before the radio waves return to a receiver and the change in the radio waves' energy upon return to a receiver provide information about a cloud. For example, shape can offer clues to differentiate natural-occurring cumulus clouds from cigar-shaped ones (difficult to determine visually at night), which are indicative of aerosol release from a single source such as a plane or a moving vehicle.

Another tool for cloud detection and recognition, LIDAR, is based on the same physical principles as radar, except instead of bouncing longer wavelength radio waves off a target, higher energy light waves are used. An acronym for "Light Detection And Ranging," LIDAR is occasionally attributed to "Laser Identification and Ranging" by those who want to emphasize the recognition feature. Using lasers that generate light waves in the infrared, the ultraviolet and the visible portion of the electromagnetic spectrum, the multiple energy wavelengths of LIDAR furnish more detailed information, including three-dimensional imaging. Limitations on detection distance and resolution are due to the collection and processing portions of the detector. The more specific the level of data desired, the closer the instruments must be located to the cloud. . . .

The U.S. Army's Long Range Biological Standoff Detection System (LR-BSDS) uses LIDAR-based technology to detect aerosol clouds from long distances. The Short Range Biological Standoff Detection System (SR-BSDS) combines infrared LIDAR with ultraviolet light reflectance (UV). The latter provides enhanced discrimination capabilities. . . .

Recent laboratory work using laser-induced breakdown spectroscopy (LIBS) has demonstrated the ability to remotely detect aerosolized and surface-adhered (on soil, rock, etc.) bacteria. The LIBS-based systems not only detect the presence of an agent but also differentiate among bacterial species and among potential biological interferents (pollen, molds) with one instrument.

Point Detectors

Detectors that pass directly through or to which a potential biological agent-containing sample is introduced are referred to as "point" detectors. These require that the instrument, and usually the operator, physically enter a cloud and obtain a sample.

Weaponized biological agents have characteristic physical dimensions. In order to be effective, agents must be small enough to not drop out of the cloud. Respirable particles have diameters between 0.5 and 20 μm [micrometers] (10^{-6} m). These are the particles which have the physiological potential to embed in the narrow passages (alveoli) or upper portions of the lung. Particles larger than 100 μm fall from the cloud; particles smaller than 0.5 μm are easily respired and do not remain in the lungs. Aerosol particle sizers (APS) take advantage of those size characteristics for detecting BW [bioweapon] agents. A strongly uniform particle distribution in the size range associated with an inhalable risk or a substantial increase in numbers relative to a typical background may be indicative of the release of a biological agent. At the heart of APS instruments, nonetheless, is simply an attempt to detect higher than normal concentrations of airborne particles.

In APS systems, particles are drawn through an orifice into a steady high-speed air flow. The velocity of the carrier air remains constant throughout. The introduced particles accelerate at rates proportional to their size. Particles impact a collector or pass through a laser light beam to characterize the size. While most particle sizers are fairly large and heavy systems, hand-held analyzers are commercially available. . . .

Detecting Particular Diseases

Immunoassay-based detectors mimic the human body's natural immune system. The immune system produces highly specific proteins, called antibodies in response to antigens from foreign bacterium, toxins or other microbiological organisms. Antigens are molecules on the surface of the foreign microbes. Antibodies form strong and specific interactions with antigens. This specific response is the foundation of immunological detectors.

Disposable hand-held assay (HHA) test kits, such as enzyme-linked immunosorbent assays (ELISAs), or tickets for detecting biological warfare agents have been available since the early 1990s. Using laboratory-produced monoclonal antibodies, HHA tickets recognize the antigen in a sample to which that antibody would be produced if human infection occurred. This technique is pathogen-specific, i.e., one agent per test strip.

Immunoassays need some sort of optical signal generator—something that will "glow" when the detecting antibodies encounter a "hit." Typically, this is done with a fluorescent or chemiluminescent dye molecule that is chemically bonded to the detecting antibodies. . . .

False Readings

Some immunochromatographic tickets [strips that change color in the presence of certain germs] have exceedingly high reported false positive rates. False positives are responses to something which the detector is not supposed to respond. A common false positive is response to a nonpathogenic "nearest neighbor" bacterial species found in the environment, i.e., mistaking *Bacillus thuringiensis* for *B. anthracis*. The flipside are false negatives, which are incidents in which an actual release is not detected. Such tests are both single use and respond to a single pathogen.

Among the disposable test strips currently available on the market, individual prices average approximately $20. While requiring less than twenty minutes for analysis and being easy-to-use, the antigen-antibody binding based tests are not sensitive. Illustratively, one of the best commercially available test strips for *Bacillus anthracis* requires greater than 10,000 spores for a positive reading, which is above the number the U.S. Army Medical Research Institute of Infectious Diseases (USAMRIID) cites as necessary to cause infection. Additionally, cross-reaction with non-virulent related species generating false positives is frequently cited as a leading problem. Interfacing with a portable test strip reader permits more rapid analysis (less than five minutes) and simultaneous screening against multiple (greater than eight) agents. Multiplexed immunoassays are being developed to detect multiple pathogens.

Another approach involves combing immunoassays with flow cytometry. Individual microspheres or microfibers are labeled with both a specific antigen and multiple color-coded dyes to provide semi-quantitative assessment of multiple biological agents collected in a single sample.

The Biological Detector (BD) portion of the U.S. military's Biological Integrated Detection System (BIDS) includes immunoassay-based sensors as part of its suite of detectors. Providing immunoassay tests for ten BW agents, including *B. anthracis, Yersinia pestis,* botulinum toxin A and staphylococcal enterotoxin B (SEB), the portable system requires substantial power, reagents, warm-up time, and is portable (135 lbs) only as far as the generator-carrying vehicle on which it is mounted can travel. Complete disclosure of the agents detected by BIDS has not been made available for security reasons.

Genetic Detection

In genetic-based detectors, DNA or RNA isolated from a sample is exposed to nucleic acid sequences, or oligonucleotides, which correspond to a suspected biological agent. These sequences are commonly referred to as "probes," as one can imagine a sequence "probing" a sample, seeking its genetic match. Similar to antibodies in immunoassay tests, these specific pieces of genetic material are typically tagged with an optical signaling molecule in order to indicate a positive result.

It is critical that probe sequences—the region of DNA or RNA targeted—be chosen well. If overly specific, a genuinely pathogenic strain may be missed yielding a false negative. Concurrently, if the chosen sequence is widely shared among a species or genus, it has the potential to respond to vaccine strains or to nearest-neighbor species, leading to false positives for innocuous non-pathogenic microbiologicals. A wise approach is to use oligonucleotides that target the virulence encoding DNA portion. In this way, genetically engineered species may also be identified. Simple genetic-based ticket detectors are pathogen-specific, like the immunoassay counterparts.

Genetic-based detection is typically combined with an amplification technique, such as polymerase chain reaction (PCR) in order to generate larger quantities of genetic material in a shorter time frame than if the material were cultured. Although many traditional instruments require a minimum of two to four hours, significant breakthroughs in thermocycling and microfluidics have led to reported analysis times of less than ten minutes. The amplified DNA can subsequently be compared to a library of unique oligonucleotides in order to identify the pathogen.

PCR and other DNA amplification techniques, while extremely powerful, are not without drawbacks. They are labor intensive, require consumable reagents, are restricted to liquid samples, offer marginal portability (typically exceeding 50 lbs), are demanding on power resources and are expensive. Different sample preparations are required for hardy anthrax spores than for a comparatively delicate filovirus. Currently, there is also a minimum of thirty minutes for protocol optimization.

Leading commercial manufacturers are advertising portable and handheld devices that combine PCR with genetic-based detection.

While having significant advantages in terms of specificity and detection limits over immunoassays, each suffers from limitations. Drawbacks that affect this type of system are the critical need for proper preparation, including thermal cycling for amplification, auxiliary reagents, high costs and highly trained operators of the devices. It is crucial that the pathogen sample be clean in order to differentiate from benign biological material in the environment. Nucleic acid probes also have finite life spans and generally require controlled storage conditions (e.g., freezers).

DNA microarrays or "chips" are being investigated for biological agent detection application. Allowing for parallel exposure of the potential pathogen to hundreds of specific substrate-immobilized oligonucleotides, these detection systems have significant potential.

While immunoassays are limited by typically being single agent specific, the biggest liability for nucleic acid-based detectors is susceptibility to interferents. Isolation and purification of the sample are critical. Occasionally overlooked or underplayed in the excitement of innovative instrumentation is the criticality of sampling in BW agent detection. The way a sample is obtained and how it is handled can significantly affect the result, especially toward minimization of false positive responses. In addition to extricating biological agents from the surrounding environment, concentration of a sample can greatly enhance the ability to identify agents that are dilutely dispersed (but still of high enough concentration to have a deleterious effect on exposed humans).

Mass Spectrometry

The ability to characterize potential BW agents has been further enhanced by the use of mass spectrometry (MS) instruments. With this type of detection system, the sample of interest is fragmented into progressively smaller charged pieces ending with constituent amino acid or protein pieces. The charged fragments have different masses permitting physical differentiation. Furthermore the chemical groups yield characteristic fragment patterns—like fingerprints. While it is possible to solve small molecule fragmentation patterns manually, fingerprint libraries for comparison with known patterns are requisite for large molecules such as biologicals. Simple algorithms can provide reasonable "guesses," with estimations of uncertainty. Another approach uses mass spectroscopy to monitor the production of unique enzymatic metabolites generated by bacteria, fungi or rickettsia; the latter approach does not apply to viruses.

MS requires the separation of mixed samples, which is typically accomplished by subjecting the sample to a chromatographic separation prior to injection into the mass spectrometer. Chromatography refers to the separation of a mixture based on the component's physical interaction with a surface—typically the internal surface of a long column through which the mixture is pushed by a gas (GC) or a liquid (LC). The addition of chromatography significantly enhances the functionality of many detectors. Chromatography technically is not a means of detection, instead it is a means of separation. A detector is placed at the end of a chromatograph to analyze the outcome. GC can be used with either gaseous or liquid state samples. Tandem mass spectrometry, two sequential mass spectroscopy runs, is another method to separate sample mixtures, although less routine. The first MS run is used for separating the parts of a sample; the second MS run is used for detection.

GC-MS can detect, identify and differentiate diverse agents—bacteria, toxins and viruses. For example, analysis of *Yersinia* species pathogens has been demonstrated. In other works, the volatile biomarkers of *B. anthracis* and a nearest-neighbor species, *Bacillus cereus*, have been identified and differentiated using GC-MS and MS-MS techniques. Pyrolysis GC-MS, in which the sample is heated to a gas but not burned, can provide rapid analysis of intact, complete microbiologicals. It is a comparatively harsh technique and not suited for detection of volatile biomarkers.

Commercial gas chromatography services, GC instruments and GC databases specific to detection of biological agents are available. Although exquisitely sensitive, current GC instruments are nevertheless bulky (and therefore, usually, remote from initial response sites), expensive ($30,000 to $150,000), require sample preparation and associated reagents and necessitate trained laboratory personnel.

Surface Acoustical Wave Sensors

Surface Acoustical Wave (SAW) systems are based on piezoelectric materials (those that produce an electrical current when subjected to pressure or mechanical stress) coated with antibodies or complementary nucleic acid sequences. Binding of the target material causes a change in the mass of the piezoelectric sensing crystals which in turn changes the frequency at which the crystal vibrates under an electric current. This change in frequency is measured and alerts to the presence and, perhaps, the identity of the BW agent. Sensitivities on the order of $10^5 - 10^6$ cells have been reported. . . .

Further Improvements Needed

In this article, the intent has been to provide an overview of currently employed technologies for detection of chemical and biological agents. As new technologies emerge, there remains a need to insure third-party validation of the results and pursue significant real-world testing. There is little doubt of the value in developing new and better instrumentation, much of which may arise from fundamental research. In a funding flurry and a ripe political climate, new devices and new experimental techniques need to be subject to extensive scrutiny and validation procedures. Among the foremost reasons are to limit false negatives and false positives at real-world sites. Excessive false positives can lead to response fatigue and ignoring a real incident; a false negative that fails to detect a CBW [chemical or biological weapon] agent release could cause a disaster of the highest order—the loss of human life.

There currently exist a wide variety of techniques that provide excellent detection capabilities for CBW agents. Each, however, has drawbacks and limitations. The prospect of a single detector amenable to all CW and BW agents is laudable, although unrealistic with current technology. Layered detectors and sensors that function together in a web-like manner to monitor progressively more refined levels—from cloud and particle detection to differentiation between biological and nonbiological components to concentration information—are a near-term approach to unified and comprehensive CBW detection. This strategy involves the development of vertical sensor webs in which different levels of detection are optimized in addition to a horizontal sensor web (the same detector distributed spatially). An additional component should be intentional redundancies to limit false positives and false negatives. Integrating systems to synergistically operate will be a significant technical challenge as most devices have been designed and manufactured as stand-alone instruments. There is also a considerable political challenge in the design and implementation of such a sensor system.

A MILITARY VIEW OF DEFENSE AGAINST BIOWEAPONS

Robert P. Kadlec

The challenge of defending against bioweapons begins with the gathering of intelligence, writes Robert P. Kadlec in the following selection. Ideally, the military would be able to obtain specific information about what an enemy planned to do with bioweapons. However, it is difficult to uncover such information. Kadlec writes that the next best protection against bioweapons is to develop a comprehensive assessment of the scientific, medical, and engineering capabilities of potential enemies. Additionally, diplomatic effort needs to be made to prevent countries or organizations from exporting critical materials to potential bioweapons producers. Diplomatic effort is also required to encourage countries to comply with existing bioweapons treaties and agreements. Furthermore, Kadlec writes, the United States must also prepare for a well-coordinated response in the event a bioweapons attack occurs, he says. A major part of this effort will be medical. Soldiers must be vaccinated against likely bioweapons threats, and stockpiles of vaccines for civilian use in case of attack must be built up. To meet these goals, Kadlec argues, government-run vaccine production facilities are warranted. Robert P. Kadlec is a physician who holds the rank of lieutenant colonel in the U.S. Air Force. He was part of a United Nations inspections team that searched for biological weapons in Iraq and served on the U.S. delegation to the Biological Weapons Convention from 1993 to 1996.

How do we meet the BW [bioweapons] threat in the twenty-first century? What policies will help solve the likely BW challenges? How should the United States counter-BW programs be prioritized and integrated?

Incomplete or absent intelligence about a suspected proliferant's BW program is a likely source of trouble. Not having specific informa-

Robert P. Kadlec, "Twenty-First Century Germ Warfare," *Biological Weapons: A Primer*, edited by Steve Bowman. New York, NY: Novinka Books, 2001. Copyright © 2001 by Novinka Books, an imprint of Nova Science Publishers, Inc. Reproduced by permission.

tion about the status of a BW program, or locations of production and storage, or methods of delivery, or the specific agents could result in an incomplete assessment. This could directly impact the development of United States strategy, policy, and capabilities to meet the threat.

A comprehensive anti-BW intelligence effort must collect information relating to the basic science, medical, and bioengineering capabilities of a potential proliferator. Short of having reliable human intelligence with direct access to an adversary's BW program, this type of information is required to assess the biological capability of that nation.

Intelligence collection and analysis are critical for future United States BW counterproliferation efforts. Determining the intent to develop BW, locating suspect facilities, and assessing the nature of the offensive program are essential elements of the intelligence effort. The importance of specific BW agent intelligence for medical and detection capabilities deserves emphasis. Even if the intelligence community collects and validates this information, there may be a significant lag time, years or even decades, before safe, effective counter-measures can be developed and fielded.

Wide Intelligence Net

Intelligence about the anticipated means of delivery and its doctrine of use is also important. This information allows development of US active defense capabilities to interdict and destroy delivery vehicles. Facility-related intelligence also allows for identification and targeting of production and related facilities for counteroffensive strikes.

The ability to identify BW-related organizations and proliferants is important to optimize the utility of export controls and the ability to interdict shipments of related equipment destined for suspected BW countries or organizations. The ability to focus limited diplomatic and economic resources to dissuade, pursue arms control, and bring international pressure on suspected proliferants is, therefore, also intelligence-dependent.

The likelihood that national technical means can identify any or all of the three key BW intelligence components—intent, location, and nature—is small. Dual-use facilities may not emit characteristic signatures, but still be capable of producing military significant quantities of biological agents. As alluded to earlier, the availability of human-source intelligence will be a critical element in providing information related to BW proliferation. Assessment of BW-related information requires trained personnel experienced in matters relating to biology, biotechnology, medicine, and agriculture. Balancing the technical component of the intelligence analysis process is the need to integrate the expertise and experience the intelligence system.

Because of the greater relative intelligence challenges and the myriad of related areas associated with BW versus nuclear proliferation, adequate resources must be applied to the problem. Increasing collection priorities should also necessitate a concomitant increase in the analysis resources devoted to the problem. There should be an assessment and if necessary a redistribution of assets to reconcile the disparity between the effort against nuclear proliferation and that of BW.

Planning Responses

Beyond the collection and assessment of intelligence, policy development and integration of the many functions are required to respond to BW proliferation. The domestic vulnerability to covert or clandestine acts of BW terror should be assessed. There must be executive-level interest and involvement to oversee the development of a crisis response system to domestic BW incidents. While the federal response to terrorist acts is well delineated, the time-sensitive health care demands created by an act of biological terror must be assessed. It is beyond the scope of the single agency identified in the Federal Emergency Response Plan, the Department of Health and Human Services, to mount the necessary reaction to deal with the health consequences and prevent unnecessary loss of life.

A historical example illustrates the scale of the effort required to respond to an act of BW terror in a major metropolitan area. In 1947, an American business man traveled to New York City from Mexico City. During his bus ride, he developed a fever, headache, and rash. Though ill upon his arrival in New York, he went sight-seeing. Over a period of several hours, he walked around the city and through a major department store. His illness, smallpox, progressed and he died nine days later. As a result of this single case, 12 other cases of smallpox and two deaths occurred. Because of smallpox's ability to be transmitted from person to person, this handful of cases was deemed so serious by public health officials that 6,350,000 persons in New York City alone were vaccinated in less than a month.

Unlike 1947, Americans have not been routinely vaccinated against smallpox since 1980. A significant proportion of the US population is susceptible to this virus. The number of cases expected to occur as the result of a deliberate act could be in the thousands or tens of thousands. Even though the World Health Organization declared smallpox eradicated, North Korea has been identified as one possible country retaining cultures of this virus to use as a biological weapon.

Devastating Potential

Even if a noncontagious agent were used, the public health consequences could be overwhelming. If several kilograms of an agent like anthrax were disseminated in New York City today, conservative estimates put the number of deaths occurring in the first few days at 400,000. Thousands of others would be at risk of dying within several days if proper antibiotics and vaccination were not started immediately. Millions of others would be fearful of being exposed and seek or demand medical care as well. Beyond the immediate health implications of such an act, the potential panic and civil unrest created would require an equally large response. Local law enforcement agencies would be overwhelmed and would need the assistance of state and federal agencies. The complete vulnerability of the United States if exposed to this type of terrorism would prompt other terrorists to attempt the same type of attack for extortion or additional terror impact.

Prior to a domestic incident such as this, a capable, practiced, and coordinated response mechanism must be in place. The Federal Emergency Management Agency (FEMA) provides this coordination function, but its actual familiarity and practice associated with biological terrorism is not known. The health-related support functions found in the Departments of Health and Human Services, Veterans Affairs, and Defense would have to be integrated into a single response plan.

Stockpiles of necessary antibiotics, immunoglobulins, and vaccines would have to be procured, maintained, and be readily available to administer within hours after recognizing an incident. An additional critical element of this response would be the management of information to allay fears and avoid unnecessary panic. The effort required to respond to a biological act of terror rivals that needed for an accidental or deliberate detonation of a nuclear device.

Arms Control

The BWC [Biological Weapons Convention] clearly represents the "lock which keeps the honest man honest." It serves a vital function by establishing an international norm against BW proliferation. Efforts should be made to provide both disincentives and incentives for current states to comply with the BW treaty. Nonsignatories should be leveraged to participate in the convention. Strengthening the BWC by enhancing transparency of biological activities is stated US government policy. . . . Like the warning to consumers—*caveat emptor* [buyer beware], subscribers to the convention must understand that complete verification is not just elusive but impossible.

During the original proposal of the BWC by the United Kingdom, the Soviet military strongly opposed any limitation of offensive BW. The Soviet Foreign Minister Andrei Gromyko felt that, for propaganda purposes, a prohibition on biological weapons would be useful. Without international controls, the Politburo and the Soviet military both endorsed the "toothless" convention in 1972. The Soviet Union was one of the three depositories of this treaty. Recent disclosures by President Boris Yeltsin regarding former Soviet and Russian violations of the Biological Weapons Convention highlight the limits of that treaty. . . .

Diplomatic Limitations

Current DOD [U.S. Department of Defense] counterproliferation policy emphasizes use of public diplomacy, positive and negative security assistance, and identifying the economic, political and military costs of proliferation. Denial of certain equipment or technologies used in BW is problematic. Export controls, interdiction, or disruption of supply networks will have limited impact given the dual-use legitimate nature of the biological materials and equipment.

Diplomatic efforts to prevent or control BW proliferation will have similar limits. States that are parties to the BWC, but are committed eventually to developing secret offensive biological weapons capabilities, can do serious BW research and development legally for a time within the current treaty framework. Nations who are not signatories can refuse entry and pursue offensive programs as well. Given the low likelihood of detecting violations, nonsignatories could take advantage of economic incentives or foreign assistance programs for joining the BWC, yet pursue clandestine offensive BW programs. There are reasonable indications that diplomacy alone can do little to prevent BW proliferation.

Nevertheless, diplomatic and economic pressure can serve a useful purpose in inhibiting a proliferant's activities by invoking sanctions, export controls, or publicly disclosing violations. One must realize that invoking these measures depends on timely and accurate intelligence. Diplomatic measures which try to control proliferation may, in the short run, delay a proliferant's efforts. In the long term, they may motivate determined proliferants to conceal or deceive their true intent and activities. Of course the perfect solution to proliferation is correcting the underlying reasons why nations choose to develop biological or nuclear weapons. Clearly, BW is a symptom of a deeper security need.

Military Countermeasures

Once proliferation occurs and an adversary attains an offensive BW capability, the focus changes to mitigating its perceived advantage and deterring its use. The range of counteroffensive capabilities and strategies must include deterrence, preemption, and destruction. During Desert Storm speculation occurred regarding the implicit use of nuclear weapons in response to BW attack. Both President George [H.W.] Bush and Secretary of Defense Richard Cheney publicly stated that any attack on US forces with chemical or biological weapons would be met with "massive retaliation." The accuracy and credibility of this policy option are subject to much debate.

Determining the culpable party after a covert or clandestine BW attack has occurred may be impossible. The circumstances following the bombing of Pan American Flight 103 [in 1988] highlight the potential difficulties of a forensic investigation following an act of terror. Before implicating Libyan intelligence operatives, both Iran and Syria and several terrorist groups were suspected. Finding a "smoking gun" and proving who is responsible for a future covert biological warfare attack could be difficult or impossible.

There will be times in the future when the US president may have to consider military preemptive strikes against a terrorist state or group to protect the United States and allied governments against BW attacks. Preemptive activities or anticipatory self-defense can range from efforts that occur during nonhostilities to open armed conflict. . . .

Destruction of the means to produce, process and deliver biological weapons is the final element of the counteroffensive strategy. There is a potential risk of collateral damage when striking BW-related facilities or delivery systems. Theoretically, a downwind hazard could occur if bulk storage of BW agents were struck when meteorological conditions were favorable to their dissemination. While no specific confirmed reports of collateral damage were documented during Desert Storm, there was one news report that implicated the occurrence of illness and death in Iraqi guards at an unidentified BW facility south of Baghdad after coalition bombing.

Another partial answer to the BW threat would be to deploy theater ballistic missile defenses capable of intercepting enemy BW warheads while enroute to their targets. Ideally, interception and destruction would occur during early boost phase of the enemy missile launch to lower the risk of friendly casualties. Good ballistic missile defenses are not enough, since the United States and its allies must also respond to the challenge posed by future enemy cruise missiles equipped with biological weapon warheads. Of course, such missile defenses are defenses of the last resort. The greatest probability of minimizing collateral damage would be realized if special forces or other means of preemption allowed the United States or its allies to destroy the enemy BW capability prior to an adversary filling the weapon or launching the attack.

Means of Defense

The last element of the BW counterproliferation strategy is medical and nonmedical passive defensive measures. The importance and problems of BW detectors have already been identified. A priority effort exists to develop and field a BW detector that can provide stand-off warning and real-time detection of attack.

Another nonmedical defensive measure that deserves emphasis is the employment of collective protective systems. Hardened shelters and work areas for rear-echelon troops as well as filtered over-pressurized systems for combat vehicles, ships, and planes could minimize the effects of both chemical and biological weapons.

Medical measures to protect against biological threats include short-term and long-term methods of protecting US military forces. Even when detectors become available, medical measures will play an important role in both protection and treatment against BW attack.

Efforts should be focused first on developing, testing, and producing Food and Drug Administration-approved vaccines to immunize soldiers against the most likely BW threat agents. The availability of suitable vaccines and other medical products must remain a priority.

On 26 November 1993, Undersecretary of Defense William Perry signed the DOD immunization policy for BW threats. It establishes the requirement for both peacetime and contingency use of vaccines against validated BW threats. Each theater commander-in-chief (CINC) is required to determine the regional threat and provide the chairman of the Joint Chiefs with requirements. Integral in meeting the regional CINC's requirements is the development of a DOD-dedicated vaccine production infrastructure.

The liability concerns of the US pharmaceutical industry have affected development and production of public health vaccines. The controversy associated with the liability risk of immunizing children against Pertussis is illustrative. Congress mandated a government-subsidized fund to defray court awarded damages resulting from severe neurologic sequelae [side effects] from the Pertussis vaccine. The rationale behind this effort was to protect the vaccine companies from large cash awards resulting from litigation, so to preserve their profitable production of important public health vaccines.

Role of Vaccines

The commercial or public need for vaccines against biological warfare agents short of an act of terror is virtually zero. Yet, should a high-confidence warning of an attack on our population occur, substantial amounts of these products would be necessary to respond to minimize illness and death. The peacetime military need exists as result of the DOD immunization directive.

The ability and desire of the pharmaceutical industry to commit its facilities for dedicated vaccine development are questionable in light of profit and liability concerns. A US government vaccine facility has value for both BW and public health considerations. Such a facility should remain a high priority project in developing capability to respond to BW proliferation.

Besides the actual protective effect gained by BW vaccines, certain elements of deterrence can be garnered by minimizing the effect of an adversary's BW agent. Immunizing US forces and having the ability to protect others will minimize an enemy's ability to coerce the United States and its allies. They will also lessen the potential impact of a BW attack on the United States or its allies.

Therefore, the perceived or actual benefit derived by the BW proliferant will be lessened. Finally, vaccines and medical countermeasures can contribute the means to maintain the war-fighting capability of US military forces as well as providing for the survival of US citizens.

A Major Challenge

The proliferation of biological warfare weapons offers less developed nations a capability as lethal and potentially devastating as a nuclear device. The ease and relative low cost of BW production, coupled with spread of dual-use legitimate biotechnology, will facilitate and accelerate BW proliferation in the short-term and well into the twenty-first century.

Biological weapons can be employed in noncombat settings under the guise of natural events, during operations other than war, or can be used in open combat scenarios against all biological systems— man, animal, or plant. Deliberate dissemination of BW agents may be afforded possible denial by naturally occurring diseases and events. The low probability of detecting the development and production of terrorist and militarily significant quantities of BW agents lessens the effectiveness of diplomatic measures such as dissuasion, denial, and international pressure.

The limitations associated with treaty verification leave little optimism for the long-term effectiveness of the Biological Weapons Convention. Ascribing to the BWC may offer further potential of plausible denial if proliferants sought to use membership as a cover for their prohibited efforts.

Expectations for preventing BW proliferation must be grounded in reality. The likelihood of preventing or deterring a determined proliferant from obtaining biological weapons is relatively small. The outlook for the future of biological weapons proliferation is discouraging. "Brain drain" from the former Soviet Union may create volatile opportunities for breakthrough proliferants.

Future US policies against BW proliferation need to be based on integrated governmental policies and capabilities to deter, preempt and defend against this threat. No single element of the program is adequate to deal with the BW problem. Together, however, these elements can lower the risk and mitigate the potential impact of BW.

In addition, the problem of biological warfare cannot be narrowly focused on its ability to kill or render people ill. Biological warfare's potential to create significant economic loss and subsequent political instability with plausible denial exceeds any other known weapon. Germ warfare at the end of the twentieth and inception of the twenty-first century directly threatens the security of the United States and the achievement of a peaceful, prosperous, and stable post-cold war era.

THE THREAT OF BIOWEAPONS JUSTIFIES RESTRICTIONS ON LIBERTIES

Thomas May

The anthrax attacks of late 2001 on the Senate and various news outlets prompted new federal legislation for biodefense. They also led to the creation of the controversial Model State Emergency Health Powers Act, which various states have been considering. In the event of a public health emergency, the act would allow officials to collect and share individuals' health information, impose compulsory vaccinations, quarantine, and treatments, and require health care professionals to treat and monitor infected people. In the selection that follows, bioethicist Thomas May acknowledges that some people regard the act as an infringement on civil liberties but he argues that such restrictions on liberty are justified. May contends that when the exercise of individual freedoms puts others at risk, then the government has the right to set limits. Freedom of speech, for example, does not entitle a person to deliberately cause a panic. The model act's provisions for forcible quarantine and treatment are similarly justified, May argues. He discounts arguments that giving government such powers will lead to overreaction and abuse by officials. Instead, he points to the need to make such crucial decisions about civil liberties in a crisis before a crisis occurs. Thomas May is associate professor of bioethics at the Medical College of Wisconsin. He frequently writes about legal and ethical issues surrounding bioterrorism.

The 'War on Terror' in the aftermath of Sept. 11th, 2001, has resulted in a number of government actions that are controversial for their perceived threat to civil liberties. In the health arena, the most controversial is the Model State Emergency Health Powers Act (MEHPA), a model law (currently under consideration in a number of states) that is designed to facilitate response to a bio-terror attack. The preamble of the Model Act states ". . . in the event of the exercise of emergency

Thomas May, "Harm, Public Health Threats, and the Model State Emergency Health Powers Act: Bio-Terror Defense and Civil Liberties," Joint Services Conference on Professional Ethics, January 2003.

powers, the civil rights, liberties, and needs of infected or exposed persons will be protected to the fullest extent possible consistent with the primary goal of controlling serious health threats." Nonetheless, the Model Act has been criticized both by conservatives and liberals for potential violation of civil liberties. In this paper, I propose to examine both the need for emergency health powers legislation, and criticisms of the MEHPA as a model for such legislation.

The key provisions of the Act that are perceived as a threat to civil liberties are these: in circumstances of a health emergency, the Act authorizes the official collection and sharing of an individual's health information; gives state officials the authority to appropriate and use property (including health care facilities) as necessary for the care and treatment of patients, or for the destruction of contaminated materials; gives state officials the authority to appropriate necessary vaccines and medications to treat infected or exposed individuals; allows forced vaccination, treatment or quarantine of individuals deemed to pose a public health threat; and allows the state to require participation of health care professionals in the treatment and monitoring of infected individuals. All of this is necessary, it is argued, because existing public health laws are obsolete, and inadequate for addressing public health crises that night arise from a bio-terror attack.

Criticism of the MEHPA focus on the violation of civil liberties themselves, as well as on the specific system to be employed in the event of a public health emergency as recommended by the Model Act, as I will discuss below. There can be no question that the powers granted under the Model Act, if adopted, pose a threat to many civil liberties we have come to regard as "rights" in our daily social lives. The issue debated concerns the advisability of legislation that would allow violation of these rights in the event of a public health emergency such as a bio-terror attack. It is my opinion that such legislation is advisable, for two related reasons: First, our political system has long recognized the need to restrict civil liberties when such restriction is necessary to prevent significant harm to the public at large; second, how these liberties should and should not be restricted for the purposes just mentioned should not be left for consideration at the time a public health emergency arises. An outline for restriction of civil liberties should be publicly debated, then recognized through the official sanction of the legislative process. In this context, I believe the restriction of specific civil liberties themselves is justified in circumstances of public health emergencies such as a bio-terror attack.

The Harm Principle

The most basic justification for restriction of civil liberties in U.S. society stems primarily from a philosophical idea known as "the harm principle." The Harm Principle is a liberal principle that seeks to protect individual autonomy while simultaneously recognizing that in some cases, the exercise of one person's autonomy can threaten another person's freedom to structure their own life and values. Thus, The Harm Principle seeks to balance conflicting rights between individuals, and in this provides a basis for limiting rights on liberal grounds other than mere social utility. [Nineteenth-century British philosopher] John Stuart Mill, the principle's most famous champion, described the principle in this way:

The only purpose for which power can be rightfully exercised over any member of a civilized community, against his will, is to prevent harm to others."

The prominence of this principle can be seen in the way the court struggles to base review of legislation on it. Even legislation that seems straightforwardly paternalistic, such as laws requiring motorcycle helmets or seat belt laws, have been upheld by courts on grounds that [law professor] Ken Wing describes as "tortured judicial logic.". . .

Mill's basic formulation of the Harm Principle illustrates the tension between public health good and the exercise of individual freedom. This principle holds that individual freedoms should not be restricted *unless* the exercise of a person's freedom poses a threat of significant harm to other people. One example of the application of this principle can be seen in the restrictions that might be placed on the exercise of free speech: this right does not allow one to, for example, shout "Fire!" in a crowded theater in order to cause a stampede. Application of this idea to public health has been recognized in several U.S. Supreme Court decisions, most notably the case *Jacobson v. Massachusetts*.

Vaccination Policy

Such restriction should only be employed, however, when necessary to prevent significant public harm. The health dangers posed by a bio-terror attack pose such a harm, as I will discuss below. In the context of the Harm Principle, it is important to recognize that the dangers imposed by refusal of public health services are not wholly individual. Vaccination provides a good example: Vaccines are not 100% effective. The effectiveness of vaccination programs relies on a concept of "herd immunity," which holds that if a high enough percentage of people *are* immune to a given disease, even those who do not achieve immunity from vaccination gain protection because they are unlikely to be exposed to the disease. Without a very high rate of participation in the program, however, there will be a percentage of people who have been vaccinated that remain susceptible to vaccine-preventable diseases in cases of an outbreak. For example, during a measles outbreak in Utah, it was determined that the significant percentage of exempted people in a particular region led to an environment which made it possible for a six (viral) generation-long outbreak. More than half of those who eventually contracted the disease had been vaccinated. Similarly, in the Netherlands, a 1999 measles outbreak began with a cluster of children enrolled in a religious school whose members routinely decline vaccination [and] grew into a ten-month-long outbreak, with 2961 reported cases. A large percentage of those who contracted the disease, and whose vaccination status was known, had received at least one dose of the Measles Mumps and Rubella (MMR) vaccine.

The relevance of these facts can be clearly seen in the justification of the MEHPA in the context of a bio-terror emergency whose containment or control requires the participation of a large segment of the population. According to MEHPA author Lawrence Gostin, et al, the justification of the Act relates to the fact that there "may be a need to exercise powers over individuals to avert a significant threat to the public's health . . . Although the vast majority of people probably will comply willingly (because it is in their interests and/or desirable for the common welfare), some compulsory powers are necessary for those who will not comply. Provided those powers are bounded by legal safeguards, individuals should be required to yield some of their autonomy, liberty, or property to protect the health and security of the community." Gostin continues: "Compulsory power has always been a part of public health law, because it is sometimes necessary to prevent or ameliorate unacceptable threats to the common good."

Too Open to Interpretation

Despite this strong justification clearly grounded in the widely accepted "Harm Principle," criticisms that the MEHPA is too broadly defined may well be correct. As it stands, for example, implementation of the MEHPA is justified if a governor believes that any of the following harms are posed: (i) a large number of deaths in the population; (ii) a large number of serious or long-term disabilities in the affected population; or (iii) widespread exposure to an infectious or toxic agent that poses a significant risk of future harm to a large number of people in the affected population. The third condition, in particular, leaves a lot of latitude for interpretation. Consider one example raised by critics: although the Act is intended to apply in circumstances of immediate urgency like a bio-terror attack, the wording of the third condition (widespread exposure to an infectious agent that poses significant risk of future harm to a large number of people) could be interpreted as allowing implementation of the Act to appropriate and use medical facilities and medications, force treatment, and quarantine individuals to address HIV infection, or even the annual flu epidemics.

Underestimating the Threat

The primary concern, here, is that the powers granted under the Act may be abused through the implementation of the Act as an overreaction to "crises" that do not warrant significant violation of civil liberties. In response to these concerns, Jurist Richard Posner argues:

"It will be argued that the lesson of history is that officials habitually exaggerate dangers to the nation's security. But the lesson of history is the opposite. It is because officials have repeatedly and disastrously underestimated these dangers that our history is as violent as it is."

Posner points to examples including the Civil War, the Japanese attack on Pearl Harbor, the invasion of South Korea, and Soviet espionage that accelerated the Soviet Union's acquisition of nuclear weapons. These problems, Posner argues, resulted from the failure to recognize dangers posed to national security in advance, and to take steps to address these possible dangers. Working now to recognize the possible dangers that bio-terror may pose is a prudent course. Once the danger posed by bio-terror is recognized, debate can turn to the specific circumstances that the powers that are called for, and to safeguards that can limit abuses of the Act's implementation without threatening its effectiveness.

Our best estimates of the dangers posed stem from several exercises designed to simulate how a bio-terror attack would play out. One of these exercises, dubbed "Dark Winter," simulated a smallpox attack in Oklahoma City, OK. Due to the inherent latency period of smallpox symptoms following exposure and the covert nature of the initial attack, public health and government officials had difficulty identifying the original location (or locations) of the attack(s) and pinpointing the number of people initially exposed in time to fully contain a smallpox outbreak. Consequently, the twenty initially confirmed smallpox cases in Oklahoma City rapidly expanded to 16,000 cases in 25 states with 1000 deaths, reported cases in 10 additional countries, widespread public panic, government destabilization, and still no clear answers of how to contain further spread of the disease.

Another exercise, dubbed "TOPOFF," simulated a bio-terror attack using plague in Denver, CO. In that exercise, a number of difficulties hindered efforts to contain the spread of disease and treat exposed victims. Travel by fearful individuals away from the site of outbreak facilitated spread of the initial outbreak to areas of Colorado outside Denver (the site of simulated attack), several other states, and even foreign countries. Lack of adequate facilities and supplies contributed to an epidemic that resulted in more than 4,000 cases of pneumonic plague and between 950–2,000 deaths in just a four day period (when the exercise was terminated).

The result of both exercises dramatically underscored the difficulties of containing a bio-terror attack without strong political leadership backed by significant legislative powers. Our best estimates, then, call for recognition of a need for strong legislatively recognized authority in times of a bio-terror emergency. The MEHPA is informed by the needs identified in these exercises. It is important that the lessons learned from these exercises not be overlooked.

Perhaps Posner's strongest argument in favor of *some degree* of suspension of civil liberties in times of crisis concerns the uncertainty that invariably faces decision-makers at the time of crisis:

> It is true that when we were surprised and hurt, we tend to overreact—but only with the benefit of hindsight can a reaction be separated into its proper and excess layers. In hindsight we know that interning Japanese-Americans did not shorten World War II. But was this known at the time?

Need for Advance Planning

Waiting until a crisis occurs to outline how civil liberties are restricted in times of emergency poses a greater danger to civil liberties than any proposed legislation. Off-the-cuff reaction (and over-reaction) seldom result in good public policy strategy. One important historical illustration that decision-making in the context of (perceived or real) crisis is the "Swine Flu Affair" of 1976. In February 1976, public health officials discovered at an Army base in New Jersey what they believed may have been an outbreak of the same strain of virus that caused the Great Influenza Pandemic of 1918. In the face of a vociferous media appeal for access to vaccinations, the Centers for Disease Control recommended to President Ford that a mass immunization program take place. Policymakers believed that, in spite of the vagueness of the outbreak threat, vaccination against this potentially serious disease was the more prudent approach to protecting public safety. Following a Congressional appropriation to pay for the shots, and a modification of the Federal Tort Claims Act to shelter the vaccine manufacturers for liability arising out of use of the vaccine, the federal government undertook a voluntary mass immunization campaign. President Ford, in an attempt to encourage vaccination and to allay fears about potential side effects arising from the shots, made an appearance on prime time television with his family to receive the shots. By late 1976, over 40 million Americans had received the shots. However, the feared outbreak never occurred, and in fact the vaccination itself led to more than 1000 cases of Guillain-Barré syndrome, a paralytic disease. On December 16 of that year, the program was reluctantly ended. Some believe that the Administration's handling of this public health emergency directly impacted the 1976 presidential election.

Drill Reveals Confusion

Avoiding reactive decision-making requires that circumstances of "emergency" are clearly outlined, and that clear lines of authority are identified and recognized. The May, 2000 TOPOFF exercise conducted by the Department of Justice is perhaps the clearest to establish a need for advance bio-terror planning in this regard. Chief among the factors identified as obstructing public health efforts was a lack of clarity in lines of authority and questions about decision making authority to impose curfews on the general public and quarantine infected individuals, close city and state borders, triage medical resources, and maintain security at, and access to, healthcare facilities. For example, some individuals and agencies treated state public health agencies as the highest authority, others looked to CDC personnel, while the FBI was perceived as looking to the state Attorney General's office as the highest authority. The result was a lack of coordination and consistency in approach. Stated one participant: "Decisions made on Saturday were reversed on Sunday, then reversed again on Sunday afternoon," and another: "Reversing decisions back and forth is the antithesis of crisis management and efficient decision making."

The MEHPA is designed, above all else, to establish clear lines of authority in times of bio-terror emergencies. The Act outlines procedures for implementation, areas of enforceable powers and the scope of required participation among health professionals, health-related organizations, and the public at large. While the concerns of civil libertarians should be considered in refining the Model Act for use in practice, these concerns should not inhibit the adoption of legislation based on the Model Act. Such legislation is necessary if we are to avoid reactive decision-making in times of crisis, and develop effective procedures for controlling disease outbreak in the event of a bio-terror attack.

THE BIOWEAPONS THREAT HAS BEEN EXAGGERATED

Philip Alcabes

In the aftermath of the 2001 terrorist attacks, the federal government made enormous changes in U.S. public health programs. Congress authorized new restrictions on civil liberties and vast new expenditures on biodefense. In the selection that follows, public health expert Philip Alcabes questions whether such measures are justified. He argues that throughout history plagues have been blamed on foreign enemies, but rarely with just cause. Even under the threat posed by international terrorism, he argues, mass casualties from a bioweapons attack are extremely unlikely. Taking smallpox as an example, he argues that the virus would be hard to obtain and easy to stop, thanks to large stocks of a vaccine that can be effective even after infection has taken place. Anthrax, the only bioweapon that has been used against American targets in recent years, produced less than two dozen illnesses and only five deaths, he points out. By comparison, he says, ordinary infectious diseases kill about 10 million people annually. The real threat, he suggests, comes not from bioweapons but from naturally occurring diseases such as the flu, which at any time may take on new and deadly forms. Biodefense efforts, he argues, are costly and likely to be ineffective against the real threat of a natural epidemic of some new pathogen. Philip Alcabes is an associate professor in the Urban Public Health Program at Hunter College in New York.

Since the fall of 2001, when America embarked on a "war on terrorism" and federal officials started warning us about the next plague, here are some events that have not happened: a U.S. epidemic of sudden acute respiratory syndrome (SARS), a widespread anthrax outbreak, any smallpox attack, the discovery of hard evidence of a biological weapons program in Iraq. Yet the talk about "biopreparedness"

Philip Alcabes, "The Bioterrorism Scare," *The American Scholar*, vol. 73, April 1, 2004, p. 35. Copyright © 2004 by Philip Alcabes. Reproduced by permission of the publisher.

continues. Some people in Washington want the Centers for Disease Control and Prevention to be transferred from the Department of Health and Human Services to Homeland Security. There is even a professional journal, Biosecurity and Bioterrorism, devoted to learned discussions of the topic. Is it sound public policy to rush to protect the country against the threat of attack with germs that could cause an epidemic? Does the bio in biosecurity mean that we should turn our public health into a matter of civil defense? Or have we Americans been sold a bill of goods?

Throughout history, the responses to both actual communicable disease and the threat of it have been guided by the metaphor of the stranger as the spreader of contagion. Allegations that epidemic disease was caused by foreigners are ancient. Thucydides reported that his contemporaries, in the fifth century B.C., attributed the Plague of Athens to Ethiopians. . . .

Spaniards Bring Smallpox to the Americas

Sometimes, of course, epidemics have come from the enemy foreigner. Clearly, [Spanish conquistador Hernan] Cortes was able to conquer Mexico because of smallpox. The disease appeared among the Taino on Hispaniola in 1518, brought by Spaniards who had colonized the island; later, it would contribute to the Taino's extinction. By 1519 smallpox was in Cuba. Cortes, who was secretary to the governor of Cuba, left to take Tenochtitlan from the Aztec chief Montezuma; either Cortes's Spanish troops or those of Narvaez, who led a relief expedition against the Aztecs after they repulsed Cortes's initial sallies, brought smallpox to the Aztecs. The disease, to which the Aztecs were immunologically naive, so diminished their numbers that Cortes had only to finish them off. Smallpox thence spread southward, killing the Incan emperor Huayna Capac and then his son in 1524–25, and plunging their people into civil war. Francisco Pizarro had little more to do to vanquish the Incas than march into Cuzco. . . .

Remote Chance of Attack

In connection with humans deliberately causing epidemics, the smallpox germ, variola virus, is the one we hear most about. It enjoyed a five-hundred-year career as a natural epidemic pathogen, from roughly the late fifteenth century until the late twentieth. Then smallpox was eradicated from the earth. Variola killed several hundred million people in the first half of the twentieth century alone—a public-health menace to be reckoned with. No doubt because of its fearsome reputation, it is the subject of a great number of speculative scenarios about how it might be resurrected as an epidemic scourge.

In fact, though, none of those scenarios is even remotely likely. First, not many people have access to viable smallpox stocks. Second, the disease that variola virus produces is fairly easy to diagnose. Third, vaccination will prevent disease even in already-infected contacts of smallpox cases, and vaccine stocks are reasonably large nowadays. The hubbub about smallpox has had the effect of sharpening physicians' diagnostic skills (indeed, so much so that instances of overdiagnosis produced false alarms) and expanding the supply of available vaccine. At this point, standard public health procedures, including case diagnosis, contact investigation, and immunization of possibly infected individuals, would be adequate to prevent an outbreak in the unlikely event that some individuals were deliberately infected.

Overblown Anthrax Threat

Anthrax is the second most popular topic of bioterrorism conversation. We have seen intentional anthrax infection—the much-ballyhooed postal anthrax events that took place in the fall of 2001. Three characteristics of that outbreak are of note: very few people became ill; very, very few died; and it was almost certainly not produced by a stranger.

Environmental studies in mailrooms indicated that many hundreds of people were probably exposed to anthrax spores that fall, yet only twenty-two people got sick. And of those twenty-two, half had cutaneous anthrax, the rarely-life-threatening skin form of the disease. Only five died. In the jargon of epidemiology, anthrax turned out to be neither very infectious nor very pathogenic. That experience should tell us that spraying anthrax spores from crop dusters or releasing them from aerosol cans into the subway is highly unlikely to make many people ill.

Speculation about subway attacks stems from a real event in March 1995, when the Japanese religious cult Aum Shinrikyo released the nerve toxin sarin in the Tokyo subway system. Twelve people died. Two subsequent attempts to release toxins in the Tokyo subways were foiled. Note that Aum was using a gas, which does not have to be sprayed; it diffuses by itself. This is not how germs are disseminated, and it is a distinction worth bearing in mind. And even that ignores the more central question of likelihood. Large-scale poisonings are not easy to carry out well.

The light death toll from mailed anthrax was a result of the low pathogenicity of the bacteria—half the cases were not pulmonary and were therefore unlikely to be fatal—and the comparative treatability of anthrax disease once detected. Do five deaths constitute a public-health crisis? Along with his colleagues, Victor Sidel, Distinguished Professor of Social Medicine at Albert Einstein College of Medicine in New York, has noted that a fraction of our nation's expenditure on biopreparedness would pay for effective treatment of tuberculosis for all of the two million people who get TB each year in India, thereby preventing close to half a million deaths a year. Half a million deaths because commonly available antibiotics are not affordable—now there's a public-health problem.

Plagues Unlikely

The other microbe that is on the lists of virtually all the bioterrorism watchers is the plague bacillus. It is true that [Japan's] Unit 731 produced plague outbreaks in China by dropping infected fleas on towns. But at that time plague was a recurring problem in Asia: a ferocious epidemic struck Manchuria in 1910, and another occurred in 1921. (It still is a problem: a large outbreak caused many deaths in India as recently as 1994.) By contrast, despite the presence of Yersinia pestis, the plague bacterium, in wild rodents in the Western Hemisphere, there has never been an extensive epidemic of human plague in this country. Even when plague epidemics moved out of Asia through much of South America, circa 1900, the U.S. saw only a small outbreak in San Francisco's Chinatown. The reason is not that Americans are immune to plague; it is that the urban arrangements that we have been accustomed to for the past two hundred years are inhospitable to the rat-flea-bacillus ecosystem. Such reforms as garbage removal, pest control, and better housing explain why plague disappeared from eastern Europe in the early 1700s and has never troubled us seriously here. Since epidemics of plague are unlikely, should we then worry that terrorists will produce isolated cases? Perhaps, but garden-variety antibiotics are very effective at treating the disease and interrupting transmission. There is no potential for the next catastrophe there.

Other pathogens have been mentioned as possible bioweapons—for example, the agents of tularemia, botulism, and Q fever. These organisms are not generally transmitted from person to person, so they carry little or no outbreak potential. Hemorrhagic fever viruses are sometimes transmitted by mosquitoes or by the bite of infected animals. It has never been shown that they can be manipulated into transportable weapons and then elude standard mosquito—and animal-control programs.

All in all, there is little evidence that terrorists are more likely, or better able, to use microbes as part of their armamentarium than ever before. . . .

The Lessons of SARS

Our most recent experience with so-called emerging infections has been SARS [Severe Acute Respiratory Syndrome]. It appeared suddenly in southern China in late 2002, the causative virus probably having entered the human population through people who had substantial contact with domestic animals. Although SARS affected more than 8,000 people worldwide and killed more than 700, it was a negligible problem in the U.S. (eight cases, no deaths) and produced no more than a mild epidemic in most other countries: despite the high case fatality ratio (people diagnosed with SARS had about one chance in ten of dying from the disease), only in China, Hong Kong, Singapore, and Canada were there more than five SARS deaths. Only nineteen countries saw more than a single SARS case. In all the affected areas, the outbreak was brought under control within about six months of its onset.

Two aspects of the SARS experience are important. First, though it is easy to acquire the virus by inhaling respiratory secretions from a SARS sufferer, it also turns out to be easy to prevent or control an outbreak. The key is to use standard infectious-disease-control measures, including case finding and reporting, active surveillance at points of entry to the country, isolation of possible cases, and recommendations against travel to heavily affected regions. None of these measures requires cutting-edge technology; all have been used in controlling communicable disease for well over a century.

Second, SARS made news partly because it was not the expected epidemic. For six months before the advent of SARS, Americans had been worrying very publicly about smallpox. Urged toward apprehension by the federal government, we had alarmed ourselves about the possibility that the long-defunct disease would be reborn in the hands of bioterrorists. The administration made ready, in mid-2002, to vaccinate half a million armed-services personnel and half a million health-care workers. The former plan it came close to accomplishing; the latter was abandoned because so many health-care workers refused to show up for vaccination. All of it repeatedly made the headlines and the evening news reports. Yet what happened in the end was not smallpox, or smallpox prevention; it was SARS. Had our faces not already been turned toward epidemic disease and our anxieties about infection elevated, had the news hours not been hungry for new news after a month of relentless coverage of the Iraq war, SARS might not have made such big headlines.

The lesson we should learn from our experience with SARS is that if we are vigilant about spotting new disease outbreaks and equally vigilant about applying public-health programs to curtail their spread, we can limit them, although we cannot ward them off completely. We cannot make life risk-free. Had we dealt with AIDS and West Nile encephalitis the way we dealt with SARS (which, of course, may return in the future and therefore requires continued vigilance), their course might have been different. West Nile, ending only its fifth season in the U.S. as I write, is already virtually a national epidemic; AIDS went national within six or seven years of its appearance. But in its initial season, 1999, in New York City, West Nile virus caused forty-six cases of encephalitis and seven deaths: not negligible, but a public-health problem more minor than Lyme disease (and far less extensive, in New York, than asthma or lead poisoning). AIDS began with a handful of cases—there were only a few hundred in 1981, the first year it was recognized—and the U.S. might have kept the toll fairly small had we had the political nerve to do something about it at the time. The point is that, at the outset, none of these "plagues" were cataclysmic. Epidemics do not work that way. Errant microbes do not find their way into the human ecosystem and wipe out most of the population unannounced. The Andromeda Strain is fantasy.

Bioterrorism Is Unlikely to Succeed

The crystal ball with which we divine epidemic mayhem is no clearer now than it used to be, and no clearer than the vision with which we try to foresee the coming plague. No one can dispute, after the events of September 11, 2001, that some people wish us harm. However, that harm is not likely to come from bioterrorism. To worry that the Middle Easterner, the Arab, or any Muslim—however the Stranger is configured—will use germs to attack us would be to pretend that we can indeed foresee great epidemics. For two reasons, that is certainly not the case.

First, humans, even ill-tempered and badly behaved humans, have never been able to use germs or weapons to the terrible degree of mortal effect that nature always has been able to use germs. Just four communicable diseases—malaria, smallpox, AIDS, and tuberculosis—killed well over half a billion people in the twentieth century, or about ten times the combined tolls of World Wars I and II, history's bloodiest conflicts. Even today, with good vaccines and effective antibiotics to stop them, infectious diseases kill about 10 million people each year.

The worst catastrophes the world has seen have been not the genocides, however gruesome, but the cataclysmic disease outbreaks. When a few million people are killed by design with Zyklon B, the machete, or the machine gun, it is a horror and an outrage; it shakes our moral faith. But the Black Death killed a third of Europe's population in just four years in the mid-1300s. Smallpox wiped out entire tribes of American natives after Europeans arrived in the 1500s. Plague killed over 50,000 in Moscow alone in just a few months in 1771. The Spanish Flu killed between 20 and 40 million in sixteen months in 1918–19.

And that suddenness is the second point. Prevision is of little help against epidemic disasters. Each of the disasters I just mentioned, and every other great epidemic of history, was unimaginable until the moment it began. But neither is prescience necessary: each epidemic, even the ones that turned out to be most terrible, began slowly, percolated a while, and could have been stopped with conventional public-health responses had anyone acted in time. SARS reminded us of that.

Distraction from Real Threat

Whether or not the Stranger is an enemy avowedly bent on terror, casting him in the role of microbial evildoer has the perilous effect of distracting us from realizing two truths: the disheartening one that the epidemic crystal ball is always cloudy, and the uncomfortable one that it is usually social circumstances that make epidemics possible and public-health funding that stops them.

Worrying about the germ-bearing Stranger, we forgo the upkeep of a workaday public-health apparatus in favor of fabricating modern wonders. The CDC now operates what it calls a "war room." From there, it can coordinate activities around SARS, West Nile virus, and other infections, as well as bioterrorism—if it can be found—using high-tech communications equipment. The war room is in an "undisclosed location." Once, CDC officials knew they were running a public-health agency. Now, apparently, they must act as if they are in charge of national defense.

After the U.S. Department of Health and Human Services scotched the 2002 plan to vaccinate health-care workers, the CDC announced it would continue its effort to vaccinate police officers and firefighters, despite numerous reasons to stop: several deaths directly attributable to the vaccine; several more possibly attributable; evidence that people who might be predisposed to heart disease (something like 10 or 15 percent of the middle-aged population) can be harmed by the vaccination; certainty that people with HIV infection (a sizable percentage of the adult population in some big-city neighborhoods) must not be vaccinated; and of course the complete absence of natural smallpox infection anywhere in the world for the past twenty-five years.

Vast Federal Spending

Federal grant money, under President Bush's multimillion-dollar Project BioShield program, has been allocated to technologic innovation for bioterrorism prevention. By 2003, according to *The Chronicle of Higher Education*, the National Institutes of Health were supporting almost seventy extramural research projects on anthrax alone. The NIH has funded two new National Biocontainment Laboratories and new facilities at Regional Biocontainment Laboratories, most at major universities, to the tune of $360 million in start-up costs. The University of Pittsburgh just lured the top staff of the Center for Civilian Biodefense Strategies away from Johns Hopkins by offering to set up a Center for Biosecurity with a $12 million endowment. The University of South Florida recently received $5 million in federal grant money for its Center for Biological Defense, which has projects like "Photocatalytic Air Disinfection" and "Aquatic Real-time Monitoring System (ARMS) for Bioterrorism Events." And Auburn University received a million-dollar federal biopreparedness grant for something called a Canine Detection Center.

When Harvard received a $1.2 million federal grant in 2002 to set up a program for detecting "events possibly related to bioterrorism" by electronically linking 20 million patient-care records from around the country (an endeavor called syndromic surveillance), the grant was a mere drop in the bucket: Congress soon allotted $420 million to Homeland Security for a larger linked health-monitoring network. A consortium led by the New York Academy of Medicine then developed software for syndromic surveillance. The new software allows public health officials to monitor what are called "aberrant clusters health events"—translation: more than the expected number of cases of some symptom that might be related to a disease that might be produced by an organism that might be in the possession of terrorists. Syndromic surveillance works fine if someone knows what to look for. But it is of no help at all with the unexpected. When there really was bioterrorism in the U.S.—the anthrax attacks in fall 2001—linked databases were useless; it took a smart clinician to figure out that anthrax was around, and old-fashioned shoe-leather epidemiology quickly worked out which people had been affected. West Nile virus, ditto. A friend who is an official of a local health department tells me that the syndromic surveillance experts find it works well for predicting the first influenza outbreak each year. But anyone's grandmother can predict the first influenza outbreak where I live, in the New York City area, since the symptoms are always the same and flu always starts here in the two weeks preceding Thanksgiving. For all its meager productivity, the syndromic surveillance software also throws out plenty of false-positive "clusters" that waste investigators' time. It is our new and expensive white elephant, justified by the fear of evildoers and germs. . . .

Costs of Biopreparedness

The core issue here is that the Stranger Spreading Germs is a metaphor, and largely an empty one. Bioterrorism is not a public-health problem, and will not become one. The next plague, whatever it is, will not decimate us unheralded. In signing the contract on biopreparedness, we have bought a confection, a defense against the chimeric stranger with the metaphorical germs.

And the costs of buy-in? When our public-health "leaders" corroborate government rhetoric about bioterrorists by reassuring us that our state or municipal health department is ready for any smallpox, anthrax, or plague attack, they legitimate both their own efforts and the standing of their offices. The planned result is that we will not question spending tax dollars so those officials can continue to defend us, even when it means closing down municipal clinics or shortchanging programs for the poor, and even if such biodefense is not what we most need or want.

The biopreparedness campaign goes to work. It discredits the simple logic of public health. Lose the distinction between the minuscule risk of dying in an intentional outbreak and the millionfold-higher chance of dying in a natural pandemic, it says. Ignore the hundred-fold-higher-still change of dying of cancer or heart disease. Defund the prenatal-care clinics, the chest clinics, the exercise and cancer screening and lead abatement programs. Ignore the lessons of history: forget that human attempts to create epidemics have almost always failed, and dismiss the repeated ability of a well-funded public-health apparatus to control epidemic disease with time-tested measures. Just think about germs, and tremble.

The lesson of history that we ignore at our peril is this: nobody can tell us how the next epidemic will happen. New germs come and go, epidemics wax and wane, but national catastrophes happen rarely. And when they do, it is never because of a stranger spreading germs. Anyone who promises certain protection from the next plague is selling us a bill of goods.

CHAPTER 5

EMERGING THREATS AND DEFENSES

STATE-AIDED TERRORISTS POSE A SERIOUS BIOWEAPONS THREAT

Elisa D. Harris

The 9/11 terrorist attacks on the United States were followed within days by anonymous anthrax attacks on Congress and the media. The first known anthrax letters, addressed to major news organizations, were postmarked September 18, 2001. The timing led many people to suspect that both attacks were planned by the Islamist terrorist group al Qaeda. However, no evidence of a link emerged. As national security expert Elisa D. Harris argues in the following selection the horrific events of that autumn led the United States to reconsider the threat of bioterrorism. Specifically, she writes, the U.S. government has recognized that the threat posed by national chemical and biological weapons programs and the threat posed by terrorist organizations that want to use these weapons are listed. More than a dozen nations, she notes, are thought to have bioweapons programs. Without assistance from these nations, terrorist organizations would have difficulty mounting a bioweapons attack. Therefore, she writes, new measures need to be taken to discourage nations from developing chemical and biological weapons and to keep existing ones out of the hands of terrorists. The international treaty banning chemical and biological weapons needs strengthening, she argues. A new treaty to make the use of bioweapons by individuals an international criminal offense is also needed, she says. Elisa D. Harris is a senior research scholar in the Center for International and Security Studies at Maryland at the University of Maryland. From 1993 until 2001 Harris was the National Security Council's director for nonproliferation and export controls.

Before the terrorist assaults of September 11 [2001] and the anthrax letter attacks that followed, U.S. officials often drew a distinction

Elisa D. Harris, "Chemical and Biological Weapons: Prospects and Priorities After September 11," *Brookings Review*, July 1, 2002, p. 24. Copyright © 2002 by Brookings Institution. Reproduced by permission.

between the threat posed by national chemical and biological weapons programs and the threat posed by terrorists using chemical and biological weapons. The two threats were seen as separate problems, requiring separate solutions. In the intervening months, however, it has become clear that the two proliferation problems are closely linked, in that assistance from national programs is likely to be critical to terrorist efforts to acquire and use chemical or biological weapons successfully, particularly on a large scale. This underscores the urgency of pursuing nonproliferation measures that delegitimize such weapons and complicate the efforts of both nations and terrorist organizations to acquire them.

Threat from National Programs

According to U.S. government officials, about a dozen countries are believed to have chemical weapons programs and at least 13 are said to be pursuing biological weapons. These national programs pose a direct threat to U.S. military forces and to friends and allies in the two regions where proliferation has been most widespread—Northeast Asia and the Middle East. They also pose an indirect threat as a possible source of chemical and biological weapons expertise or materials to other national or terrorist programs.

In recent months [2002], both President [George W.] Bush and Secretary of Defense [Donald] Rumsfeld have called attention to the nexus between proliferation and terrorism, warning that countries that seek weapons of mass destruction and support international terrorism may assist terrorists in getting chemical, biological, or nuclear weapons. This emphasis is on the mark. And it is borne out by last fall's [2001] anthrax attacks, which killed five people and injured some 17 others. As of May [2002], the perpetrator of these attacks had not yet been apprehended. But the nature and quality of the anthrax—highly virulent and weapons-grade—contained in the letters sent to selected media outlets and members of Congress indicate it almost certainly originated in the U.S. biological defense program.

As the General Accounting Office concluded in a 1999 study, terrorists who lack assistance from a national program face daunting technical and operational hurdles in weaponizing and delivering chemical or biological weapons, especially on a large scale. During the early 1990s the Aum Shinrikyo's attempts at mass terror in Japan through chemical and biological weapons had only limited success despite $1 billion in assets and access to university-trained scientists. In April 1995, the doomsday cult released sarin gas on the Tokyo subway at the height of the morning rush hour, but killed only 12 people and injured 1,000. Nine other attacks using biological agents, including anthrax and botulinum toxin, failed to produce even a single casualty.

Absent assistance from a national chemical or biological weapons program, most terrorists are likely to continue to rely on lower-tech methods of attack involving industrial chemicals or common poisons. As a report to Congress by the Central Intelligence Agency last January [2002] made clear, terrorist groups are "most interested in chemicals such as cyanide salts to contaminate food and water supplies or to assassinate individuals." Such groups also have "expressed interest in many other toxic industrial chemicals . . . and traditional chemical agents, including chlorine and phosgene," which are widely used in industry. Biological materials are of less interest, the report said, except for "small-scale poisonings or assassinations." The best known instance of low-tech biological terrorism was the 1984 effort by the Rajneeshee cult to influence the outcome of a local election in Oregon by contaminating salad bars with salmonella. No one was killed, although 750 people were injured.

One cannot rule out the possibility that terrorists will obtain chemical or biological weapons on their own. CIA Director George Tenet has warned that al Qaeda has tried to acquire some of the most dangerous chemical agents and toxins and that documents recovered from al Qaeda bases in Afghanistan show that Osama bin Laden has pursued a sophisticated biological weapons research program. This past March [2002], U.S. military officials confirmed the discovery of a laboratory, believed to be intended to produce anthrax and other biological agents, under construction near Kandahar, although there is no evidence that al Qaeda ever produced such agents. As with other terrorist groups who have attempted chemical or biological attacks, U.S. intelligence officials reportedly believe that al Qaeda would need help from foreign experts or governments to mount an effective weapon-of-mass-destruction program.

Prevention Efforts Are Needed

Since September 11, the Bush administration has responded to concerns about the use of chemical or biological weapons against the United States with a variety of proposals to defend against and manage the consequences of such attacks. The administration has asked for $4.5 billion in new bioterrorism funds for fiscal year 2003 alone to strengthen state and local health systems, increase the national pharmaceutical stockpile, improve coordination among federal, state, and local agencies in an attack, and develop new vaccines, medicines, and diagnostic tests.

The dangers posed by national chemical and biological weapons programs, however, require a response based on more than just defense. New prevention efforts also are needed to reinforce the international norm against chemical and biological weapons and to impede the acquisition of such weapons by those who would use them. Such a strategy should include: strengthening treaties that outlaw chemical and biological weapons, tightening international controls over chemical and biological materials, expanding nonproliferation efforts in the former Soviet Union, and criminalizing chemical and biological weapons activities by individuals.

Strengthening Existing Treaties

The 1993 Chemical Weapons Convention, the cornerstone of the chemical weapons nonproliferation regime, requires parties to eliminate all stocks of chemical weapons and permit international monitoring of both government and commercial facilities to verify compliance. In force for only five years, the treaty has already made progress toward reducing the threat from national chemical weapons programs. Nine of the countries previously identified by the United States as chemical weapons proliferation concerns—Russia, China, Iran, Ethiopia, South Korea, India, Pakistan, Sudan, and Vietnam— have become parties to the convention. Two countries that had not acknowledged possessing chemical weapons, South Korea and India, have now declared stockpiles, and 11 countries, including Russia, China, Iran, South Korea, and India, have declared current or past production facilities.

But numbers tell only part of the story. The Chemical Weapons Convention also faces several critical challenges. Of most immediate concern is the crisis in its implementing body, the Organization for the Prohibition of Chemical Weapons (OPCW). This past April, the United States succeeded in removing the director general from office, accusing him of mismanaging finances and proposing ill-considered initiatives related to the war on terrorism. Other concerns focus more squarely on the integrity of the treaty itself—particularly whether some parties have made inaccurate declarations or are continuing offensive activities. Russia, Iran, China, India, Pakistan, and Sudan have all been identified by the United States as having not divulged the full extent of their chemical weapons programs.

Both the management problems and the concerns about treaty non-compliance must be addressed. For its part, the United States must acknowledge that much of the OPCW's budget problem is a consequence of the nominal-growth budget imposed on it by the United States and other major funders. Delays in payment (and nonpayment) of annual assessments and inspection costs by many of these same countries have exacerbated the budget problem, ultimately resulting in major cuts in planned verification activities. The United States should work with the OPCW and other parties to ensure adequate funds for carrying out all necessary verification activities. The United States also should be prepared to use challenge inspections to address serious compliance concerns, especially in countries where bilateral consultations have been unsuccessful or are not appropriate.

The 1972 Biological and Toxin Weapons Convention was widely viewed as a milestone in the history of arms control, because it was the first international treaty to outlaw an entire category of weapons of mass destruction. The treaty, however, included no provisions for enforcing compliance. At the time, little was known about other countries' biological weapons programs.

Based on defectors' reports and other information, we now know that the Soviet Union breached the treaty from the outset. During the early 1970s, it launched a massive effort to supplement its existing work on biological weapons at military facilities with research and development at civilian facilities managed by an organization known as Biopreparat. Three other countries—North Korea, Egypt, and probably Israel—also had biological weapons programs at the time the treaty was concluded. Iraq began its program in the mid-1970s, South Africa in 1981. By the late 1980s, China, Iran, Syria, Libya, and Taiwan had been publicly identified by the United States as also having biological weapons programs. Except for Israel, all were either signatories or parties to the treaty.

In 1994, with the support of the United States, an Ad Hoc Group was established to develop new measures, including a legally binding protocol, to strengthen the convention. In July 2001, the Bush administration announced that it opposed not only the draft protocol introduced the previous April but also any subsequent protocol effort. The administration argued that such an approach was both too weak and too strong—too weak to catch cheaters, too strong to avoid putting at risk US. biological defense or trade secrets. At the treaty's five-year review conference in November 2001, the United States emphasized the need to develop more effective ways to deal with noncompliance, but the proposals it put forward focused largely on voluntary, national efforts. On the last day of the conference, the United States stunned and angered its allies by trying to force through a decision to disband the Ad Hoc Group and terminate its mandate. Desperate to avoid a complete collapse of this meeting aimed at bolstering the convention, parties agreed to suspend work until November 2002, having done nothing about the noncompliance problem. . . .

Tightening Controls on Hazardous Materials

Following Iraq's use of chemical weapons against Iranian military forces and its own Kurdish population during the Iran-Iraq War, the United States and other Western countries imposed export controls on equipment and materials that could be used to make chemical, and subsequently biological, weapons. Today, 33 countries make up the so-called Australia Group, an informal body that seeks to harmonize national export controls over chemical and biological-related exports. The Australia Group's success has led proliferators to turn increasingly to other suppliers, particularly companies in India, Pakistan, and China, for equipment and materials.

Since 1997 the United States has also required facilities that send or receive particularly dangerous biological materials—the 36 microbes and toxins on the Select Agent List—to register with the Centers for Disease Control and Prevention in Atlanta and to report all domestic transfers of select agents. As the anthrax incidents last fall have shown, however, US. facilities that sent or received select agents before 1997, or that simply possess them, are not subject to the reporting requirement. Moreover, most of the more than 1,500 culture collections worldwide make biological cultures available to researchers with few restrictions or controls.

Last October [2001] Congress tightened domestic controls over access to biological materials by passing legislation prohibiting felons, illegal aliens, people from terrorist countries, and other restricted individuals from possessing or transferring items on the Select Agent List. Other curbs on biological agents, including a requirement that facilities that possess select agents register with the CDC, were enacted into law in late May.

The United States should capitalize on new relationships it has forged with New Delhi, Islamabad, and Beijing since September 11 to shut down the alternative suppliers that have emerged in the wake of the Australia Group's success. The United States should also take advantage of the heightened international concern about biological weapons to secure tighter international controls on culture collections and other repositories of biological materials and to strengthen oversight of laboratories to prevent deliberate or inadvertent use of biotechnology for destructive purposes.

A Focus on the Former Soviet Union

Since the early 1990s, the United States has used a variety of nonproliferation assistance programs to ensure that former Soviet chemical and biological weapon scientists, equipment, and materials do not contribute to foreign chemical and biological weapons efforts. Under these programs, the United States is helping design and build Russia's first nerve gas destruction facility, at Shchuch'ye, and dismantle or convert to peaceful purposes former chemical weapons production facilities at Volgograd, Russia, and Nukus, Uzbekistan. The world's largest anthrax production facility, at Stepnogorsk, Kazakhstan, has been dismantled, and thousands of former biological weapons scientists have received funding for collaborative research with U.S. scientists on both public health and biodefense-related projects. Security has also been tightened at culture collections around the former Soviet Union. But much more remains to be done.

Russia has already informed the OPCW [Organization for the Prohibition of Chemical Weapons] that it cannot meet its April 2007 deadline for destroying its chemical weapons stockpile. If Russia is to have a chance at meeting the April 2012 extension deadline, work at the Shchuch'ye facility will need to be accelerated and expanded. Efforts also should be undertaken to dismantle or convert other chemical and biological weapons production facilities, expand collaborative research on global diseases such as HIV and tuberculosis, broaden collaborative work on vaccines and other medical countermeasures to biological weapons, facilitate commercialization activities at former biological weapons facilities, and strengthen security at culture collections and other sites that maintain biological materials. The task will not be cheap—upwards of $1 billion in additional funds will be required over the next five years. But keeping critical elements of the former Soviet programs from facilitating national or terrorist chemical or biological weapons efforts is essential.

Updating Criminal Laws

Although both the chemical and the biological weapons conventions require parties to prohibit on their territory any activities that are banned under the treaty, both conventions focus principally on the actions of states, not individuals. And neither requires parties to establish criminal jurisdiction over foreign nationals on their territory who have engaged in prohibited activities elsewhere or to conclude extradition arrangements.

To help fill this gap, the Harvard Sussex Program has drafted a treaty making it a crime under international law for anyone knowingly to acquire or use chemical or biological weapons or to help others do so. At the end of April, the British government endorsed the negotiation of such a treaty. As provided by treaties on aircraft hijackings, hostage taking, and the theft of nuclear materials, anyone committing a prohibited act would be subject to prosecution or extradition if apprehended on the territory of a party to the treaty. The United States should work with the UK to press for an international convention criminalizing chemical and biological weapons activities by individuals.

ENGINEERING DEADLY GERMS

Jon Cohen

Unintended consequences arise in every field of invention, but few have greater lethal potential than those created by genetic engineering. In the following selection, author and science journalist Jon Cohen explores the implications of a startling discovery by two Australian scientists. They set out to find a way to curb the infestation of mice that their country periodically suffers. During their investigations, they accidentally discovered how to make already deadly viruses far more deadly. Worse yet, their research seemed to indicate that genetic engineering might be capable of producing a variant of the smallpox virus that could bypass the immunity provided by current vaccines. Cohen examines the dilemma the scientists faced over whether to publish or suppress their findings. In the end, they did publish. Cohen suggests that this was the right decision, in part because it alerted the scientific community and defense planners to the possibility of "designer bugs," and in part because such variants may be found in nature anyway. Furthermore, the Australians' project may yet prove useful in alleviating the hunger and poverty that may give rise to terrorism. Cohen quotes an expert who says the research may be effective in suppressing the rodents that destroy food-stocks and spread disease in many poor countries. If science must be suppressed, Cohen argues, individual scientists should be the ones to make that decision. A veteran science journalist, Jon Cohen is the author of *Shots in the Dark: The Wayward Search for an AIDS Vaccine*, published in 2001 by W.W. Norton.

Four years ago a team of Australian scientists, attempting to create a genetically engineered virus to combat common pests, stumbled across a mechanism that could potentially increase the killing power of a host of human diseases. Their findings, published last year [2001] amid great controversy, bring to the fore a question of increasing urgency: Might technologies intended to improve the world provide terrorists

Jon Cohen, "Designer Bugs," *The Atlantic Monthly*, vol. 290, July 1, 2002, p. 113. Copyright © 2002 by Atlantic Monthly Company. Reproduced by permission of the author.

and rogue nations with the means to build the ultimate bio-weapon?

In 1859 a wealthy Australian . . . named Thomas Austin imported for sport thirteen wild English rabbits to his estate near Geelong, in Victoria. The rabbits did what rabbits do, and within three years 14,253 of them had been shot on Austin's land. By 1869 more than two million had been killed on a neighbor's property. Soon hundreds of millions of rabbits formed what became known as a "gray blanket" across the continent, destroying native plants, competing with native animals for food and shelter, and savaging grazing lands. In 1950 the government agreed to wage bio-warfare against them, and scientists released myxomatosis, a rabbit–specific pox virus from South America, into the wild. The virus quickly killed 99 percent of the country's rabbits. During the next three years, however, the kill rate among the initial survivors and their descendants dropped to 95 percent; it continued to decline until, eventually, it leveled off at about 50 percent. "It was a classic example of the co-evolution of virus and host" Frank Fenner told me recently. Fenner, a virologist at the John Curtin School of Medical Research, in Canberra, headed the studies analyzing why myxomatosis became less effective. In essence, he said, "you've got this arms race" in which the virus becomes weaker and the rabbit more resistant.

In 1988 a young virologist named Ron Jackson began working at what would later be called the Pest Animal Control division of the Cooperative Research Centre, in Canberra. His goal was to devise a solution that would sidestep those evolutionary forces and work indefinitely. Specifically, he hoped to produce a genetically altered virus that would sterilize rabbits.

Going After Mice

Jackson initially planned to use myxomatosis, but he couldn't easily get the rabbit genes he needed to engineer the virus. So he switched to mice and a virus called mousepox, intending to perform a "proof-of-concept" experiment that would allow him subsequently to proceed with rabbits. When the project showed early signs of success, he realized that the strategy might also be applied to mice, which bedevil Australia almost as much as rabbits do.

Every four years or so Australian mouse populations explode, causing what is referred to as a plague of mice. Each mouse plague costs the grain industry roughly $75 million in lost production. "So we view it very much that we're working on industry's behalf," Tony Peacock, the head of the Pest Animal Control division (essentially, Australia's Minister of Pests), told me recently. Mouse plagues also affect the general population, causing annoyances large and small; for example, mice are expert at chewing through electrical wires in people's homes.

And then there are rats, which cause widespread damage in Australia and destroy up to 20 percent of the world's rice crop—$4.5 billion worth—each year, and which carry some sixty viruses that can infect human beings. Research into contraceptives for rabbits and mice might ultimately have the added benefit of pointing to an effective strategy for controlling rats. Back in 1988 there seemed no reason not to pursue it.

Ten years later, on January 27, 1998, Ron Jackson's day began, like many of his days, with a drive along the winding roads of the Australian National University campus in Canberra. Eventually Jackson pulled up in front of the brick buildings of the John Curtin School, located across town from his own lab at the Cooperative Research Centre. The school is one of the few places in the world where researchers can work with mousepox. Although it is closely related to variola, the virus that causes smallpox in human beings, mousepox cannot harm people. It can, however, wipe out entire colonies of mice. An accidental release of mousepox among laboratory mice could ruin months' or even years' worth of experiments, so the school takes many precautions to ensure that the mousepox used there stays there.

Jackson came first to the outer door of the animal lab. Next to it a sign warns, in block red letters, NO ADMITTANCE. HIGHLY INFECTIOUS AREA. After swiping his key card, he walked down the hall and entered the "clean room," a small vestibule lined with bright-green surgical gowns. He donned a gown and snapped on a pair of powder-blue polypropylene shoe covers. He then opened the door to the "dirty room:' a facility with negative pressure to prevent air from escaping. Inside the dirty room, amid the odors of mouse food and urine, he padded over to two metal cages, each of which held five mice of the strain known in lab shorthand as Black 6.

Vaccinating Against Pregnancy

Jackson and his fellow researchers, who included Ian Ramshaw, an immunologist at the Curtin School, were working with a genetically engineered mousepox that should have caused no serious harm to Black 6, which can survive even the most lethal known strain of the virus. Ideally, female mice infected with Jackson and Ramshaw's virus would become sterile and would also infect other females, sterilizing them as well. The virus would work like a vaccine, preventing pregnancy much as a vaccine prevents illness.

Mice, like human beings, coat their eggs in a jelly composed of several proteins. The jelly helps sperm to implant and protects the fertilized egg as it makes its way through the fallopian tube. Female mice normally do not mount an immune response to their own eggs; but Jackson and Ramshaw reasoned that if female mice became flooded with high doses of an egg-jelly protein, the mice's immune systems would "break tolerance" for the protein: the protein would, in effect, look like foreign material, triggering an antibody attack against the eggs. Because the protein is neither infectious nor transmissible, it would have to be carried by another agent—a sort of Trojan horse. Genetically engineered mousepox would serve as the Trojan horse.

Earlier that month Jackson and Ramshaw had published a paper suggesting that their virus could work: in one strain of mice it had sterilized 70 percent of the females they had tried it on. There was a big catch, however: it failed to work in two other mouse strains. To reduce mouse populations significantly, a sterilizing vaccine would, of course, have to work in many strains. The researchers decided to tackle the problem head on, refocusing their efforts on the most recalcitrant of the other two strains—Black 6.

Jackson and Ramshaw theorized that the immune system in Black 6 was so effective against mousepox that it was destroying the Trojan horse before it could breach cellular walls and deliver the protein. They decided, therefore, to tweak the immune system in two ways, simultaneously boosting its attack on the protein and blunting its attack on the mousepox. The researchers were encouraged to pursue such seemingly contradictory aims by the fact that the immune system has a seesaw-like mechanism. On one end of the seesaw are Y-shaped antibodies, which latch onto proteins and render them inert. On the other end are so-called killer cells, which target and destroy cells infected by foreign invaders. Tilting the seesaw toward a greater antibody response should, theoretically, push it away from producing killer cells, allowing more mousepox to survive long enough to deliver the protein.

In an effort to tilt the seesaw in this way, Jackson and Ramshaw inserted a gene for interleukin-4 into their mousepox. IL-4 is a chemical, secreted by the immune system, that boosts the production of antibodies in both mice and human beings. On January 21 the team injected ten Black 6 mice with the new version of mousepox. Six days later, when Jackson checked on the mice, he found that the IL-4 had had a vastly different effect from what he'd expected. One mouse was dead, its tissues badly swollen—a classic symptom of mousepox. Several others were hunched up and quiet. Two days later three more mice died; by the end of the month all ten were dead.

Increased Lethality

Jackson and his colleagues immediately realized the implications with respect to smallpox and its potential as a biological weapon. "We'd come up with, at least with mousepox, a highly effective mechanism for increasing lethality of a virus for genetically resistant animals," he explains. In short, they had stumbled on what might prove a relatively simple way to bolster the killing power of smallpox, already one of the most feared viruses of all time.

Soon the researchers would have data that were even more alarming. The mice, they realized, had died because the IL-4 had undermined their production of killer cells too well, leaving the animals vulnerable to a disease they were normally able to resist. What would happen, they wondered, if they vaccinated Black 6 mice against mouse–pox before injecting them with the IL-4 version of the steriliz- ing virus?

By November, Jackson had the results: even in vaccinated mice the mousepox with IL-4 was lethal 60 percent of the time. He immedi- ately went upstairs to Ramshaw's office to convey the news. "Oh, boy," Ramshaw said. "What have we created here?"

Again, the implications regarding smallpox were inescapable. The vaccine against smallpox was so effective that the World Health Orga- nization eradicated variola from the human population more than two decades ago, and routine vaccinations were halted. All stockpiles of the virus were destroyed, save for two: one in a laboratory in Atlanta, Georgia, the other in a lab in Koltsovo, Russia. Mass vaccina- tion would be our most effective defense should terrorists (or "rogue nations") obtain smallpox and use it as a weapon. But a version of variola containing IL-4 might render that defense useless.

Jackson and Ramshaw knew that the bio-weapon they had created to combat common pests—a weapon whose mechanism might be used to intensify a host of human diseases, not just smallpox—funda- mentally altered the world's terror equation, much as suicide hijackers did again three years later. What they did not know was how to han- dle their findings, or even whether to publish them at all—a quandary that molecular biologists will increasingly face. Their uncertainty would be borne out: when they did publish their results, in February of last year [2001], they found themselves at the center of a media storm that distorted many of the details and implications of their work. People would soon begin imagining the worst: terrorists un- leashing a virulent disease and public-health officials mounting enor- mous vaccination campaigns, only to see those vaccinated rapidly succumb; health-care workers dying by the hundreds; panic sweeping the populace, with some people blocking access to their communities and others taking to the backwoods with food and weapons in an effort to escape. Moreover, the media's handling of the story would muddy a vital discussion about how to gauge the threats posed by natural and engineered bio-weapons and how to determine what steps scientists, policymakers, and the public should take. . . .

Colleagues Consulted

[Smallpox expert Frank] Fenner's position was clear; he thought the researchers should share their findings. "There was no point in hold- ing up publication, because other people would do the same sort of thing," he told me. And although the results surprised him, he did not see much reason for alarm. "I thought it probably wouldn't work in a way that would make smallpox a more deadly bio-terrorist weapon than it already is," he explained. "If you have something that kills twenty-five percent of the unvaccinated population and spreads reasonably well, then what more can you ask from a bio-weapon?"

Fenner believes that anyone attempting to use a smallpox-IL-4 virus as a weapon would face three main obstacles. First, what worked with mousepox might not work with variola—and terrorists would have no way of testing their construct short of conducting experiments on human beings. Second, a virus that can defeat vaccination poses serious risks for the scientists who engineer it and for anyone who tries to release it. Third, even if terrorists could engineer and release an IL-4-containing variola that mimicked the mouse-pox-IL-4 results, the virus would probably kill people so quickly that they would be unable to spread the infection to others, thus negating one of the qualities—contagiousness—that makes smallpox an attractive bio-weapon to begin with. (Bio-terrorists, wanting to be able to control their attacks, have traditionally favored diseases that are not easily spread from person to person, such as Q fever, plague, tularemia, botulism, and anthrax. The relatively recent interest in smallpox and other contagious diseases reflects the increasing recklessness of would-be bio-terrorists.)

Over the next few months Ramshaw polled other colleagues. No one advocated withholding the mousepox data. . . .

Jackson and Ramshaw finished their experiment, analyzing the various immune responses discernible in the blood of surviving mice and in the organs of dead ones. By the time they solicited advice, applied for a patent to protect their invention of an infectious contraceptive vaccine, and drafted a manuscript, more than a year had passed. When they did submit the manuscript, to the *Journal of Virology* in July of 2000, it said nothing about the link between their work and potential bioweapons. "What we wanted was a presentation of just cool scientific fact" Seamark says. Neither the editors of the journal nor either of the independent scientists who reviewed the paper raised the larger implications.

Media Storm

In December of 2000, a few weeks before the paper was set to appear online, Ramshaw was interviewed by Rachel Nowak, a reporter for *New Scientist* magazine, about AIDS-vaccine work—the main focus of his lab. Nowak asked him if he had anything else interesting under way. In an unguarded moment he told her about the upcoming *Journal of Virology* paper, and even spelled out the dilemma it posed. Nowak shifted gears and pursued the mousepox story full bore.

After the interview Ramshaw realized that his comments might concern his colleagues, so he called Seamark, who says that he expected some uproar but was not upset. "Things like that excite me," he told me. "It's a test of your ability to manage." Seamark then spoke with Nowak, as did Jackson.

On January 10, [2001] a few days before the publication of Nowak's mousepox story, *New Scientist* faxed its piece to Seamark, as agreed: the researchers has asked for time to prepare for questions from journalists. Upon seeing the slant of the piece ("Killer Virus: An engineered mouse virus leaves us one step away from the ultimate weapon") and of an accompanying editorial ("The genie is out: Biotech has just sprung a nasty surprise. Next time, it could be catastrophic"), the Cooperative Research Centre prepared a press release, with its own spin, for issue the following day: "Discovery Prompts Call for Biowarfare Review." In it Seamark was quoted as saying that the "best protection against any misuse of this technique was to issue a worldwide warning." The release also highlighted the need to strengthen the Biological Weapons Convention, a thirty-year-old agreement among nearly 150 nations not to develop, produce, or stockpile biological-warfare agents except for peaceful purposes. (The treaty has been blatantly violated by several signatories—for instance, the Soviet Union started its bio-weapons program the year after signing it—and attempts at crafting verification measures have largely failed. The United States, fearing that drug companies would be forced to reveal trade secrets, has been among those resisting such measures.)

The Cooperative Research Centre release fanned media attention. When Jackson turned on the television on the morning of January 12, he heard a reporter saying that he and his colleagues had re-created smallpox. During the next two weeks the story reverberated across Australia and the world. Jackson found himself fretting about his reputation, the time he was spending talking to reporters, even his family's safety.

Ramshaw had a more philosophical reaction. "I'm a great believer in the rice-grain hypothesis," he says. "You have a pile of rice, and if you add one more grain, you can have a massive avalanche. Minor things make a big difference. There are minor things that created this whole issue, such as the publication in *New Scientist*, a reporter coming along to talk." But he, too, was unprepared for the onslaught of attention. And he experienced some disapprobation: one colleague came up to him and asked, point-blank, "Why did you do this experiment?"

Most of the media reports twisted some aspects of the story and neglected others. Some writers implied that the researchers sat on their data for more than two years as they wrestled with the question of whether to publish. (That probably delayed them no more than six months.) Smallpox with IL-4 is surely not the ultimate bio-weapon; as Fenner argues, it may not even be a very good one. An emphasis on the accidental nature of the discovery—especially coming at a time when debates raged over genetically modified plants, mad-cow disease, and foot-and-mouth—created the mistaken impression that once again arrogant scientists had bumbled, this time creating a Franken-virus. But most disappointing of all to the Australian researchers is that many stories failed to examine the very question that Ramshaw's colleague had confronted him with: Why did they do this? The impulse informing their work was largely ignored. . . .

Preparing for the Likeliest Threats

Until last November [2001], D.A. Henderson, Frank Fenner's collaborator, directed the Center for Civilian Biodefense Studies at Johns Hopkins University, in Baltimore. After the anthrax attacks he accepted an appointment as director of the newly created Office of Public Health Preparedness, at the Department of Health and Human Services. Henderson well recognizes the threat posed by designer bugs. But he is a practical and blunt man who has studied these issues longer and harder than most, and he speaks with the certainty and inclemency of a soldier who has seen battle. "One can come up with all sorts of what-ifs," he says. "You can play the Armageddon game very easily. At this point we need to get ourselves prepared to deal with two biological agents: smallpox and anthrax. If we do that, we're going to be ready to deal with a lot of things.". . .

In the long term, Henderson and others argue, even strengthening international agreements won't be as effective as simply helping the developing nations of the world. In this vein it is not hard to imagine that the very technologies that might lead to bio-terrorism might be used to reduce the threat of it. For instance, although the Canberra researchers abandoned the idea of making a sterilizing vaccine with mousepox plus IL-4, they may try to use it, or some version of it, to kill mice. "It probably could be developed to be one of the best rodenticides on the market," Bob Seamark says. "And using similar ingredients, you might develop one for rats." In that case the mousepox experiment might lead not to a nastier smallpox but to a means of increasing the food supply, and the prosperity, of millions of the world's poor—thus reducing one of the factors that may motivate terrorists. Sitting in his living room, enjoying a glass of whiskey at the end of a fine summer's day, Frank Fenner smiled broadly at the notion. "It's a lovely idea," he said, tinkling the ice in his glass. "It really is.". . .

The Folly of Censorship

On occasion scientists and journalists withhold what they know. Scientists routinely do this if they have yet to file a patent application for a discovery. Journalists often omit troop locations and other sensitive details from their stories, for reasons of national security. But in such instances the decision to withhold is made by individuals or the institutions they work for. And so it should continue.

But if scientists do not stand up for themselves, the government will step in; indeed, it has begun to do so. In February [2002], *The New York Times* revealed that the Bush Administration had quietly removed from public access thousands of long-available federal reports about germ warfare, and had begun drafting a new "information security" policy. White House science advisers have had exploratory discussions with the American Society for Microbiology, which publishes ten journals, including the *Journal of Virology*, about the possibility of withholding potentially dangerous articles, or at least excising details that would allow other labs to replicate the work described.

Mandating that review panels assess which scientific studies should be censored would reek of the way things worked in the former Soviet Union—and it would surely backfire. Such policies are ham-fisted and, in the end, counterproductive. Knowing the mousepox data, scientists can now work on fashioning vaccines and drugs to combat an enhanced version of smallpox, should it ever surface as a weapon. The experiment also crucially raised our awareness of the threats posed by designer bugs and garden-variety pathogens alike. On balance, then, the publication of the mousepox data and the intense discussions surrounding it have in all likelihood made the world a safer place.

AMATEUR "BIOHACKERS" COULD POSE A SERIOUS THREAT

Chappell Brown

The development of the Internet has led to the rise of electronic viruses—self-reproducing packages of code that are engineered to infiltrate—or "hack into" computers. According to the following selection, a similar problem could arise from the development of biotechnology, the emerging field of genetically engineered organisms. Technology journalist Chappell Brown writes that the development of automated systems to manipulate genetic code will give rise to a wide variety of novel and possibly dangerous life forms. To a limited extent, such artificial life has already been created by so-called transgenic technologies, in which genes from one species are spliced into the genome of another. For example, a bacterial gene that produces insecticide has been transferred into the genome of corn to make insect-resistant crops. At present, gene splicing requires great expertise and institutional resources. However, Brown predicts that automation will soon make it possible for "biohackers" without a great deal of specialized knowledge to create potentially deadly new microbes. To defend against this threat, experts say it may be necessary to create licensing and tracking systems for the oligonucleotides— discrete sections of DNA—that are used in genetic engineering. Whether such restrictions will work, Brown notes, remains to be seen. Chappell Brown is a longtime staff correspondent for *Electronic Engineering Times*, where he also serves as managing editor for technology and systems design.

Design automation systems tailored to the task of genetic engineering could prove to be double-edged tools. While they represent a central thrust of the emerging synthetic biology movement, they also can lead to the accidental or deliberate creation of pathogenic biological components.

Chappell Brown, "Experts: Synthetic Biology May Spawn Biohackers," *Electronic Engineering Times*, June 28, 2004, p. 45. Copyright © 2004 by CMP Media LLC, 600 Community Drive, Manhasset, NY 11030, USA. Reproduced by permission.

One expert in the field, Harvard University genetics professor George Church, compared the potential misuse of synthetic biological designs with the danger posed by nuclear weapons. But there is one important difference, in his view—it is much harder to build a [nuclear] fusion device than to genetically engineer a pathogen. And the complexity of biological processes also increases the danger of accidents.

By reducing the molecular biology of the cell to a list of standard modules with predictable behavior, professional biodesigners could engineer molecular machines in much the same way that system-on-chip designers create silicon systems. Just as a circuit designer does not need to be an expert in silicon physics and manufacturing processes, the future biodesigner will not need a detailed knowledge of biochemistry to effectively create complex biochemical machines.

Artificial Biological Agents

"Even if we don't have bioterrorists and teen-age biohackers, we will still create things that do not have the properties that we thought they would," Church said. The problem is that the body has not evolved a general ability to fend off artificial biological agents. "Even if you are genetically resistant and even if you are recently immunized you will have problems with this type of bug."

Church chaired a panel on the problems and opportunities of DNA synthesis at the recent Synthetic Biology 1.0 conference, held at the Massachusetts Institute of Technology earlier this month [June 2004]. A critical question for researchers and entrepreneurs getting into the new field is what form regulation of the technology should take. Church suggested that anyone designing systems with synthetic biological components be required to have a license, which would entail passing basic competency tests.

Licensing might head off the possibility of unintended side effects by maintaining a level of competency among the people in the profession, but would do little to prevent deliberate attempts by terrorists or hackers to create pathogens. The continuing problems the Internet is experiencing with computer viruses that are released secretly give some indication of the problems that synthesized self-replicating systems pose. While the barrier to entry for building a computer or network is very high, once built, it becomes a vehicle for much smaller bits of code that someone with only a low level of expertise can release into the system.

Biological synthesis becomes fairly easy once the basic building blocks—the oligonucleotides—have been built, so the regulation of the whole process could be centered on licensing and tracking them.

"Our experience with computer viruses is that people that do this kind of thing are rather sloppy, they're not very good at covering their tracks," said Tom Knight, who directs MIT's BioBrick wet lab in the Computer Science and Artificial Intelligence Laboratory. "There is an opportunity here because the oligonucleotides contain a lot of information which can be used to track and monitor what is being done with them."

As an experiment, Knight assembled a list of the oligonucleotides used in his lab and asked himself whether he would be able to predict what was being built with them. "It's not a double-blind experiment, because I already know what we are building with them, but I managed to convince myself that it would be easy to determine that even if I didn't know," he said.

Keeping Tabs on Ingredients

The situation is similar to the nuclear industry, where difficult-to-produce fissionable material is closely tracked and stored in secure facilities. Something similar could be done for oligonucleotide production and distribution.

The potential for danger in this new technology really depends on how effective the emerging techniques will be in actually creating viable biomachines like artificial viruses. The conference attendees seemed to assume that the field will proceed along the same time line as the semiconductor industry. The current state of the art for synthetic biology corresponds to the first steps engineers took to put a few gates on a chip, thus kicking off the integrated circuit revolution.

One factor that could speed up the process is the experience that has been gained with electronic design systems throughout the 40 years of VLSI [Very Large Scale Integration] advances. Today's digital circuit designers are uniquely positioned to take advantage of the new field's decoupling of design and implementation. An accident of nature makes it possible to describe cellular processes in terms of the familiar AND, OR and NOT logic operations of digital circuits. So if successful, the synthetic biology movement could lower the entry barrier for electrical engineers for a novel nanotechnology arena-one with broad applications in industry and particularly in medicine. Prototype biodesign systems are already emerging.

Timeline Remains Unknown

But the larger unknown is the speed of the implementation phase. First, standard biochemical modules with standard inputs and outputs will have to be defined. Then some automated, highly parallel manufacturing system will have to be designed that can take a description of a system in terms of standard parts and crank out actual biological components.

"My impression is that biology is still in the dignified style of the English countryside," Knight said. "Practitioners go into the lab and if something works, that's great and if it doesn't, they come back the next day and try again. . . . We have an opportunity to take that stately pace and accelerate it a lot," he said. "Some people here have already developed many of the tools to do that. There is a lot of power and danger here, but I would like to think that the advantages that come with the power outweigh the dangers."

Market pressures are already prompting biotech companies to speed up the DNA synthesis process. Another panelist, John Mulligan, a genetic engineer who started Blue Heron Inc. (Bothell, Wash.) based on his own automated DNA synthesis line, discussed some of the basic enabling technologies that are based on microfluidic chips and robotics.

Mulligan pointed out that speed of synthesis does not just involve the problem of how fast a string of amino acids can be assembled. Chemical reactions are prone to errors, and a major barrier that slows down DNA synthesis is the need to correct errors and verify the correctness of a molecule that can have hundreds of millions of base pairs, Mulligan said.

The large pool of expertise that has been gained by the semiconductor industry in its successful bid to crank out chips with hundreds of millions of transistors is of no use to biological synthesis, however. In fact, the self-replicating nature of biological systems is a built-in manufacturing system, although one that is prone to variations in the form of mutations.

The danger in biosynthesized systems stems from the ability of biological processes to easily support self-replication. Some observers believe that self-replication itself should be strictly banned as the only way to fend off the threat of some engineered molecular system running rampant. But such a restriction would take away much of the power of synthetic biology. And with the pace of innovation, it may already be too late to put the self-replicating genie back in the bottle.

THE UNITED STATES LAUNCHES PROJECT BIOSHIELD

Frank Gottron, as interviewed by Ira Flatow

Vaccines are the most promising line of defense against bio-weapons, but most pharmaceutical companies have been reluctant to produce new ones. The industry regards them as costly, risky, and comparatively unprofitable. In the following transcript, National Public Radio's Science Friday host Ira Flatow interviews congressional science analyst Frank Gottron about the federal government's response to this dilemma. They discuss the proposals of Project Bioshield, a ten-year, $6 billion effort to fortify the nation against future bioweapons attacks. The most important aspect of the project, according to Gottron, is a government guarantee to buy the relevant vaccines as they are produced. He explains that the Secretary of Health and Human Services will have the power to authorize emergency use of unproven vaccines. Flatow and Gottron also discuss Bioshield II, a possible successor to the initial Bioshield proposal. Gottron says that it may contain provisions to protect manufacturers from lawsuits and to nurture the emerging biodefense industry. On July 21, 2004, two months after the interview took place, President George W. Bush signed the first Bioshield bill into law. Frank Gottron is a science and technology policy analyst in the Congressional Research Service, where he researches, among other topics, biological and chemical warfare. Ira Flatow is the host of National Public Radio's program Talk of The Nation: Science Friday. He was NPR's science correspondent from 1971 to 1986.

Ira Flatow: There aren't effective countermeasures, vaccines or treatments for many bioterror agents, and that's because there's no commercial market for these drugs. Drug companies won't spend the money to develop and produce them if no one will buy them, and unless there's a bioterror attack, no one is likely to do that. Well, faced with that situation and the need for available drugs in the event of an attack, President Bush announced Project Bioshield in his 2003 State of the Union address, a 10-year, $6 billion program to spur research, development, production and stockpiling of vaccines and treatments for biological and chemical weapons and other dangerous pathogens.

Congress earmarked money for this effort last year [2003], but the Project Bioshield legislation hasn't been passed yet. Many companies can't or won't put up the money to develop these drugs without the backing from the federal government. But all that may change soon. This week [May 21, 2004], the Senate passed a 10-year, $5.6 billion version of the bill. The House passed its bill last summer. And a final version of the bill could be on the president's desk sometime next month.

What will Project Bioshield do for companies working on anti-terror drugs? And will this law be enough to protect us against a biological or a chemical attack?. . .

Let me introduce my guest. Frank Gottron is a Science and Technology Policy analyst in the Resources, Science and Industry Division at the Congressional Research Service in Washington. He joins us by phone.

Welcome to the program, Dr. Gottron.

Dr. Frank Gottron: Thank you.

Flatow: Yesterday, [National Institutes of Health infections disease expert] Dr. Anthony Fauci said that he was sure that the US will suffer a bioterrorist attack. He said the question is not whether, he said, but when. Will this Project Bioshield be effective in counter—you know, being a deterrence for that?

Dr. Gottron: Well, I'm not—there's a disagreement on whether it will serve as an effective deterrent, but it will certainly, most people agree, help us respond to an attack. And you could think that our ability to respond could deter use of certain agents. So if the bad guys know that we can stop the agent they're going to use, then maybe they won't attempt it.

Provisions of Project Bioshield

Flatow: Right. Tell us what the Senate legislation that passed [May 19, 2004], what does that incorporate?

Dr. Gottron: Well, there's three main provisions in Project Bioshield in both the House-passed and the Senate-passed versions. The first and most important, getting the most attention, is the guaranteeing of a government market. And as you described, it will allow industry some assurance that if they successfully develop a product, that there will be someone to buy it. There are a couple other provisions that are important as well, something that's referred to as the emergency use provision, which would allow in the case of an emergency, an attack, for instance, that the secretary of Health and Human Services could allow drugs or contermeasures that have not yet fully completed the

FDA approval process to be used. Now that would only be in dire circumstances and if that's the only thing that's available.

Flatow: You mean, so drugs that are under test but show promise won't have to go through the long . . . [approval process].

Dr. Gottron: Exactly.

Flatow: Right.

Dr. Gottron: And it would be a temporary measure, something that's going through testing, for instance, it could be rushed to market to deal with an emergency.

Flatow: And the third point?

Dr. Gottron: The third point is some flexibility for the Department of Health and Human Services with regards to certain types of purchases and grant making.

Flatow: And how did the government determine exactly what kind of drugs that they want to stockpile?

Dr. Gottron: Well, it's an ongoing process. The legislation talks about the secretaries of Health and Human Services and the Department of Homeland Security deciding what goes into the stockpile. In practice, there is a multiagency subcommittee, called the Weapons of Mass Destruction Medical Countermeasures Subcommittee, that is looking at this. And what they're doing is—well, they have representatives from the Department of Homeland Security, the Department of Defense, the Department of HHS, as well as some representation from the intelligence community. As you can imagine, it's not just strictly a defense issue, it's not strictly a public health issue. But intelligence may play a factor as well.

Flatow: Could you make, you know, an educated guess of what kinds of drugs they're looking at?

New Anthrax Vaccine

Dr. Gottron: Well, they're publicly stated that they're looking at a new anthrax vaccine, some anthrax treatment products that could be used in addition to antibiotics that are currently used, a next-generation smallpox vaccine, maybe botulism anti-toxin, a new plague vaccine, some anti-radiation drugs and some other vaccines. They've said publicly that they think that it's likely that those will be able to be procured under Bioshield.

Flatow: And are the drug companies pretty happy with this legislation?

Dr. Gottron: I think everybody agrees that this is at least a good first step. But I also think that it's fair to say that most people don't believe that it's a panacea. It's a very complicated problem that we're facing, and, you know, it would be rare that a problem this complicated would be solved with, you know, a single piece of legislation. There's already been talk, some lawmakers have been quoted as saying that, you know, there may be some need for a Bioshield II, if you will.

Flatow: Even before Bioshield I.

Dr. Gottron: Well, now that it's passed, now they're talking about— or almost passed. . .

Flatow: Right.

Dr. Gottron: . . . that it's maybe more incentive.

Flatow: Oh, I see. So what would that have in Bioshield II, for example, that might not happen in Bioshield I?

Dr. Gottron: Well, some of the other policy options that have been discussed include idemnification. Industry would be very eager to be idemnifed if they assume a large liability of . . .

Flatow: Right.

Dr. Gottron: . . . one of their drugs being used and adverse reaction to it. So that—several companies have said that that is holding up them from getting into this field.

Flatow: They're afraid of a big lawsuit.

Dr. Gottron: Exactly.

Flatow: They may be sued for a bad batch of drugs or something.

Dr. Gottron: Right.

Flatow: And so the Congress would then insure them or would say, 'You can't sue them'?

Safeguarding Manufacturers

Dr. Gottron: It's unclear. There are several provisions that have been discussed. It's pretty early in the process, I think. But there is some precedent for it similar to what was done with smallpox vaccine, where the manufacturers were indemnified in that case.

Flatow: And that's basically what Bioshield II would be or . . .

Dr. Gottron: Maybe, yeah.

Flatow: Maybe.

Dr. Gottron: It's very in the nascent stages. People have also talked about ways to encourage the existence of a dedicated biodefense industry through encouraging more venture capital into this particular area of research. So it's still early days.

Flatow: Is this a pretty good chunk of money, about $6 billion?

Dr. Gottron: It's a lot of money to me.

Flatow: Yeah.

Dr. Gottron: I guess the question is: Does this really get everything we want?

Flatow: Right.

Dr. Gottron: How far does $5.6 billion go?

Flatow: Right.

Dr. Gottron: Our sister agency, the Congressional Budget Office, has put out some estimates just to give you a flavor. They thought over the 10 years, a new anthrax vaccine would maybe—the government would maybe spend $1.4 billion on that for over 10 years. So a new smallpox, maybe 1 to $2 billion over 10 years. So it's a lot of money, certainly, but these are also expensive treatments and things. So it's not clear how much more that we'll be able to get from it.

Flatow: You know, 10 years is a long period of time to wait considering the state of the world these days.

Dr. Gottron: Sure, sure, And the idea is not that we're going to wait the 10 years to spend it. The government has already started looking at the new anthrax vaccine and in theory things will be bought much sooner than the 10 years. So it will be sort of a rolling procurement process. . . .

Flatow: You mentioned that new anthrax vaccine. What's wrong with the old one?

Dr. Gottron: Well, it's not ideal for responding to an attack. The current one has several doses over a long period of time, and ideally what you'd want is a single dosage so they could just give you one shot in the arm or some alternative delivery method and then you'd be immune. The current course is not like that. It's several injections over a long period of time before you get immunity. So obviously in an emergency situation, it's not ideal. Under circumstances for the military, you could vaccinate the people before they get to the theater. So it's a little different problem for a civilian market.

No Funds for Personnel

Flatow: Is there any money in the Project Bioshield to pay for the hospital workers, the additional hospital workers and people who will have to dispense the drugs to the general population during an emergency?

Dr. Gottron: No, actually this is just a procurement of drugs to actually go into the stockpile. So there's no money for the . . .

Flatow: It's like buying the bullets without having the guns for them, isn't it?

Dr. Gottron: Well, there are separate appropriations for managing the stockpile, and those wouldn't be included in the 5.6 that are covered under Bioshield.

Flatow: So there—because we hear from hospitals all the time, they're saying, 'We don't have the money,' you know, it's not filtering down, the funding to the hospital level to take care of the people should there be another attack. Is there a separate—You're aware of separate funding that would get there?

Dr. Gottron: Well, there's certainly efforts to increase the infrastructure that would allow for surge capacity and funding of that sort. So there are efforts ongoing.

Flatow: Yeah, but you have to have I guess the people, more than the effort.

Dr. Gottron: Yeah.

Flatow: They've got to be in the hospital. To have an effort, the people have got to be there to give out the stuff because we don't know when that might happen. It could happen tomorrow. It could happen, God forbid, some other time, you know?

Dr. Gottron: Sure.

Flatow: So what happens with the states of these two bills? How far apart are the Senate and the House versions?

Conference Committee

Dr. Gottron: Well, the version that passed the Senate is fairly close to what passed the House. Some of the congressional leaders have been quoted as saying that they think that it's going to go pretty quickly. It's not clear if there will be an actual conference committee or if the House will vote on the Senate version and then just pass it directly on to the president for his signature.

Flatow: So nothing major there.

Dr. Gottron: No. This obviously took quite some time since the president announced it in 2003, the State of the Union address. And what's been happening is the legislation has been evolving through many different versions, and now what's passed the Senate is fairly close to what was passed by the House. So all of the major disagreements have been taken care of.

Flatow: So let's say we get a bill signed into law. Does that mean it's a free-for-all for the drug companies?

Dr. Gottron: No.

Flatow: Yeah, get 6 billion bucks out there.

Dr. Gottron: Right. No. What will happen is the government will say, 'Look, we really want a countermeasure for disease X. We want a new treatment for anthrax,' let's say. And companies will submit proposals and the government will end up picking a proposal. So there will be this sort of dialogue that goes on and then a decision. And once the decision's made, the government's essentially saying, 'Company A, we really like your treatment. You say it's going to be ready in three years. You'll be ready to deliver so much of it to us to put into the stockpile. Here, let's write a contract today that says if we get it in three years, we will pay you X amount of money for X number of doses.' So everything is written into the contract.

Flatow: Right.

Dr. Gottron: And then with that, then the company can say, 'Well, that justifies us finishing the research and development on it.'

Body Temperature Could Become an Early Warning System

Robert Armstrong, Patricia Coomber, and Stephen Prior

The federal government has begun to put air-sampling sensors in key locations within major cities in an attempt to detect the release of dangerous pathogens. The project, known as Bio-Watch, seeks to alert authorities to the presence of known biological threats. In the selection that follows, Robert Armstrong, Patricia Coomber, and Stephen Prior, three experts affiliated with the National Defense University, evaluate the likely effectiveness of the surveillance systems. They conclude that in the event of a terrorist bioweapons attack static biosensors are unlikely to be sufficient. To supplement them, they propose using human detectors. Specifically, they propose that the police, firefighters, and emergency medical technicians of a city be tested every day for changes in body temperature. According to the authors, the human immune system triggers a rise in temperature within hours of exposure to pathogens. A change in one person would not be significant, but if a cluster of people who had all been in the same location suddenly displayed an elevated temperature, that might be a sign of an outbreak. Robert Armstrong and Patricia Coomber are senior research fellows in the Center for Technology and National Security Policy at the National Defense University. Coomber is also a colonel in the U.S. Air Force. Stephen Prior is a distinguished research fellow in the center, and also serves as director of the National Security Health Policy Center at the Potomac Institute for Policy Studies.

As a nation, we are investing a significant amount of money in sensors as part of the BioWatch program. Recent press reports have described a $60 million sensor network deployed in 31 cities with a proposed increase to $118 million for 2005 to cover additional cities. Details of the program are understandably classified, but there has

Robert Armstrong, Patricia Coomber, and Stephen Prior, "Looking for Trouble: A Policymaker's Guide to Biosensing," *Defense & Technology Papers*, June 2004. Copyright © 2004 by Center for Technology and National Security Policy, National Defense University. Reproduced by permission.

been local acknowledgment of sensors in New York, Washington, Chicago, Houston, San Francisco, San Diego and Boston. Government officials will not confirm what agents the system screens for, but they say it is less than a dozen. That most likely limits it to the candidate agents listed in CDC's Category A list.[1]

The BioWatch program has not been universally accepted and has plenty of critics. Calvin Chue, a researcher at Johns Hopkins University, points out that BioWatch would likely be effective only in detecting a major atmospheric release. Small-scale attacks, or attacks delivered through food or water, that could result in hundreds—or thousands— of victims would probably go undetected. Moreover, as Chue comments, BioWatch sensors do not monitor any indoor environments. In this case, an indoor release will only be detected once it leaves the building and encounters a BioWatch sensor. The Director of the Center for Biological Defense at the University of South Florida—Jacqueline Cattani—summed up her feelings as follows: "If you saw planes going over and releasing major clouds of this stuff, there's a chance that people would get suspicious a long time before anybody checked the filters."

Other critics further emphasize the fact that the sensors only cover one-half of the U.S. population. They point out problems with positioning of the sensors and question the amount of air sampled. Additionally, they cite the high labor costs involved with the system. The filters have to be collected and processed by trained laboratory technicians.

Reliability Is Doubted

Even the proponents of the program make statements that are somewhat self-damning. One EPA [Environmental Protection Agency] executive was quoted as saying that *if* an attack were close enough to a sensor, authorities could know about it within 12 hours. He rightly pointed out that 12 hours is quicker than if we waited for victims to develop symptoms. However, that *if* is a major point and raises the issue of spatial distribution and placement, as well as meteorological conditions. It is worth noting that an EPA sensor was in place just blocks from the World Trade Center towers, but following the collapse on September 11th [2001], it did not register the incident—only when the wind direction changed on September 12th did the sensor become "aware" of the incident.

The problem of false alarms (positive or negative) must also be considered for the BioWatch sensor network. One senior government official was quoted as saying that of the nearly 500 sensors nationwide, not one had ever raised a false alarm. That is so statistically unlikely as to be considered impossible.

---

1. The U.S. Centers for Disease Control, or CDC, has classified potential bioweapons threats. Category A pathogens present the most severe threat.

Even 500 sensors are far too few for the coverage sought by Bio-Watch. The Federal Government is seeking to increase the number of collectors per city. According to Congressional testimony by Department of Homeland Security Under Secretary for Science and Technology Dr. Charles McQueary in late February 2004, the "average" city covered by the current BioWatch program only has ten collectors. Studies indicate that 40–60 would provide the optimal coverage. In addition, according to Dr. McQueary, cities have requested more collectors to cover key facilities, such as transit systems, airports, and stadiums. . . .

Chances of an Unknown Pathogen

What is the likelihood an unknown agent will be released on the population? Would it be viral? Bacterial? Contagious? Actually, the human population deals with this issue frequently. An analysis of pathogenic microbes and infectious diseases reveals that, on average, for the 30-year period between 1973 and 2003, one new (i.e., previously unknown) disease emerged annually. These new diseases did not appear only in remote corners of the world. Some of the more memorable ones that impacted the continental United States and Canada include Legionnaires' disease (1977), HIV/AIDS (1981), West Nile virus (1999), and SARS (2003). . . .

Medical reporting also ranks high when dealing with known biological agents. This suggests that rather than spending additional money on a sensor-based system that has applicability primarily for known agents, why not expand the system to include a medical component that has applicability across both known and unknown agents? (While DHS [U.S. Department of Health and Human Services] is attempting to develop an integrated, real-time, human-animal-plant surveillance system, as part of its Bio-Surveillance Program Initiative, such a complete system is many years off. The sensor-based BioWatch component is currently a major part of the initiative.) This medical approach seems particularly prudent, given that we are investing in a system designed to detect both the possible (known agents) and the probable (unknown agents). Such a system-of-systems would then be useful both against bioterrorism and for general public health.

Human Detectors

The JASON study[2] noted that we already have roughly 300 million biosensors in the U.S.—our population. Not only do humans sample the air when we breathe, but we also concentrate the sample, and our immune systems and innate responses to insult from biological challenges act as a detector. These responses are both highly specific and

---

2. The JASON Review Committee is an independent panel of senior scientists and technical experts that advises the U.S. Department of Defense on matters of defense, science, and technology. It was established in 1960.

highly sensitive. If a sample of the population were monitored for the first signs of symptoms of challenge (regardless of route of infection), then the information gleaned could also be timely.

On the basis of these observations and our wargame analysis of the utility of the existing technology solutions, we propose that police-men, firemen, and mail carriers be used as a sentinel population to monitor for possible outbreaks of known or unknown agents. Statisti-cally, they provide a better sample of air than stationary collectors, because they are more uniformly distributed across a metropolitan area. Unlike the current systems, they are not subject to the vagaries of microclimates. Also, during the course of their duties they encounter both outdoor and indoor environments. Their daily routes and move-ments are fairly well-defined, making it easy to pinpoint affected areas.

Although the performance characteristics of the BioWatch collec-tors remain classified, it is relatively easy to estimate their capacity to sample the air. Current EPA "high-volume" environmental air sam-plers are rated at taking in 40–60 cubic feet of air per minute (cfm). Assume a "very-high-volume" capacity for the BioWatch collectors at 100 cfm (equal to 2,832 liters/minute). At that rate, the collectors sample the equivalent of one large room (24.5' × 24.5' × 10') per hour, or approximately 170,000 liters of air.

Focusing on Washington

Take the metropolitan Washington, DC, workforce as a sentinel popu-lation. There are 12,110 police and sheriff's patrol officers, 4,900 fire-

---

Figure 1. The selected workforce is uniformly distributed across the city and encounters both indoor and outdoor environments.

A Hot Idea

Metropolitan Washington, DC workforce
• 150 parking enforcement workers
• 12,110 police and sheriff's patrol officers
• 4,900 firefighters
• 5,940 mail carriers
• 400 EMS workers
TOTAL POPULATION: 23,500 people
In one hour, each member samples 480 liters of air.[3] Per hour, the entire workforce samples 11,280,000 liters.
• Roughly equivalent to 66 high-volume samplers.[4]

3. Assume an average breathing rate of .5 liters per breath, with 16 breaths per minute.   4. Assume a "very-high-volume" capacity for the BioWatch collec-tors at 100 cubic feet of air per minute (cfm).

fighters, 400 EMS [Emergency Medical Services] workers, 5,940 mail carriers, and 150 parking enforcement workers for a total population of 23,500 people. Assume an average breathing rate of .5 liters per breath, with 16 breaths per minute. (That is a conservative breathing rate, as it is derived from "at rest" figures. Given their level of physical activity, this population is very likely breathing more than that.) So, in one hour each member of this sentinel population samples 480 liters of air. Per hour, the entire workforce samples 11,280,000 liters of air. That is roughly the equivalent of 66 very-high-volume samplers.

These samplers are highly specific and highly sensitive, and they have no false positives. What data could be efficiently and economically collected from them, to assess the results of their sampling? Considerable work is being done on identifying various blood components that would indicate the earliest signs of disease. These components would be non-specific and alert us that the body is in the early stages of an immune response. Further blood tests would be needed to identify the agent. Urine, sweat, or breath might also be tested. The perfection of these early identification tests (often referred to as pro-dromal states) is still well in the future. Plus, there will likely be considerable logistics and economic factors to consider.

Body Heat as Indicator

At the moment, of all the potential parameters that can be readily measured, body temperature offers the most efficient and economical approach. Moreover . . . medical information is the preferred data when dealing with an unknown agent. Body temperature is a primary piece of medical information.

The technology for measuring body temperature was widely used during the recent SARS epidemic. Various approaches were used, including infrared thermal imagers, oral or ear fever thermometers, and forehead, or temporal artery, infrared thermometers. All focused on measuring specific body temperatures for analysis of any elevation above the expected norm.

The most efficient method for monitoring a workforce is most likely the infrared thermal imagers. While they are not considered the most precise method of measurement, they are good at detecting if someone appears hotter—or colder—than another person.

Every member of a shift could be scanned as he/she came to work. They could all be scanned again at the end of their shift. If members of a shift were exposed near the end of their tour, their temperature might not be elevated by the time they are scanned prior to going home. However, it is likely that the next shift coming on will also be exposed—this time at the beginning of their shift—and will have a measurable temperature increase by the end of their shift. (Baseline data could be stored on all employees and individual temperature variations could be easily accounted for.)

In general, the immune system will register the presence of a foreign agent by increasing the body temperature within a matter of hours. One person showing an elevated temperature might not warrant further investigation, but a cluster would suggest the need for further blood tests.

An Idea Worth Testing

Given the cost of purchasing and maintaining the systems proposed under BioWatch, it seems worth the time and effort to conduct a test of the feasibility of thermal imaging as a medical monitoring technique. It certainly appears to offer a rapid, simple, and cost effective capability for disease detection that is currently ignored.

By contrast, the military presents a different set of problems, when considering the detection of bioagents. Forces in the field need a standoff detection capability. Not only does it provide them with a detect-to-warn capacity that would not be practical in a civilian setting, it also provides them with a reconnaissance capability. There is no argument that the continued development and deployment of biosensors is critical for combat operations.

The Department of Defense is scheduled to award a $1.1 billion contract for its Installation Protection Plan (IPP). Ultimately, the IPP is to establish a network of chemical, biological, radiological and nuclear-detection sensors at 200 military installations worldwide. While the chemical, radiological and nuclear-detection sensors may be important and necessary parts of the Guardian program, this study suggests that the biosensor component might be modified to include thermal imaging. As with the BioWatch program, a short test of this idea seems fiscally responsible, prior to embarking on this five-year effort.

AMERICA SHOULD LEAD A GLOBAL BIOSECURITY EFFORT

Lauren T. Hickok and Reynolds M. Salerno

The dangers of bioweapons are such that it is far better to prevent them from being deployed than to try to respond to them after an attack. In the selection that follows, biosecurity experts Lauren T. Hickok and Reynolds M. Salerno review the case for a global strategy to prevent such attacks. They explain that biosecurity means taking steps to prevent bioterrorism before it starts. Such steps can only be achieved, they argue, if the international community collaborates on a global scale. Biotech industries are springing up in Eastern Europe and Asia, they point out, increasing the possibility of a clandestine bioweapons effort. Even more worrisome, they argue, is Southeast Asia, where both high-tech economic growth and terrorism are rife. U.S. allies could take a step in the right direction by passing biosecurity legislation, the authors say. However, few countries have passed such legislation to date. Moreover, the nations participating in the Biological Weapons Convention—the main international treaty limiting bioweapons—have not agreed on a definition of biosecurity. To remedy these shortcomings, the authors argue that the United States should exert global leadership by drafting model legislation, sharing expertise, and offering resources to at-risk nations. Lauren T. Hickok is a biosecurity analyst at Sandia National Laboratories in Albuquerque, New Mexico. Reynolds M. Salerno is a principal member of the Sandia Technical Staff and director of Sandia's biosecurity program.

The anthrax attacks in the U.S. in fall of 2001 were a reminder that bioterrorism is no longer a matter of science fiction. These incidents and the rapidly expanding global biotechnology industry have redefined bioterrorism as a credible threat to human security and certainly to U.S. national security. However, the world has been slow to wake up to the new challenge.

The U.S. policy to mitigate the biological weapons threat encompasses a number of initiatives, among them the national implementation of biosecurity—that is, security systems and practices to protect dangerous biological materials in legitimate research facilities from theft and sabotage. By mitigating the biological weapons threat at the source, biosecurity aims to stop bioterrorism before it starts. In 2003, the U.S. Government published regulations requiring facilities and individuals that use, store, and/or transport any of 82 Select Agents to register with either the Centers for Disease Control and Prevention or the Animal and Plant Health Inspection Service. These regulations demand that such facilities and individuals adhere to specific biosecurity procedures designed to maintain oversight and control over those materials.

However, securing only U.S. bioscience facilities does not adequately address the threat. Dangerous pathogens can be acquired from overseas labs, made into weapons, and easily transported to the U.S. or other countries, where they can then be deployed. Thus, efforts to achieve biosecurity domestically are only effective if the U.S. is committed to international biosecurity as well.

The Need for Global Efforts

Implementation of biosecurity on a global scale is particularly important given today's rapidly expanding biotech industry, and its corresponding proliferation of biological materials, technologies, and expertise. Many countries are looking to biotech, and with good reason: the industry holds great promise for improving human health and well being. Recent years have brought the development of new vaccines and therapies, and such advances will accelerate. What's more, the decoding of the human genome may provide the ability to prevent many forms of human suffering. And the rise of genetically modified organisms may bring agriculture to a new frontier, where hardier crops provide poorer countries opportunities to develop as never before.

Given such possibilities—and the associated economic benefits—developing countries have chosen to enter the global biotech race in increasing numbers; many consider it the silver bullet that could provide recession-hit industrial sector a new fillip. In countries as diverse as Brazil, South Africa, and Bulgaria, the trend is taking root. Biotech is booming in Eastern Europe and more still in Asia, where numerous countries—Singapore, India, China, Taiwan, Japan, and South Korea, to name but a few—have allocated billions of dollars to promote bioscience research.

Regrettably, by increasing the availability of dangerous biological materials, the biotech revolution has inadvertently increased the risk of bioterrorism, in any part of the globe. The result is a need to protect the dangerous biological materials in these many emerging markets—and that's the domain of biosecurity.

Terror Comes to Southeast Asia

For a contemporary example, consider Southeast Asia. Biotech has exploded in the region. There, heavy government subsidies are the norm—take Malaysia's $26 million investment to build three institutes in the new Biovalley Malaysia, an enormous public/private bioscience park that is part of a plan to attract at least $10 billion in investment in biotechnology by the decade's close. Singapore, a more developed neighbor, in 2001 embarked upon "One North," a 15-year plan that allocates $8.2 billion to make Singapore a high tech hub with a strong focus on biotech. The plan's specific biotech-related expenditures include the $500 million Biopolis Complex, opened in 2003 and touted as a gem among the region's industrial bioparks. These promising developments have inspired other Southeast Asian nations to jump on the trend. Indonesia—among others—sees biotech as the new solution and plans to expand its existing infrastructure, which includes three Inter-University Centers on Biotechnology as well as numerous research facilities and culture collections.

Yet recent years have also brought an increase in terrorist activity to the region. Recall the Bali bombings of 2002, which claimed over 200 lives. Similarly sobering was this past August's [2003] bombing in Jakarta, which claimed 10 lives and suggested that terrorist ambitions had not dimmed. The group Jemaah Islamiah is held responsible for both, and is allegedly linked to Al Qaeda.

To be sure, a penchant for terrorism does not mean a penchant for bioterrorism. But we would do well to be wary. The increasing ease and decreasing cost of producing a biological weapon may motivate terrorists to introduce and spread highly infectious disease as well as rely on conventional explosives. Even today, a knowledgeable and skilled individual could easily remove a microscopic amount of a pathogen from a lab, then grow, process, and deploy that material as a weapon using commercially available equipment. Because of this, the conjunction of expanding biotech and increased terrorist activity amounts to a serious concern for international security. Biosecurity is an important part of the solution.

Few Countries Have Responded

So where does that leave us?

Despite concerns about bioterrorism and the propagation of facilities that house dangerous pathogens and toxins, the concept of protecting those materials from theft and sabotage—that is, biosecurity—has not been widely embraced. Currently, only a handful of countries have promulgated comprehensive biosecurity legislation, let alone fully implemented the requirements therein.

One reason for the general lack of biosecurity is that the concept is in fact relatively new. In the United States, biosecurity regulations went into effect less than a year ago. The international community has only just begun to address the issue. Although the subject was discussed at recent meetings of the States Parties to the Biological Weapons Convention in Geneva, these preliminary discussions have yet to produce a consensus on a clear definition of biosecurity. No international biosecurity standards currently exist.

But protecting dangerous pathogens and toxins from theft and sabotage should not be postponed until an international organization establishes biosecurity guidelines. Individual nations can and should take responsibility for securing their own collections of high consequence biological agents. And the United States, a leader in the new field of biosecurity, can help. By sharing expertise with interested nations, the U.S. can expand the reach of biosecurity and enhance national and international security.

U.S. Leadership

Establishing national biosecurity legislation worldwide will be a critical first step, and the U.S. can greatly improve global biosecurity by helping interested countries to draft such laws. These laws should establish standards for both facility security and the secure transport of dangerous biological materials; they should also establish regulations governing exports of materials and technologies that could be used in biological weapons proliferation.

Many U.S. government agencies—all with various experiences in this new field—can collaborate to develop a comprehensive U.S. policy for international biosecurity. The policy should address a range of issues, from the specifics of implementing biosecurity at a facility to the general principles of establishing biosecurity nationwide. To bring these issues effectively to an international audience, the U.S. will need to demonstrate that biosecurity will bring great benefits for both national and international security. The U.S. must also be prepared to provide resources to critical nations that cannot achieve adequate levels of biosecurity without international assistance. Only when such measures have been put in place can the U.S. state with confidence that appropriate action has been taken to stem the international proliferation of biological weapons.

GLOSSARY

aerosolization: The process of making solid or liquid particles small enough to spread in an invisible airborne mist. (See also weaponize.)

anthrax: A deadly bacterium frequently associated with sheep's wool. Highly valued in bioweapons programs because it is both deadly and durable but not contagious from person to person. (See also cutaneous, inhalational, and spore.)

antibiotic: Any one of numerous medicines used to kill bacteria but ineffective against viruses.

bacterium (plural, bacteria): A tiny single-celled organism lacking a nucleus. Bacteria reproduce by dividing into two, sometimes as often as every twenty minutes. Many are benign, but some can be deadly.

bioagent: A bacterium, virus, or biological toxin that has the potential to be turned into a bioweapon.

Biological and Toxin Weapons Convention (BWC): The 1972 international covenant governing biological weapons. The BWC prohibits all activity associated with offensive biological weapons production but lacks any enforcement provisions.

biosafety: Technically, the term refers to the levels of biological containment set by the Centers for Disease Control. Biosafety levels 1 through 4 have been established. The higher the level, the stronger the requirement for protective measures, such as isolation suits, special ventilation, and decontamination showers.

bioweapon: A biological weapon involving a bacterium, virus, or biologically produced toxin encased in some type of delivery system.

bubonic plague: An infectious disease caused by the bacterium *Yersinia pestis* and characterized by dark swellings (called bubos) on the skin. Natural outbreaks killed millions in Europe during the Middle Ages. Japan allegedly deployed bubonic plague as a bioweapon against Chinese civilians during World War II. (See plague.)

CBW: A commonly used abbreviation for chemical and biological weapons.

Centers for Disease Control (CDC): The U.S. agency principally responsible for the study and control of infectious diseases.

cutaneous: Infection through the skin. Among the bioagents that can infect cutaneously are anthrax and smallpox.

epidemic: An outbreak of a contagious disease that spreads rapidly and widely.

epidemiology: The branch of medicine that studies the spread, incidence, and prevention of disease.

infection: The invasion of the body by a self-reproducing pathogen.

inhalational: A form of a disease such as anthrax that infects when breathed into the lungs.

latency: The period between exposure to a pathogen (bacterium or virus) and the onset of symptoms. Some diseases such as smallpox are infectious during latency, making their containment especially difficult.

microbe: A microscopic life form also known as a microorganism, especially a bacterium that causes disease.

milling: A mechanical process in which an inert substance is mixed with deadly bacteria or viruses and then ground into a uniformly sized powder that can be easily inhaled and lodged in the lungs.

pandemic: The spread of a disease throughout an entire population or throughout the entire world. The common cold is a pandemic disease.

pathogen: A disease-causing agent, especially a microorganism such as a bacterium or virus.

plague: Generally, any widespread and deadly outbreak of disease; more precisely, one of three forms of disease (bubonic, septicemic, or pneumonic, afflicting the skin, blood, or lungs respectively) caused by the bacterium *Yersinia pestis*.

public health: To protect and improve the health of a community or population through scientific measures such as vaccination, sanitation, monitoring, and quarantine.

pulmonary: Relating to the lungs. Certain diseases, such as plague, have a pulmonary form that is especially deadly.

quarantine: The enforced isolation of people or animals imposed to prevent the spread of contagious disease.

ricin: A deadly toxin derived from the castor bean plant and used as a bioweapon in attacks on individuals.

sepsis (or septicemia): The presence of pathogenic organisms or their toxins in the blood.

smallpox: A highly contagious and deadly disease caused by the variola virus. Responsible for countless deadly plagues throughout history, smallpox was eradicated in nature through an international vaccination campaign that ended in 1980. However, some of the virus remains in the United States and Soviet stockpiles.

spore: A dormant state into which some bacteria can lapse. As a spore, the bacterium ejects most of the water in its cell and takes on a hard-shelled form in which it can survive tough conditions for many decades. Anthrax is especially hard to kill when in spore.

toxicology: The study and treatment of toxins and other poisons.

toxin: An organic substance capable of causing harm or death when introduced into bodily tissues. (See ricin.)

transgenic: Relating to an organism whose genome has been altered by introducing genes from another organism. A transgenic biological agent can, in principle, be more dangerous than the natural form of the pathogen.

tularemia: An infectious disease caused by the bacterium *Francisella tularensis* that causes flulike symptoms and swellings of the lymph nodes but is rarely fatal. Carried by rodents—especially rabbits—it may be transmitted by contact with infected animals or insect bites.

vaccine: A preparation of a weakened or killed pathogen or a portion of the pathogen's DNA that, when introduced into the body, creates immunity against later exposure to the disease. Vaccination is considered the most effective public health countermeasure for many biological agents.

virulence: The capacity of a pathogen to produce disease and spread to others. The more virulent a disease, the deadlier its consequences.

virus: A parasitical biological particle that enters a living cell and takes over its genetic machinery to make copies of the virus, which then burst out of the cell to infect others.

weaponize: The process of turning a bioagent into a weapon. Usually involves methods of keeping the bacteria or viruses virulent and devising a method of delivery. May also involve genetic manipulation of the bioagent. (See also milling, transgenic.)

World Health Organization (WHO): A United Nations agency, headquartered in Geneva, Switzerland, that serves as the primary coordinating body for global health programs and policy.

ORGANIZATIONS TO CONTACT

The editors have compiled the following list of organizations concerned with the issues debated in this book. Descriptions are derived from materials provided by the organizations. All have publications or information available for interested readers. The list was compiled on the date of publication of the present volume; names, addresses, phone and fax numbers, and e-mail/Internet addresses may change. Be aware that many organizations take several weeks or longer to respond to inquiries, so allow as much time as possible.

American Academy of Emergency Medicine (AAEM)
555 East Wells St., Suite 1100, Milwaukee, WI 53202-3823
(800) 884-2236
Web site: www.aaem.org

The American Academy of Emergency Medicine is a specialty society representing academic and practicing emergency physicians. As an organization, it seeks to give physicians, rather than organizations, primary control over the delivery of emergency medical services. It maintains a bioterrorism task force and publishes the *Journal of Emergency Medicine (JEM)*, whose contents are available online at its Web site.

American Biological Safety Association (ABSA)
1202 Allanson Rd., Mundelein, IL 60060
(847) 949-1517
Web site: www.absa.org

The American Biological Safety Association was founded in 1984 to promote biosafety as a scientific discipline and serve the growing needs of biosafety professionals throughout the world. ABSA publishes and distributes the quarterly journal *Applied Biosafety* and a number of other biosafety publications. ABSA also conducts an annual Biological Safety Conference to keep members informed of current biosafety issues and regulatory initiatives.

American College of Emergency Physicians (ACEP)
1125 Executive Circle, Irving, TX 75038-2522
(800) 798-1822
Web site: www.acep.org

The American College of Emergency Physicians promotes quality emergency medical care. It was founded in 1968 and represents more than twenty-two thousand members. Its Web site includes extensive informational links and guidance on responding to possible bioterrorism attacks.

Association for Professionals in Infection Control and Epidemiology (APIC)
1275 K St. NW, Suite 1000, Washington, DC 20005-4006
(202) 789-1890
Web site: www.apic.org

APIC is a multidisciplinary international organization with over ten thousand members. Its purpose is to improve the quality of health care through the practice and management of infection control and the application of epidemiology in all health settings. The organization, based in Washington, D.C. was started in 1972 out of recognition of the need for an organized, systematic approach to the control of infections. It publishes the *American Journal of Infection Control*, whose past issues are available online at the APIC Web site.

Centers for Disease Control and Prevention (CDC)
Office of Bioterrorism Preparedness and Response Planning
Mailstop C-18, 1600 Clifton Rd., Atlanta, GA 30333
Web site: www.bt.cdc.gov

The Centers for Disease Control form the nation's main public health entity. Within the CDC, the Office of Bioterrorism Preparedness and Response Planning offers guidance to the public, to state and local officials, and to health care providers on response to bioweapons. It also tracks reports of biological-agent exposure and plans for emergencies. The CDC produces many reports, notices, and periodicals, some of which are available online, notably *Morbidity and Mortality Weekly Report (MMWR)* at www.cdc.gov/mmwr.

Federal Emergency Management Agency (FEMA)
500 C St. SW, Washington, DC 20472
(202) 566-1600
Web site: www.fema.gov

The Federal Emergency Management Agency, now part of the new Department of Homeland Security, is tasked with responding to, planning for, and recovering from disasters. FEMA's Office of National Preparedness has been given responsibility for helping to ensure that the nation's first responders are trained and equipped to deal with weapons of mass destruction, including bioweapons. FEMA has an online library at its site that includes agency directives, circulars, and policy statements.

Infectious Diseases Society of America (IDSA)
66 Canal Center Plaza, Suite 600, Alexandria, VA 22314
(703) 299-0200
Web site: www.idsociety.org

The Infectious Diseases Society of America represents physicians, scientists, and other health care professionals who specialize in infectious diseases. IDSA communicates between its members, the international experts on infectious diseases and bioterrorism, and U.S. policy makers. IDSA worked closely with Congress and the administration to respond to the anthrax attacks in 2001 and provided expert advice concerning the development and implementation of the National Smallpox Immunization Plan. It publishes an online newsletter and an electronic journal, *Clinical Infectious Diseases*, both available on its Web site.

Institute for Biosecurity
Saint Louis University School of Public Health
3545 Lafayette, Suite 300, St. Louis, MO 63104
(314) 977-8257
Web site: www.bioterrorism.slu.edu

The institute seeks to provide public health and health care facilities with the tools needed for preparedness, response, recovery, and mitigation of intentional or naturally occurring outbreaks, as well as to deter the use of biological agents by terrorists. It maintains an electronic library of news and journal articles from many sources at its Web site.

National Center for Biodefense

George Mason University, 10900 University Blvd., MS4E3, Manassas, VA 20110
(703) 993-4263
Web site: www.gmu.edu/centers/biodefense/index.html

The National Center for Biodefense promotes awareness of the national and international security challenges and medical and public health threats posed by biological terrorism and biological weapons proliferation. Its scientists are engaged in biomedical research to develop unique approaches and techniques for warding off and treating infectious diseases and other biological threats. It maintains a list of faculty publications on its Web site.

National Emergency Management Association (NEMA)

PO Box 11910, Lexington, KY 40578
(859) 244-8000
Web site: www.nemaweb.org

The National Emergency Management Association is a nonpartisan, nonprofit association dedicated to enhancing public safety by improving the nation's ability to prepare for, respond to, and recover from all emergencies, disasters, and threats to our nation's security. It primarily represents state emergency management directors. NEMA provides organizational news at its Web site.

Stockholm International Peace Research Institute (SIPRI)

Project on Chemical and Biological Warfare
Signalistgatan 9, 169 70 Solna, Sweden
Web site: www.sipri.org/contents/cbwarfare

SIPRI is an independent foundation established by the Swedish government in 1966 to promote peace. The SIPRI CBW Project studies actual, alleged, or potential uses of chemical and biological warfare and the associated weapons and technologies. The project began shortly after the establishment of SIPRI. It aims to prevent the hostile use of biological and chemical technologies, whether by states or by terrorist or criminal organizations. SIPRI publishes a well-respected annual yearbook, and its site includes a variety of relevant publications that can be ordered online.

U.S. Department of Homeland Security

Washington, DC 20528
Web site: www.dhs.gov or www.ready.gov

The Department of Homeland Security, initiated by an executive order from President George W. Bush and created by Congress in 2002, consolidates twenty-two agencies and 180,000 employees, unifying once-fragmented federal functions into a single agency dedicated to protecting America from terrorism. Among its functions is to coordinate biodefense efforts. The site includes up-to-date news releases and advisories.

World Health Organization (WHO)

Preparedness for Deliberate Epidemics
Web site: www.who.int/csr/delibepidemics/en

The World Health Organization is the United Nations' health agency. WHO's objective, as set out in its constitution, is the attainment by all peoples of the highest possible level of health. In 2002 member states passed a resolution calling on WHO to develop a strategy for response to, among other things, a deliberate epidemic. The WHO has prepared extensive information in this connection. WHO publishes a vast array of information, both online and in print.

BIBLIOGRAPHY

Books

Yonah Alexander and Milton Hoenig	*Super Terrorism: Biological, Chemical and Nuclear.* Ardsley, NY: Transnational, 2001.
Sidney D. Drell, Abraham D. Sofaer, and George D. Wilson, eds.	*The New Terror: Facing the Threat of Biological and Chemical Weapons.* Stanford, CA: Hoover Institution, 1999.
Madeline Drexler	*Secret Agents: The Menace of Emerging Infections.* Washington, DC: Joseph Henry, 2002.
Richard Falkenrath, Robert Newman, and Bradley Thayer	*America's Achilles' Heel: Nuclear, Biological, and Chemical Terrorism and Covert Attack.* Cambridge, MA: MIT Press, 1998.
Laurie Garrett	*The Coming Plague: Newly Emerging Diseases in a World Out of Balance.* New York: Farrar, Straus, and Giroux, 1994.
Jeanne Guillemin	*Anthrax: The Investigation of a Deadly Outbreak.* Berkeley, CA: University of California Press, 2001.
Donald A. Henderson et al.	*Bioterrorism: Guidelines for Medical and Public Health Management.* Chicago: American Medical Association, 2002.
Institute of Medicine	*Chemical and Biological Terrorism: Research and Development to Improve Civilian Medical Response.* Washington, DC: National Academies, 1999.
Roland E. Langford	*Introduction to Weapons of Mass Destruction: Radiological, Chemical, and Biological.* Hoboken, NJ: Wiley-Interscience, 2004.
William H. McNeill	*Plagues and Peoples.* New York: Anchor, 1998.
Judith Miller, Stephen Engelberg, and William J. Broad	*Germs: Biological Weapons and America's Secret War.* New York: Simon and Schuster, 2001.
Meryl Nass	*Anthrax: A Practical Guide for Citizens: What You Should Know, What You Can Do, and How It Came to This: A Compilation of Public Materials Intended to Serve as a Practical Citizen's Guide.* Belmont, MA: Harvard Perspectives Press, 2001.
Michael T. Osterholm and John Schwartz	*Living Terrors: What America Needs to Know to Survive the Coming Bioterrorist Catastrophe.* New York: Delacorte, 2000.
John Parachini	*Anthrax Attacks, Biological Terrorism and Preventive Responses.* Santa Monica, CA: RAND, 2001.
Jonathan B. Tucker	*Scourge: The Once and Future Threat of Smallpox.* Cambridge, MA: Atlantic Monthly Press, 2001.

Jonathan B. Tucker   *Toxic Terror: Assessing Terrorist Use of Chemical and Biological Weapons.* Cambridge, MA: MIT Press, 2000.

Raymond A. Zilinskas   *Biological Warfare: Modern Offense and Defense.* Boulder, CO: Lynne Rienner, 2000.

Periodicals

G.J. Annas   "Bioterrorism, Public Health, and Civil Liberties," *New England Journal of Medicine*, April 25, 2002.

Kathleen Bailey   "Policy Options for Combating Chemical-Biological Terrorism," *Politics and the Life Sciences*, September 1996.

Richard Betts   "The New Threat of Mass Destruction," *Foreign Affairs*, January/February 1998.

Stephen M. Block   "The Growing Threat of Biological Weapons," *American Scientist*, January/February 2001.

Christopher F. Chyba   "Biological Terrorism and Public Health," *Survival*, Spring 2001.

Jim A. Davis   "The Looming Biological Warfare Storm: Misconceptions and Probable Scenarios," *Air & Space Power Journal*, Spring 2003.

David T. Dennis,   "Tularemia as a Biological Weapon: Medical and
Thomas V. Inglesby,   Public Health Management," *Journal of the American
Donald A. Henderson   Medical Association (JAMA)*, June 6, 2001.
et al.

Helen Dewar and   "Senate Approves Bioterror Provisions: Billions
Justin Gillis   Allotted for Medical Measures," *Washington Post*, May 20, 2004.

Dee Ann Divis   "Biowar: U.N. to Expand Bioterror Powers?" *World Peace Herald*, January 27, 2005.

Laurie Garrett   "The Nightmare of Bioterrorism," *Foreign Affairs*, January 2001.

David Hagstad   "Emergency: Bioterrorism," *American Journal of Nursing*, December 2000.

Daniel Hamilton   "Facing Up to the Bioterror Threat," *International
and Tara O'Toole   Herald Tribune*, January 31, 2005.

Donald A. Henderson   "The Looming Threat of Bioterrorism," *Science*, February 26, 1999.

Mark G Kortepeter,   "Bioterrorism," *Journal of Environmental Health*,
Theodore J. Cieslak,   January 2001.
and Edward M. Eitzen

Nicholas D. Kristof   "Case of the Missing Anthrax," *New York Times*, July 19, 2002.

Steven Kuhr and   "The Threat of Biological Terrorism in the New
Jerome Hauer   Millennium," *American Behavioral Scientist*, February 2001.

Allan Lengel   "Anthrax Probers Still Seek Maryland Leads,"
                        Washington Post, July 18, 2004.

Matthew Meselson,   "The Sverdlovsk Anthrax Outbreak of 1979," *Science*,
Jeanne H. Guillemin   November 18, 1994.
et al.

P.P. Mortimer   "Anticipating Smallpox as a Bioterrorist Weapon,"
                        Clinical Medicine, May/June 2003.

Stephanie Nebehay   "WHO Begins Building Smallpox Vaccine Reserve,"
                        Reuters, January 19, 2005.

Hugh Pennington   "Smallpox and Bioterrorism," *Bulletin of the World
                        Health Organization*, October 2003.

Eugene Russo   "Bioterrorism Preparedness," *Scientist*, January 8,
                        2001.

Scott Shane   "Exposure at Germ Lab Reignites a Public Health
                        Debate," *New York Times*, January 24, 2005.

Jeffrey D. Simon   "Biological Terrorism: Preparing to Meet the Threat,"
                        Journal of the American Medical Association (JAMA),
                        August 6, 1997.

Brian Vastag   "Experts Urge Bioterrorism Readiness," *Journal of the
                        American Medical Association (JAMA)*, January 3, 2001.

Srinivas Venkatesh   "Bioterrorism: A New Challenge for Public Health,"
and Ziad A. Memish   *International Journal of Antimicrobial Agents*, February
                        2003.

Meredith Wadman   "Action Needed to Counter Bioterrorism," *Nature*,
                        August 21, 1997.

Melinda Wharton,   "Recommendations for Using Smallpox Vaccine in a
Raymond A. Strikas,   Pre-event Vaccination Program," *MMWR Dispatch*,
Rafael Harpaz et al.   February 26, 2003.

INDEX

aerosol particle sizers (APS), 111
Agent W. *See* ricin
AIDS, 136
air-sampling sensors, 168–70
Alcabes, Philip, 132
Alibek, Ken, 9, 52, 69, 81
Alibekov, Kanatjan, 39
Allies, research on bioweapons by, 25–32
anthrax, 7, 21, 43
   accident, at Sverdlovsk, 40, 50
   attack, via U.S. mail, 8, 9, 48, 87–98, 142, 143
   bacterium, 48–49
   bombs, 30–31
   cutaneous, 47, 48
   exaggerated threat of, 134
   in Exodus, 48
   forms of, 47–49
   genetically engineered, 9
   pulmonary, 47–49
   research on, 28–31, 38
   Soviet stockpiles of, 40
   used during WWI, 16–17
   vaccine, 45, 49, 102, 164–65
   victims of, 95–98
antibiotics, bioagents resistant to, 9
Armstrong, Robert, 168
Aum Shinrikyo, 8, 134, 143
Austin, Thomas, 150
Australia Group, 146–47
Australian mousepox study, 150–56
Aztecs, 133

Bacillus anthracis, 48–49
Baldwin, Ira, 36
Bali bombings, 176
Baliunas, Sallie, 47
Banting, Frederick, 26–27
Barnaby, Wendy, 25
bioengineering. *See* genetic engineering
biohackers, 10, 158–61
Biological Integrated Detection System (BIDS), 112–13
biological materials, control of, 146–47
biological weapons, 7
   in ancient times, 14–15
   bans on, 17–18, 49–50, 145–46

   during Cold War, 33–40
   dangers of, 7–9, 123–24
   defense against, 11–12, 117–23
   detection of, 109–16, 122, 168–73
   difficulty of developing, 8
   during Middle Ages, 14
   racially discriminating, 11
   safety of Soviet, 9
   taboos against, 15–16
   unpredictability of, 10–11
   used by Japanese, 18–24, 34, 76–80
   use of, against Native Americans, 14, 15, 52
   during WWI, 14, 16–17
   during WWII, 18, 19–32, 69, 76–80
   see also bioterrorism
Biological Weapons Convention (BWC), 37–38, 50, 120, 124, 145–46, 155
BioPort, 45
Biopreparat, 38, 81–85
biopreparedness, 132–33, 138–40, 144–49, 174–77
Bioshield bill. *See* Project Bioshield
bioterrorism
   with anthrax, 87–94
   dangers of, 119–20, 129–30
   defenses against, 100–108, 117–24
   is unlikely to succeed, 137
   prevention of, 132–33, 138–40, 144–49, 174–77
   state-aided, 142–48
   threat, 42–43, 47–48
      is exaggerated, 132–40
      justifies restriction of civil liberties, 125–31
BioWatch program, 168–70, 173
bioweapons. *See* biological weapons
Black Death. *See* plague
Block, Steven, 7, 12
blowback, 11
blowfish poison, 22
body temperature, 170–73
botulinum toxin, 62
botulism, 22, 43–44, 135
Britain
   bioweapons research in, 25–29
   use of bioweapons by, 14, 31, 52
British Medical Association, 14
Brokaw, Tom, 8, 88

Brown, Chappell, 158
brucellosis, 22
Bryden, John, 26, 27
bubonic plague, 22, 44, 71, 72, 73
Bush, George W., 47–48, 100, 121
Bush, Vannevar, 29

Camp Detrick. See Fort Detrick
Canada, bioweapons research in, 25–28
castor beans, 61
Castro, Fidel, 37
Category A agents, 43–45
Category B agents, 43, 45
Category C agents, 43
cattle, pathogens affecting, 29
censorship, 156–57
Centers for Disease Control (CDC), 7, 36–37, 43, 133, 138
chemical weapons, 143, 144
    ban on, 33
    control of, 146–48
Chemical Weapons Convention, 145
Cheney, Richard, 121
China, use of bioweapons in, 19–24, 34, 76–80
Chue, Calvin, 169
Church, George, 159
Churchill, Winston, 28, 30, 31
Chyba, Christopher, 12
cidofovir, 55–56
ciprofloxacin, 8
civil liberties, restrictions on, 125–31
Civil War, 50
cloud-spotting, 110–11
Cohen, Jon, 149
Cold War, bioweapons programs during, 33–40
computer viruses, 158, 159–60
contagious diseases, rapid spread of, 10–11
Coomber, Patricia, 168
Cortes, Hernan, 133
counterproliferation measures, 100–108, 117–24
criminal laws, 148
crisis planning, 129–31
Cuba, 133
culturing, of microbes, 110

Dark Winter, 7–8, 129
Daschle, Tom, 87, 88, 90, 95
Davenport, Colleen M., 42
Department of Homeland Security (DHS), 105

detection systems, 109–10, 115–16, 122
    BioWatch program, 168–70
    body temperature, 170–73
    cloud-spotting, 110–11
    genetic-based, 113–14
    immunoassay-based detectors, 111–13
    mass spectrometry, 114–15
    point detectors, 111
    surface acoustical wave (SAW) sensors, 115
diplomacy, 120–21
DNA microarrays, 114
Doppler radar, 109, 110

Egypt, ancient, 48
8-Ball, 36
Elkins, Karen, 69, 70
emergency planning, 129–31
England. See Britain
Europe, plague in, 71–72, 137
Exodus, book of, 48

Falkenrath, Richard A., 11–12
false negatives/positives, 112
Fauci, Anthony S., 100
Federal Emergency Management Agency (FEMA), 120
federal spending, on defense strategies, 138–39, 168, 173
Fenner, Frank, 150, 153–54, 156
Fildes, Paul, 28, 30
First World War. See World War I
Flatow, Ira, 162
flea bombs, 23–24, 78
fleas, 71, 72
flow cytometry, 112
Food and Drug Administration (FDA), 42, 105–107
food poisoning, 22
Ford, Gerald, 130
Forsman, Mats, 69
Fort Detrick, 30, 36
France, use of bioweapons by, 17
Francisella tularensis. See tularemia
Fraser, Donald, 27
French and Indian Wars, 52
Frist, Bill, 60, 87

gas gangrene, 22
genetic-based detectors, 113–14
genetic engineering, 9, 149–50
    biohackers and, 10, 158–61
    mousepox study, 150–55

publishing studies of, 153–57
on smallpox, 9, 10, 38, 152–54
Geneva Protocol, 18, 19, 20, 33, 34
genocide/ethnic cleansing, 15
Germany, use of bioweapons by,
    16–17
germ warfare. *See* biological weapons
glanders, 22, 45
Goebel, Greg, 19
Gorbachev, Mikhail, 84
Gostin, Lawrence, 128
Gottron, Frank, 162
Granite Peak Installation, 31
Grant, Llelwyn, 97
Great Britain. *See* Britain
Great Influenza Pandemic, 130
Grosse Ile, 29–30
Gruinard Island (Scotland), 30

hand-held assay (HHA) test kits, 112
Hankey, Maurice, 25–26, 27, 28
Hanson, Doug, 60
Harm Principle, 126–28
Harris, Elisa D., 8, 142
Harvard Sussex Program, 148
hazardous materials, control of,
    146–47
Henderson, Donald A., 51, 156
Hickok, Lauren T., 174
Hungary, 18

immunoassay-based detectors, 111–14
Institute for Biosecurity, 71
intelligence gathering, 117–19
International Declaration Concerning
    the Laws and Customs of War, 15
International Peace Conference,
    15–16
Investigational New Drugs (IND), 46,
    106–107
Iraq, 146
Ishii, Shiro, 18–24, 34
Italy, 26

Jackson, Ron, 150–55
Japan, use of bioweapons by, 18,
    19–24, 33–34, 76–80
JASON study, 170
Jemaah Islamiah, 176
Jenner, Edward, 39, 52

Kadlec, Robert P., 117
Knight, Tom, 159–61
Koch, Robert, 49
Korean War, 36–37

Kosal, Margaret E., 109
Kosovo, 67–68
Kuperman, Robert, 31

Langmuir, Alexander, 36–37
laser-induced breakdown
    spectroscopy (LIBS), 111
lasers, 109
Leahy, Patrick, 90, 95
LIDAR, 110–11
Lieber code, 15
Lincoln, Abraham, 50
livestock, pathogens affecting, 29
Long Range Biological Standoff
    Detection System (LR-BSDS), 111
Lord, Alexandra M., 33
Lukin, Yevgeny, 86
Lumumba, Patrice, 37

Malaysia, 176
Manhattan Project, 35
mass spectrometry, 109, 114–15
May, Thomas, 125
McClellan, Mark B., 100
McNaughton, Andrew, 26
medical defenses, 122–23
melioidosis, 45
Mellanby, Edward, 27, 28
Middle Ages, 14
military countermeasures, 121–22
Milloy, Stephen, 8
Model State Emergency Health
    Powers Act (MEHPA), 125–26,
    128–31
monkeypox, 54
Moreno, Jonathan, 11
mousepox, 10, 150–55
Mulligan, John, 161
Murray, E.G.D., 29

National Institute of Allergy and
    Infectious Diseases, 104
National Institutes of Health (NIH),
    104–105, 138
National Pharmaceutical Stockpile,
    45
Native Americans, spread of smallpox
    among, 14, 15, 52
N-bomb, 30
Ningpo (China), 23–24
Nixon, Richard, 37
Nowak, Rachel, 154
nuclear weapons, 7

oligonucleotides, 159–60

Operation Vegetarian, 28–29
Organization for the Prohibition of
 Chemical Weapons (OPCW), 145
orphan drug program, 45–46

Pan American Flight 103, 121
Pasteur, Louis, 49
pathogens, 7
 detection of, 109–16, 122, 168–73
 overview of, 42–45
 unknown, 170
 see also specific types
Patriot's Council of Minnesota, 63
Perry, William, 123
pharmaceutical industry, 45–46, 123,
 162–67
Pingfan Institute, 20–23
plague, 21–22, 44
 in Europe, 71–72, 137
 exaggerated threat of, 135
 forms of, 72–73
 genetically engineered, 9
 symptoms of, 73
 treatment of, 73–74
 vaccine, 74
 see also bubonic plague;
  pneumonic plague
pneumonic plague, 22, 71–73
point detectors, 111
polymerase chain reaction (PCR),
 113–14
Porton Down, 26–29
Posner, Richard, 129
Poste, George, 11
Prior, Stephen, 168
prisoners of war (POWs), Japanese
 experiments on, 19–24, 76–80
Project Bioshield, 11, 100–108, 138,
 162–67

al Qaeda, 62–63, 65, 142, 144, 176
Q fever, 45, 135

rabbits, 68–69, 150
Ramshaw, Ian, 151–56
Reed, Guilford, 29
ricin, 60–66
Ridge, Tom, 93
rinderpest, 29
Roosevelt, Franklin, 30
Rucker, Angela, 95
Russia, tularemia outbreak in, 69

Salerno, Reynolds M., 174
salmonella, 22, 144

Sandakchiev, Lev, 85–86
sarin, 62, 64
SARS (Severe Acute Respiratory
 Syndrome), 10–11, 132, 135–37
Schrage, Michael, 10
scientific findings, debate over
 sharing, 153–57
Seamark, Bob, 154, 155, 156
Select Agent List, 147
self-destruct genes, 11
September 11, 2001, 42, 142
septicemic plague, 22, 72, 73
Sherman, William Tecumseh, 50
Shinozuka, Yoshio, 76
Sidel, Victor, 134
smallpox, 7, 44
 in the Americas, 14, 15, 52, 133,
  137
 control of, 38–39, 58–59
 dangers of, 51–53
 exaggerated threat of, 133–34
 genetically engineered, 9, 10, 38,
  152, 153–54
 outbreak response, 53–54, 56–57
 simulated attack of, 7–8
 stockpiles of, 39
 transmission of, 119
 treatment of, 55–56
 use of, as bioweapon, 51–52
 vaccine, 52, 54–55, 57–58, 102
 vulnerability to, 39
South Africa, 11
Southeast Asia, 176
Soviet Union
 bioweapons programs of, 33,
  35–39, 81–85
 weapons stockpiles in, 9, 39, 40,
  52, 147–48
 see also Russia
Spaniards, 133
Spanish Flu, 137
state-aided terrorism, 142–48
Stockholm International Peace
 Research Institute (SIPRI), 15–16
surface acoustical wave (SAW)
 sensors, 115
Sverdlovsk (Soviet Union), 40, 50
Swine Flu Affair, 130

Tenet, George, 144
terrorism. See bioterrorism
terrorists, 62–63, 65, 142, 144, 176
 Russian scientists collaborating
  with, 9
 state-aided, 142–48

TOPOFF, 129, 130–31
toxins. *See* pathogens
transgenic technologies, 158
treaties
    Biological Weapons Convention,
        37–38, 50, 120, 124, 145–46, 155
    on criminal laws, 148
    Geneva Protocol, 18, 19, 20, 33, 34
Tucker, Jonathan, 9
tularemia, 7, 22, 44, 67–70, 135

Unit 731 program, 18–24, 76–80
United Kingdom. *See* Britain
United States
    bioweapons, security of, 9
    bioweapons programs, 29–37
        halting of, 37–38
    mail
        anthrax attacks through, 8, 9,
            48, 87–98, 142, 143
        ricin in, 60–61
    should lead biosecurity effort,
        174–77

vaccines
    adverse reactions to, 55–56
    anthrax, 45, 49, 102, 164–65
    compulsory, 127–28
    development of, 100–108, 122–23,
        162–67
    plague, 74
    smallpox, 39, 52, 54–55, 57–58,
        102
    tularemia, 70
vaccinia immune globulin (VIG),
    55–56, 58

van Courtland Moon, John, 15
variolation, 39
variola virus, 9
    see also smallpox
Vector, 84–85
viral hemorrhagic fever (VHF), 44–45
Vogel, Gretchen, 67
Vollen, Laurie, 10

Wallace, Norma, 95–98
war on terrorism, 132
Washington, D.C.
    anthrax attack on, 8, 9, 87–98
    workforce in, 171–72
weapons of mass destruction. *See*
    biological weapons; chemical
    weapons
West Nile virus, 136
Wheelis, Mark, 15
Wing, Ken, 127
Wong, Kate, 9
World Health Organization (WHO),
    52
World War I, 14, 16–17
World War II, 18
    Japanese experiments during,
        18–24, 33, 34, 76–80
    research on bioweapons during,
        25–32
    use of bioweapons during, 69

Yersinia pestis. See plague

Zhdanov, Viktor, 39
Zhukov, Georgi, 35